Curved Thought and Textual Wandering

Curved Thought and Textual Wandering

Gertrude Stein's Postmodernism

Ellen E. Berry

Ann Arbor

THE UNIVERSITY OF MICHIGAN PRESS

Copyright © by the University of Michigan 1900 1992
All rights reserved
Published in the United States of America by
The University of Michigan Press
Manufactured in the United States of America

1995   1994   1993   1992   4   3   2   1

Library of Congress Cataloging-in-Publication Data

Berry, Ellen E.
    Curved thought and textual wandering : Gertrude Stein's
postmodernism / Ellen E. Berry.
       p.   cm.
    Includes bibliographical references (p.   ) and index.
    ISBN 0-472-10300-8 (alk. paper)
    1. Stein, Gertrude, 1874–1946—Criticism and interpretation.
2. Postmodernism (Literature)—United States.   I. Title.
PS3537.T323Z557   1992
818'.5209—dc20   92-11657
                                                        CIP

Contents

Introduction

During her 1935 American tour, Gertrude Stein was asked by a perplexed journalist, "Miss Stein, why don't you write the way you speak?" With characteristic equanimity and an unfailing talent for the devastating punch line she replied, "Young man, why don't you read the way I write?" Stein wrote copiously and continuously for more than forty years: the Yale catalogue of her works lists over six hundred titles, many of which are only beginning to be read. Her subjects range from meditations on the nature of female identity and desire, to analyses of the psychology of dictators, to celebrations of a plate of vegetables. She explored complex aesthetic questions within what are often considered minor genres; she reshaped, subverted, even extinguished major ones in an effort to decompose nineteenth-century representational aesthetics and to compose new nonmimetic literary modes for the twentieth century, discontinuous forms that radically disrupt traditional notions of how fiction should be defined, valued, and read. Learning to read Stein's rich and varied output has proven one of the great critical challenges of the twentieth century at least in part because our interpretive frameworks have had to "catch up" with her remarkable innovations.

This book develops a case for the centrality of postmodern critical categories to an understanding of Stein's fictional experiments and, further, to a more accurate understanding of her position within literary history. It describes a number of ways, both formal and contextual, that Stein approached the modern from a direction that has come to be viewed as postmodern. In doing so it also participates in ongoing efforts to chart lines of relation or divergence between the cultural productions of a postmodern moment and those of an earlier modernist era.

Postmodernism is a capacious, often contradictory, term within whose parameters a number of conflicting definitions and heterogeneous practices circulate.[1] For the purposes of this study, it refers to "a slowly emerging cultural transformation, particularly in Western societies, a noticeable shift in sensibility, practice, and discourse formations which distinguishes a postmodern set of assumptions, experiences and propositions from those of a preceding period."[2] More specifically, "postmodern" may be conceived in at least three ways: as an interpretive framework or method of analysis that implies changed assumptions concerning the relationship between reader and text; as a range of aesthetic practices and values—evident in many contemporary artistic productions—that differ in significant ways from those of preceding eras; and as a contemporary cultural condition arising from social, economic, and ideological shifts that implies—among other things—a changed relationship between the artist and previously repudiated cultural materials. As an evolving theoretical structure by which cultural knowledge and critical procedures are being reordered, *postmodernism* as I am using it is not solely a term designating the art works of a post-1960s era. Nor is it primarily a history-transcendent avant-garde impulse that has always existed alongside dominant signifying practices. Instead it may be considered a broadly based cultural dynamic that has emerged—gradually and unevenly—over the last one hundred years from within complex processes of modernization. In a late twentieth-century moment this cultural dynamic is becoming dominant, a claim that should not be seen as incompatible with a second: that postmodern culture is itself decentered, composed of multiple competing discourses and sites of difference rather than clear and stable cultural hierarchies. This study participates in ongoing efforts to construct definitions of the postmodern through an examination of Stein's artistic practices. It also contributes to current projects engaged in historicizing the postmodern literary emergence, and, crucially, it makes a case for the centrality of gender as a largely neglected category of analysis within such historicizing efforts.

Like the postmodern itself, Stein is an unusually capacious and contradictory "category" and she has been read in a number of ways: as "a writer animated by an [extremely] conscious program"

(Steiner), and "an improvisational writer" who wrote "thousands of pages of disconnected trivia" (Bridgman); as a literary cubist (Brinnin, Dubnick, Steiner, Walker), a metaphysician (Stewart, Sutherland), a "late master of the American Sublime" in the American logocentric, Emersonian tradition (Bloom), and a destroyer of the logocentric tradition (Benstock); as the first modernist (Kostelanetz), a lesbian modernist (Stimpson, Fifer), a modernist who differed from modernism in every conceivable way (Benstock).[3] It is possible to read Stein as a postmodernist—to emphasize postmodern features in her work— first because aspects of a postmodern impulse were already incipient within literary modernism. From this perspective, postmodernism might be thought of as restructuring certain elements—marginal to, repressed by, or ignored within the modernist program—in such a way that they become focusing components within postmodern theories and practices. This process of refocalization,[4] in which postmodern features emerge from within the margins of a dominant modernist aesthetic, has been obscured in part because of the institutionalization of a canon that has privileged as definitively modern particular aesthetic features and literary values (and the authors seen as best embodying them) through the use of specific interpretive strategies. Postmodernism's (partial) emergence from within the modern becomes most apparent when it is articulated from the perspective of those writers considered tangential to a canonized modernism—as Stein clearly was. Such a process of articulation exposes the ways in which the heterogeneity of modernist expressions has been minimized in order to construct a modernist literary style or collective spirit and opens the way for more complex descriptions of modernism and its relation to postmodernism.

This contemporary recovery of emergent postmodern features has led to a postmodernization of particular modernist texts as well as to a reconfiguration of the terrain known as literary modernism.[5] In this sense then—one I explore throughout the study, most overtly in chapter 1—to "postmodernize" a text means to read it through the lens of specific new interpretive paradigms. These would emphasize such strategies and values as play with, rather than mastery of, the text; decentering moves rather than ones that promote coherence and closure; a radical indeterminacy rather than ambiguity, irony, and paradox; a renunciation of interpretative metanarratives in favor of small local strategies that generate a series of interpretive moments no one of which is definitive; an emphasis on the reader's active role in constructing multiple textual meanings.

In fact, I am referring to two things here. Conceivably almost any text might be postmodernized—as the numerous deconstructive readings of realist texts suggest (Barthes's explosion of Balzac's "Sarrasine" being perhaps the most notorious). Similarly, one can recuperate a fragmented postmodern text for realism or for a modernist aesthetic by imposing particular narrative or thematic frameworks upon it—as I suggest in chapter 1. However, I would wish to maintain a distinction—however fuzzy it may sometimes become—between the interpretive strategies applied to a text and the aesthetic features contained within it. While almost any text might be postmodernized, not all texts are postmodern since, as I indicated above, postmodern also refers to a particular set of textual practices and aesthetic values more or less consciously adopted by an author. These might include a radical suspicion of narrative form and other structures perceived as authoritarian and thus an emphasis on disruption of narrative hierarchies, causal structures, and clear teleology; promotion of acausality, nonteleological motion, fragmentation, open structures, indeterminacy, mise-en-abyme, dispersion, randomness, principles of nonselection and other modes for producing discontinuity; an emphasis on performative modes and reflexive structures; a valuing of radical changeability, multiplicity, heterogeneity, polyvocality, difference; expression of radical ontological and epistemological doubt emerging from an awareness of the dislocation of centered structures and privileged discourses; generic mixing, especially of high and low forms.[6]

In this study I both postmodernize a number of Stein's novels by emphasizing particular aspects of them and claim that in a number of instances she wrote texts whose features and aesthetic assumptions mark them as decidedly postmodern. That said, I don't mean to suggest that Stein simply cease being regarded as a modernist author (or a metaphysician, or a literary cubist) and be reassigned a securely postmodern position—although Stein's contradictions and enigmas have often evoked in critics the desire to put her in a (her) secure place. Treating an author as one point of origin for a postmodern impulse often becomes a containment strategy whereby a previously neglected writer gains importance solely for the degree to which she or he might be said to predict the work of later writers.

Such strategies may distort the complexity of the postmodern literary emergence by containing its multiplicity within a singular genealogy. They may also obscure those features of an individual author's work that might not fit comfortably within postmodern categories—in Stein's case certain residual premodern impulses along with aspects of what we currently consider to be a modernist aesthetic. Rather than situate Stein definitively within a stable position, my aim has been to display new facets of her work through the use of postmodern frameworks and, in so doing, to extend the process of reassessing Stein that has developed throughout the 1980s in work by Shari Benstock, Carolyn Burke, Harriet Chessman, Marianne DeKoven, Janice Doane, Lisa Ruddick, Catharine Stimpson, Jayne L. Walker, and others.[7] Employing a number of critical perspectives—poststructuralist, a variety of feminisms, psychoanalytic, linguistic—this contemporary renaissance in Stein criticism has opened multiple new configurations of meaning in her works thereby also demonstrating that they are rich and complex enough to support a range of critical approaches. This critical diversity is, I believe, itself a positive dimension of a postmodern cultural impulse.

Although the following areas are concerns throughout, the first chapters of this study focus most directly on questions of reading and interpretation, on the isolation of particular textual features now identified as postmodern, and on Stein's rationale for the invention of such textual arrangements and disarrangements. Chapter 1 situates Stein in relation to two feminist narratives of the reading process and demonstrates the ways in which her work challenges and exceeds such narrativizing impulses. I argue for the importance of recognizing how narrative as a powerful and persistent mode of structuring experience—including one's experience of a text—may act to obscure the difference of nonmimetic works. This then suggests both the need for and the difficulty of moving beyond narrative-based models of interpretation. In the next chapter I turn to Stein's own encounter with the narrative assumptions of nineteenth-century realist modes. "Curving Thought, Making Nonsense: The Death of Realism in *A Long Gay Book*" analyzes the strategies by which Stein moves from an adherence to realist narrative principles toward a radical dislocation of them. These strategies arise in large part from her equation between realist narrative and patriarchal modes of authority. Her efforts to radically disidentify with this authority—evident throughout her early works but most dramatically performed in *A Long Gay Book*—push her beyond modernist disruptions of realism and toward a postmodern form of the novel.

In the two subsequent chapters I analyze two distinct responses to the problematic question of how to make the novel as a genre "go on" in a twentieth-century form, i.e., without returning to a reliance on conventional novelistic categories such as plot and character. In "Metafiction and the Aesthetics of Privacy in *A Novel of Thank You*" I suggest that the radical self-reflexive strategies Stein employs in this text emerge from a complex theoretical stance and context of enunciation, one that reflects an avant-garde imperative to reformulate the basis of the novel, a gender-inflected relation to literary tradition and cultural materials, and an individual aesthetic base in which an avant-garde literary response is articulated through and in relation to a specific interpersonal dynamic. Whereas *A Novel of Thank You* is involuted or self-reflexive in its textual dynamic, *Lucy Church Amiably*, the second major postrealist novel that I examine, is incorporative. In this text, organized according to a performative rather than a mimetically-based aesthetic, Stein reconceives character (understood as agent or central consciousness) as a series of spectacularly unstable positions in textual space that defy gender categories and even those categories by which we have conventionally defined the human. Here the novel with its private dramas becomes the novel as an act of postmodern performance and the realm of the private expands to fill the world.

The remaining three chapters explore facets of another characteristic feature of postmodern culture: a changed relationship between the artist and particular cultural materials—in this case, a variety of forms emerging from mass culture and the signifying systems of everyday life. As a number of critics have noted, many postmodern artists deliberately incorporate popular materials into their works for a wide range of purposes and effects.[8] A radical discursive, stylistic, and generic heterogeneity—in part arising from an erasure of the great divide between high and low (mass) culture—is, in fact, a central distinguishing feature of a contemporary cultural milieu. Here culture no longer operates as a unitary fixed category but as a decentered fragmentary assemblage of conflicting discourses, forms, and institutions. Postmodernism's radical eclecticism, or cultural heteroglossia, contrasts sharply with a modernist desire to view culture as an autonomous space, or sphere, and to erect a stable hierarchy of cultural forms within it. This effort involved, among other things, repudiating, even pathologizing, an emerging mass culture that, as Andreas Huyssen has shown in *After the Great Divide*, was persistently gendered female. Thus, as Huyssen further notes, a characteristic feature of the modernist aesthetic is a gesture of "warding off" the threat of a developing mass culture imaged as "trivial and banal on the one hand, monstrous and devouring on the other."[9]

Whereas many modernist writers attempted to differentiate high and mass culture as a precondition to the development of a modernist aesthetic, Stein tried, in a variety of complex ways, to express the modern in relation to them both. As a means of exploring this assertion, I detail Stein's efforts to work within what were considered debased or outmoded genres (the detective novel, melodrama) and popular discursive systems (the everyday, prophecy as spurious history making) not so as to recuperate these modes for a modernist agenda but to explore the possibilities emerging from interactions between "high" and "low" within them. In many cases this means employing them to critique both realist and modernist narrative assumptions. As a corollary to this exploration, I read some central aspects of Stein's aesthetic practice—for example, her conception of twentieth-century movement—as a response to the ways in which newly emerging mass technologies were altering the aesthetic expectations and competencies of a modern reading public. Stein's aestheticization of technic—her incorporation into the art work of the technological imagination—is most clearly evident in her late novel *Ida* which I read as a postmodern melodrama. The novel's generative force, I argue, emerges from neither logical causation—the structural principle of realism—nor from a process of poetic association—the organizing principle of modernism—but rather from a postmodern process of simulation that Jean Baudrillard considers the central dynamic of postmodern culture. With this practice, and in line with the practices of many contemporary writers, Stein replaces the modernist values of originality and uniqueness with a postmodern aesthetics of expendability and reproducibility.

This study is not only engaged in reading Stein as a postmodernist in the ways I have suggested. Using Stein as an example, it also demonstrates the importance of historicizing the postmodern literary emergence from a variety of different perspectives (perspectives on difference) in particular, for this study, an analysis inflected through the lens of gender positioning. Most theorists attempting to trace the history of postmodernism, among them Ihab Hassan, Brian McHale, Fredric Jameson, and Andreas Huyssen, have done so with reference to an overwhelmingly male genealogy, a perspective that then colors their overall conception of the postmodern. For instance, Huyssen considers postmodernism to be a belated American manifestation of the 1930s European avant-garde produced in reaction to the institutionalization of those aesthetic and cultural values promoted by high modernist writers such as T. S. Eliot and Ezra Pound. This perspective generates a neat line of descent within literary history by privileging as definitive only one version of modernism and one postmodern reaction to it. In light of widespread recent efforts to reexamine the nature of literary modernism from a variety of perspectives, including feminist and ethnic positions, this is a particularly untenable critical stance. Such accounts of the modern era as Carolyn Burke's, Shari Benstock's, Marianne DeKoven's, Sandra M. Gilbert and Susan Gubar's, and Houston Baker's reveal it to be a period of intense cultural tension and ideological struggle during which a number of aesthetic tendencies circulated, many of which have been repressed and distorted by processes of canon formation. Recovering the specificity of these differing revolts against reigning norms, these different responses to "the modern," has become a central task of recent cultural criticism of the period. It now becomes possible, indeed necessary, to ask "whose modernism?" a question which also implies another—"whose postmodernism?" Because Stein's work forms such a strong counterexample to the pattern defined by Huyssen and others, because it represents such a unique response to the modern, it acts as one site through which a more expansive and accurate account of both modernism and postmodernism might begin to be theorized.

This study offers an approach to Stein that attempts to reflect both her postmodernism and her feminism. Although I have organized my readings of individual texts in a roughly chronological order, thereby retaining a conventional developmental framework, I also stress intertextual relations among them. These suggest that Stein's career as a writer, like the texts that she wrote, did not so much progress teleologically as begin again and again in a multiply reconfigurable, nonprogressive accumulation of stylistic and thematic concerns. Stein's aesthetic practice undercuts notions of an author's development as necessarily progressive or logically coherent and of individual texts as significant primarily for the degree to which they advance this narrative trajectory.

In her effort to compose an antirealist version of the novel, Stein opens a variety of new spaces of textual productivity through the composition of a new aesthetics of fragmentation and textual wandering. Her texts wander intertextually; Stein frequently grafts whole sections of previously written works into later texts in a process of self-quoting. More generally, she reworks themes and strategies in a process of using everything and beginning again and again. Thus her texts, taken together, exist in a vast intertextual dialogue—each text is a rewrite even as it is being written. Stein's texts also wander extratextually so that the work being composed and the scene of composition commingle, a process that disrupts notions of the text as a discrete entity, an autonomous work apart from everyday life. Finally, textual wandering describes an intratextual strategy whereby the organization of a work is generated by the convergence and dispersal of moments of significance, a dynamic process that stops but does not end.

My goals throughout this study have been to clarify an understanding of Stein's postmodern aesthetic practice over the course of her career and to advance theories of postmodernism in a general sense by insisting on definitions that are both textual and contextual, ones able to account for the social, ideological, historical, *and* aesthetic contexts within which processes of artistic production take place. Such expanded definitions are crucial to an accurate understanding of the complexity and diversity of postmodern cultural practices, and are nowhere more important than with a writer such as Stein.

Chapter 1

On Reading Gertrude Stein

One of the most important functions of art is to render manifest the complexity
of our desires in front of works.

—Gilbert Lascaut

Reading Plot 1

Gertrude Stein's texts leave something to be desired. Considered from one
perspective—a perspective that until quite recently has dominated
evaluations of her literary worth—this statement points to Stein's
limitations as an artist. B. L. Reid's violently negative assessment of
Stein in *Art by Subtraction*, though extreme, nonetheless typifies this
position: "Stein's true position is anti-literary, anti-intellectual, often
anti-human and anti-moral . . . her work possesses no beauty, no instruction, no passion . . . [but] her failure to communicate is the crime
for which we will finally have to hang her."[1] For Reid, Stein's fiction
lacks most of the qualities we demand of literature. It withholds,
willfully, that complex "something," failing to provide a real ground
for the satisfying literary encounter between reader and text we have
learned to desire. This encounter typically proceeds from mystery to
mastery: the reader unravels the text's enigma as he or she moves
through it, his or her mystification turning into knowledge and ultimately mastery of the reading experience.

Teresa de Lauretis's comments on the nature of narrative logic
help to clarify some key assumptions underlying this model of the
reading process:

All narrative, in its movement forward toward resolution and
backward to an initial moment, a paradise lost, is overlaid
with . . . an Oedipal logic. . . . The work of narrative . . . is a mapping of differences, and specifically, first and foremost of sexual

difference, into each text; and hence, by a sort of accumulation, into the universe of meaning, fiction, and history [including here, theories of reading] . . . to say that narrative is the production of Oedipus is to say that each reader—male or female—is constrained and defined within the two positions of a sexual difference thus conceived: Male-hero-human, on the side of the subject; and female-obstacle-boundary-space, on the other.[2]

According to de Lauretis, narrative works to authorize and legitimize the male status of the subject whose desire is for illumination (revelation of and ultimately reconciliation with the father's truth), for stable identity (perpetuation of the father's name and authority), for realization of the object of desire and closure. The linear causal structure of narrative is shot through with a "genealogical imperative," a pattern of anticipation and resolution by which "events in time come to be seen as begetting other events within a line of causality similar to the line of generations." At the point of conclusion, all possibility has been converted into necessity—"the subsequent having been referred to the prior, the end to the beginning, the progeny to the father."[3]

If we approach Stein's fiction with conventional narrative (Reiderly) expectations we are likely to seek with desire but not to find. We remain frustrated from completing the satisfying literary encounter with the text, groping blindly in the dark, failing to discover the Oedipal pleasure that Roland Barthes insists is fundamental to fictional pleasure: "to denude, to know, to learn the origin and the end."[4] Instead we come up empty-handed. "No beauty, no instruction, no passion . . ."—there is "nothing" there (the Oedipal shock). The enigma remains open, and the encounter between reader and text has come to nothing.

Reading Plot 2

Gertrude Stein's texts do indeed leave something to be desired. In contrast to Reid's position, this assessment suggests that Stein's texts leave behind something of value, something that satisfies, something we desire very much: the story of a woman de-siring the father by confronting his claims to truth and his notions of literary value. Stein's texts do not honor the father. They are anti-authoritarian, revolutionary, inscribing her sometimes playful, often painful, efforts to transgress phallocentric norms, logics, and structures.[5] To transgress, as Susan Suleiman reminds us, means to feel intense pleasure "at the exceeding of boundaries," but also intense anguish "at the full realization of the force of those boundaries."[6] Describing her efforts to escape "the thing that is just past," the weight of nineteenth-century literary tradition and conventional morality, Stein writes, "You always have in your writing the resistance outside of you and inside of you, a shadow upon you, and the thing which you must express. In the beginning of your writing this struggle is so tremendous that the result is ugly.... But the essence of that ugliness is the thing which will always make it beautiful. I myself think it is much more interesting when it seems ugly, because in it you see the element of the fight... the vitality of the struggle."[7] In her struggle to "excreate a no since," to undo common sense logical structures, and to express the "thing" inside her (including her lesbianism), Stein is forced to eat "Pain soup," to "sigh" and "cry" over sentences that are "always in their [the patriarchs'] way,"[8] always policed by patriarchal grammatical norms. The "sentences" passed on her literary worth seemed always in their way also, and, for the most part, Stein struggled alone, in often painful isolation. As Shari Benstock notes, "it is one of many pernicious expatriate myths that Gertrude Stein controlled a powerful Left Bank salon from which she dictated literary aesthetics. Gertrude Stein's Paris existence was, mostly, a separate one... she spent her time alone, writing.... Once the experiment in the Rue de Fleurus apartment had begun, however, it could not be easily stopped, even though Stein admittedly paid a high price in continuing a venture so easily misunderstood."[9] For the Mother of Us All, "Life is strife."[10]

This modernist plot (modernist in that it expresses a sensibility of struggle) is a particularly desirable one for feminist critics. It is, in effect, part of a feminist insistence that texts written by women be rewritten to tell the tale of the woman writer's struggle against, or effort to outwit, internal and external patriarchal censors. This tale of repression (that is also repressed) emerges clearly when a revisionary feminist perspective is assumed, allowing us to find the complex substance of the struggle in what was previously perceived as merely deficient or "ugly."[11] As Patrocinio Schweickart imagines it in her feminist theory of reading, female author and feminist reader are protagonists in the context of two settings. The first setting, what I've called the modernist plot, is "judicial"—"one woman is standing witness in defense of the other. . . . The feminist reader takes the part of the woman writer against patriarchal misreadings that trivialize or distort her work."[12]

Reading Plot 3

Once again, *Gertrude Stein's texts leave something-to-be-desired.* In this sense, Stein's texts give leave. They permit and affirm a kind of writing (called variously *l'écriture feminine*, women's writing from the body, or, in Marianne DeKoven's formulation, experimental writing) in which the artist unmakes patriarchal structures by inscribing an other-than-Oedipal measure of desire, a desire coded as "feminine."[13] Stein's joyful deconstructive play with logical and linguistic structures uncovers regions of experience not normally represented in fiction and the semiotic body of language itself—a body we desire in ways having nothing to do with an Oedipal rhythm of anticipation and completion (mastery). Rather, as Jane Gallop puts it in describing "female" desire, we feel "sparks of pleasure ignited by contact at any moment along the line, not waiting for closure but enjoying the touching." As a result of such "sparks," "the impatient [Oedipal] economy aimed at finished meaning, products, theses, conclusions might just go up in smoke."[14] "A feminine textual body," says Hélène Cixous, "is recognized by the fact that it is always endless, . . . it doesn't stop, and it's this that very often makes the feminine text difficult to read. For we've learned to read books that basically pose the word 'end'."[15]

Stein's own description of her relation to language suggests this other nonpredictable, nonteleological rhythm of desire also: "I found myself plunged into a vortex of words, burning words, cleansing words, liberating words, feeling words, and the words were all ours and it was enough that we held them in our hands to play with them whatever you can play with is yours and this was the beginning of knowing . . . that we would play and play with words and the words were all ours all ours."[16] Here, Stein burns/bathes orgasmically in language, claiming language as her (our) own, in an eroticized linguistic space beyond paradox, beyond the sentences of the father. She ex-creates logical structures and "excretes" a different language, one written with and of her body. As readers of her texts, we undulate in a continuous interplay between union and separation, saying and unsaying, that invites us to wander through the text (enjoying the touching) rather than penetrating it to make it beget something.

Schweickart's second feminist reading scenario comes in here. Author and reader are two women engaged in intimate conversation, a setting she distinguishes from the politics of address underlying mainstream reader-response theory.

> It does not seem unreasonable to say that the theories of reading that currently dominate reader-response criticism . . . embody characteristically male approaches to the interaction between self and other and so between reader and text. These approaches proceed from a subjectivity that is strongly invested in maintaining firm ego boundary, hence the prominence of issues of partition and control . . . a characteristic feature of the masculine mode of reading [is] the inability to play host to fundamental difference.[17]

The feminist problematic, on the other hand, is "defined by the drive 'to connect' . . . the desire for relationship . . . and the desire for intimacy, up to and including a symbiotic merger with the other," rather than by the drive that is "implicit in the mainstream preoccupation with partition and control—namely, the drive to get it right,"[18] to master the text.

This postmodern invitation to connect and play blissfully with the mother tongue is another desirable feminist plot. To play in this way is to rejoin the mother as well as to merge with the other woman (lover, sister, friend) through whom we know ourselves. This plural, fluid experience of reciprocity and sympathetic response suggests a union in which self and other often are indistinguishable, where—as Betsy Wing puts it in her very useful gloss on the term "jouissance"— "total access, total participation, as well as total ecstasy are implied."[19] Instead of sense and thematic meaning (or "beauty," "instruction," and "passion" as Reid means these terms), in this postmodern feminist narrative Stein offers us access to a linguistic utopia where nothing is denied. Marianne DeKoven names this utopia as "limitless, dense, semantic plenitude, . . . writing as erotic celebration, as liberation from the strictures of hierarchical, sensible, monologistic order."[20] To hold words in our hands, to play with them, is enough; performing our jouissance becomes our telos. The critic's hands are full of something (always to be) desired.

Must Feminist Desire Always Be (Re) Implicated in an Impulse to De-sire?

These two feminist narratives of the reading process—the modernist judicial plot of struggle against the father; the postmodernist relational plot of "escape" from the law to an intersubjective space of perfect mutuality—clearly are productive and enabling narratives. They offer theoretical perspectives that allow us to validate Stein's struggle as a woman artist and to celebrate her difference from a patriarchal textual norm rather than trivialize and dismiss her writing as Reid's Oedipal expectations allow him to do. Yet these feminist accounts still are largely confined within a metanarrative logic that positions Stein as a woman writer in a particular way and structures meaning and desire (Stein's and our own) toward particular ends: confrontation (with the law) or emancipation (from the law). The limitation here being that if narrative privileges a certain form of evolution and resolution, then points of resistance to that evolution, elements that are contradictory, inexplicable, excessive—sites of difference—all may disappear. In seeking to reread Stein from a feminist perspective, to uncover and preserve her difference, have we merely replayed what Suleiman calls "the eternal Oedipal drama of transgression and the Law—a drama which always, ultimately, ends up maintaining the latter[?]"[21] In describing Stein's and our own enactment of these plots of struggle and escape have we again positioned ourselves in the same old story, reinscribing the Oedipal plot as the-effort-to-escape-it?

Unlike more conventionally mimetic works, avant-garde texts such as Stein's make it particularly clear that any act of interpretation—even a feminist one—rests on imposition of an interpretive code that, paradoxically, may condemn to silence aspects of the female difference that we as feminists seek to reveal and understand. Perhaps all interpretation, as Barthes suggests, involves a struggle between the arbitrariness of writing and the realist plot-making motivations that contain textual excess and make interpretation possible. A narrativized account of Stein's subversions of narrative logic would appear to leave the feminist critic embedded in an old bind: how to speak difference without returning through and to an "economy of the same."[22] Perhaps one way to begin to dislocate this theoretical impasse is to adopt a, by now, familiar feminist strategy—to double back on these two feminist reading plots so as to stir up what may have been silenced within them.[23]

What has been de-emphasized in the foregoing accounts is, first, the demand posed by Stein's texts, the pains and desires evoked in the reader who seeks to read Stein carefully. Second, what remains unacknowledged is the difference of the other woman with whom we are engaged in our intimate textual dialogue.[24] What, more precisely, is involved in a desire to "watch-think-seek the other in the other" as Cixous puts it in "The Laugh of the Medusa"—to seek nonoppositional or "fundamental" difference? If "woman becomes the possibility of a different idea" (Cixous), what does it mean to desire the other woman's difference from me rather than her congruence with me, especially with my desire to believe that we are all in this together, writing and reading the same plot? Perhaps feminists inevitably, no less than any other group, have difficulty desiring difference, which is to say, among other things, difficulty confronting the otherness of the other woman and hearing *her* desire without reducing it to *our* desire. We also have more of a stake in preserving the possibility that something different might speak. What risks are involved in affirming the necessity of assuming this position, this desire for difference? The difficulty of listening to the other woman's desire is at issue in and is uncovered by any effort to read Stein from a feminist perspective. This is so because her texts speak her (multiple) desire(s) so insistently and call into question the nature of our desire so thoroughly.

An Act of Acceptance and the Nature of the Demand

In *The Making of Americans*, the narrator quips, "Some say alright all but one way of loving, another says alright all but another way of loving. . . . I like loving, I like all the ways any one can have of having loving feeling in them. Slowly it has come to be in me that any way of being a loving one is interesting and not unpleasant to me."[25] I am tempted to take this statement as a rule of thumb for reading Stein, to assert that an act of acceptance as large-spirited as this one fundamentally is necessary. But part of this act of acceptance must also involve acknowledging the demands Stein's texts make of a reader.

To begin, much of Stein's writing requires an unusual act of attention on the reader's part and invites a level of intimacy perhaps unprecedented in fiction. On the one hand, we must agree to "not solve [the text] but be in it . . . to understand a thing means to be in contact with that thing," as Stein puts it in *The Geographical History of America*.[26] Rather than approaching the text with our critical distance intact, expecting it to yield a solution, we must relinquish a position of mastery, linked to the affirmation and preservation of meaning, and give ourselves to the text ("be in it") agreeing to wander where it takes us, submitting ourselves to language as Stein herself did.[27] On the other hand, we must attempt to read carefully, alertly, with the utmost attention to every detail rather than selecting some details as more important than others since, according to Stein, "reading word by word makes the writing that is not anything be something," and "everything is something," meaningful, worthy of attention.[28]

Reading Stein's texts, then, requires a paradoxical or split act of attention—a relaxed hyperattention, an unconscious hyperconsciousness, a borderline state of awareness a little like insomnia. We must remain alert yet flexible, able to hold several perspectives nearly simultaneously; we must become comfortable with sudden shifts in the levels of textual articulation, the sense of a world going in and out of focus, of words becoming meaningful and then fading from meaning as in this piece from *Tender Buttons:*

Orange In

Go lack go lack use to her.
Cocoa and clear soup and oranges and oatmeal.
Whist bottom whist close, whist clothes, woodling.
Cocoa and clear soup and oranges and oatmeal.
Pain soup, suppose it is question, suppose it is butter, real is, real is only, only excreate, only excreate a no since.
A no, a no since, a no since when, a no since when since, a no since when since a no since when since, a no since, a no since when since, a no since, no, a no since a no since, a no since, a no since.[29]

Here, lines two and four stand out clearly as objective descriptions of objects found in the world, in sharp contrast to lines one and three where the rhythm and sound of words predominate. The final lines hover in between sense and nonsense, between now and an indeterminate linguistic elsewhere, recording the speaker's desire to undo logical structures (excreate a no since) and to remain in the present (no since when = now) even as they fade at the end of the passage into sheer repetition of sound.

The act of attention called for here describes the perspective demanded of the writer: she or he must simultaneously submit to experience and language (cease being an active, unified subject), and pull back to structure, shape, and differentiate (regain subjectivity). We must, ourselves, fully realize the (her, our) desire for language in order to read Stein. This requires what Julia Kristeva calls a "double motion of adhesion and distancing," adhesion meaning a growing together of two normally separate entities, distancing meaning to create a gap or space between them. A desire for the signifier (adhesion to the rhythmic semiotic aspect of language) is curbed through the necessary imposition of a code (distance created through an interpretative framework).[30] For the reader to realize the desire for language, she or he must confront more directly the question of who is in control: reader, writer, or language itself. While these issues of adhesion, distancing, and control undoubtedly arise in any confrontation between reader and text, Stein pushes them to the foreground by inscribing within the space of the text itself sometimes abrupt oscillations between adhesion and distancing, between perceptual indiscriminacy and commonsense selection, between preoedipal and Oedipal acts of attention.

Finally, the rhythm and mode of apprehension called for here mime the problematic trajectory of female identity itself, an unstable oscillation between self and other, between merging (loss of self) and differentiation (constitution of a separate self) according to theorists such as Nancy Chodorow. Critical identity issues of intimacy with the other woman and differentiation from her are precisely what is at stake in reading Stein, as I hope to show.

Stein multiplies the ways in which a text constitutes the figure of the author and multiplies the number of positions available to us as readers in relation to a text, a series of postures, poses, roles, and positions of address as flexible as those she assumed. In order to

begin to suggest some of this multiplicity and to analyze more specifically the nature of the demand involved in reading Stein, I turn to
an examination of four of the many types of reading moments to be
encountered in her works—all of the while attempting to read word
by word and to scrutinize my desire in relation to these texts.

Reading Moment 1: Collaboration

Roland Barthes refers to the type of doubled reading method I have
described as reading with "application"—both to merge with the text
and to apply oneself to it diligently—and "transport"—to be carried
away in ecstasy by the text but also to separate oneself from it. He
argues that it is the method most suited to an encounter with any
postmodern text, as Stein herself anticipated. Barthes's method of
reading

> skips nothing; it weighs, it sticks to the text, . . . it is not logical
> extension that captivates it, the winnowing out of truths, but the
> layering [application in the sense of applique, or layering of ma-
> terial] of significance; as in the children's game of topping hands,
> the excitement comes not from a processive haste but from a kind
> of vertical din . . . it is at the moment when each (different) hand
> skips over the next (and not one *after* the other) that the hole, the
> gap, is created and carries off the subject of the game—the sub-
> ject of the text. . . . Read slowly, read *all* of a novel by Zola, and
> the book will drop from your hands; read fast, in snatches, some
> modern text, and it will become opaque, inaccessible to your
> pleasure: you want something to happen and nothing does, for
> *what happens to the language does not happen to the discourse:* what
> "happens" . . . occurs in the volume of the languages, in the ut-
> tering, not in the sequence of utterances.[31]

There are moments in reading Stein during which we experience the
kind of pleasure Barthes describes. This pleasure arises from the
"vertical din," the layering of languages that builds in volume (both
bulk and sound), creating a pileup of words that does not necessarily
add up in discourse. Pleasure arises from the multiplicity of languages colliding with one another; in Stein's words "a single image
is not splendor." At these times, the pulse of the text—its rhythm

and speed—and my pulse feel in sync (like Jeff and Melanctha in their good moments; like Ida who learns to dance with Andrew). I conspire with the text; we breathe together.

In this passage from *Ida*, for instance, the typology of the text simulates the game of "topping hands" that Barthes describes. We are poised in the in-between, the gap created when words and voices (including our own) call and respond, are coming and going. This is the point; we are part of the joke, and we enjoy it:

> Who is careful.
> Well in a way Ida is.
> She lives where she is not.
> Not what.
> Not careful
> Of course not
> Who is careful
> That is what they said
> And the answer was
> Ida said
> Oh yes, careful
> Oh yes, I can almost cry
> Ida never did Oh yes.
> They all said oh yes
> And for three days I have not seen her. That is what somebody did say. Really somebody has said. For three days I have not seen her.
> Nobody said Ida went away.
> She was there Ida was
> So was her husband. So was everybody.[32]

The "way" that Ida is careful is that she is "not careful" (not full of care, not deliberate), just as she lives where she is not (careful) which is why nobody has seen her even though "she was there"—perhaps a warning about dependence on the visual, about expecting things to be what they seem or to stay fixed. Does Ida remain "there" because nobody says she went away or is she "not there" because someone says "I have not seen her"? Where is the locus of narrative authority, in the "I," in the "they," in the "somebody"? Where is the ground of Ida's reality? Among what temporal and logical dimensions are we floating?

The pleasure of *Ida* is the pleasure involved in the game of Chinese boxes—the "staging of an appearance-as-disappearance."[33] We become confused or irritated as readers only when we seek to stop the game, to fix Ida in one place by making her visible and coherent. As is true of Lucy Church Amiably, Ida "made many admirable reflections." Pleasure comes from multiplying the reproductions of copies, from generating more excess, more roles, not from seeking the original that would fix Ida's identity and stop the game. As Stein puts it in *Lucy Church Amiably*, "let me see who can see these replace those." What we are to "see" is the process of "painting on glass," a process in which copies reflect only copies. "When this you see," Stein promises, "you can marry me," join her in her affectionate play.[34] Although we must reflect (think seriously about what Stein is up to) we must not become refractory. We must admire but not wonder too much about what it all points to.

Another way to describe this particular textual pleasure is to say that Stein takes us through the pleasurable overload of just-one-more. Just when we think we have reached the limit (of Lucy Church's transformations, of Ida's comings and goings, of the possible permutations of Stein's insistent style), she adds one more and perhaps again just one more loop, taking us beyond where we thought she/we could go. The experience of just-one-more is to be distinguished from narrative suspense, which always works on the anticipation of closure expressed as significance. It is also to be distinguished from limitlessness, as in DeKoven's "limitless, dense semantic plenitude." Limitlessness is not as pleasurable as the tease, the anticipation of the end, and the realization of the gratuitous one more. It is a special kind of excess, a hyperbolic excess, an excess that throws us beyond . . .

Reading Moment 2: Watchful Distance

Stein's works as a whole express a strong theatrical or performative element. Celebratory, vaudevillian works such as *Ida* and *Lucy Church Amiably* in particular invite an active response from the reader, perhaps because they are such mobile restless texts. We collaborate in making the game go, in coperforming our jouissance, as Schweickart's feminist model of reading stresses. Yet there are moments in reading Stein during which an active role seems unsuitable. These texts or parts of texts seem to require no response, to demand no understanding. They invite contemplation, a certain watchful distance, not interpretation or identification or collaboration. They may be curiously affectless, emotionally uninflected, or they may describe an instant of slight emotional weight. They may border on being unreadable. Yet they are not indifferent; they do not refuse the reader. Rather they evoke a feeling of repletion or repose as if already full (not needing just one more) or merely contentedly self-sufficient. These texts offer a different kind of plentitude, a pleasure involving receptivity, a relaxation of the reader's desire in the pleasure of the other woman's.

The one line poem "Dining," in *Tender Buttons*, strikes me as such a reading moment: "Dining is west."[35] This statement is not profoundly meaningful (it does not appear to be a definition of anything), nor does it inspire linguistic play. I don't feel compelled to respond to it; in fact, I find delight in its self-assured eccentricity, its wholeness, its minimalism. Perhaps I desire it more because it appears not to require (desire) my response—it does not wish to engage me in conversation as Schweickart's model suggests it should.

At other times, the text opens on small private moments, instants in which intangibles are confessed, as in this excerpt from "A Long Dress": "Where is the serene length, it is there and a dark place is not a dark place, only a white and red are black, only a yellow and green are blue, a pink is scarlet, a bow is every color. A line distinguishes it. A line just distinguishes it."[36] *Tender Buttons*, as whole, might be said to confess small private desires evoked by the beauty of a bow in every color bisecting a dress, by the perception that yellow and blue mingle to make green, by the recognition that what culture considers a dark empty place (that which the serene length of the dress hides) is neither dark nor empty but another place of serenity. There is joy evoked by "a feather trimmed by the light," by simple, exquisitely subtle contrasts of texture and hue.

Often the perception that the speaker articulates is more concealed, not as clearly apparent to the reader as it is in the above examples:

More
An elegant use of foliage and grace and a little piece of white
cloth and oil. Wondering so winningly in several kinds of oceans
is the reason that makes red so regular and enthusiastic. The
reason that there is more snips are the same shining very colored
rid of no round color.[37]

Recognitions such as these are not quite recoverable (interpretable)
in terms of a public code. They are, in Kathleen Fraser's apt description, "not yet located in the historic design of literature" since they
issue from the "deep space of the mind where harm cannot enter,
where the true sorting out begins,"[38] the space that Nancy K. Miller
evocatively calls "the place of production that marks the spinner's
attachment to her web."[39] In these reading moments "we hear a
woman piecing it together, catching some moments of babble or per-
plexity or unidentifiable bliss."[40] Our pleasure as readers comes from
watching the process of another mind confronting the world through
language and trying to sort it out or to speak her desire. We can
recognize this process as important to the other, and yet not understand precisely why or what meaning she is trying to untangle or
produce. We participate to the degree that we reconstruct the process
of this other finding and performing *her* desire.

In the following passage from *A Long Gay Book*, for example, we
listen to a voice stretching to distinguish and articulate some corre-
spondence or insight, some joy or subtle distinction that lies, again,
in-between:

A line is the presence of a particular sugar that is not sugary
but splendid and so bland, so little and so rich, so learned and
so particular, so perfectly sanguine and so reared.
To indicate more wall flowers than there is paper, to indicate
more houses than there are houses, to indicate nothing more is
not an urgent and particular privilege, it is selected and if it is
not wanted is there any reason for losing anything. There is
what there is by the raking of the felt hats.[41]

The perception that the speaker is struggling to articulate grows out
of a negation, a sugar that is not sugary—not the essence of what
we have always taken sugar to be. "Definition" proceeds through a

series of paradoxes: this particular (singular) sugar is both splendid (exceptional, magnificent) and bland (mild, unexceptional), both little (insignificant or modest) and rich (full of, abundant), both learned (having acquired public knowledge) and particular (privately unique), both perfectly sanguine (calm, cheerful) and so reared (agitated). This sugar and the method used to "indicate" it exist in a space of paradox and excess beyond logical categories. As the second paragraph suggests, it is the excess of pattern, the one more flower than the wall paper can contain, as well as the extra substance and space, the one more house than the houses that are counted. Yet from another perspective—the speaker's—the particular sugar is not extra; it is the thing itself. This other perspective is calmly and deliberately chosen although it may be the "not wanted" or the rejected perspective from another point of view. The final sentence affirms the speaker's perspective by bestowing a tactile reality, a substance, on that which may appear to have none: "there is [substance] what there is [is substance] [known] by the raking [feeling, moving one's hands across] of the felt hats [both the material and the process of feeling]." As in the other passages described above, here we are not so much asked to share the speaker's "particular sugar" as to reconstruct and value the process by which she finds, names, and celebrates it.

Are we willing to listen very carefully to the other woman's desire, to her moments of unidentifiable bliss? What else (beyond *our* pleasure in *her* pleasure) is at stake in listening with this degree of closeness, in applying ourselves this intimately to the text? Luce Irigaray's comments on the position of the analyst in relation to the analysand are useful in beginning to answer this question: "Either the unconscious [here, the desire of the other woman, the difference of the other woman] is nothing but what has already been heard by you . . . or the unconscious is desire [difference] which attempts to speak itself, and, as analysts [feminists] you have to listen without excluding [read word by word in Stein's terms]. However much this listening to everything might bring about callings into question of your desire . . . whatever risk of your death might ensue." To listen without excluding involves the risk of loss of identity, loss of power and control, perhaps the risk of alienation or even death, according to Irigaray. If analysis [here feminism] is not to be a "process of adapting the patient [here female difference, desire] to some reigning order of discourse [an economy of the same], it must risk unseating the analyst [the feminist]."[42]

Reading Moment 3: Claustrophobia

If reading moments such as the ones I have described thus far do not seem to pose the extreme degree of risk that Irigaray describes perhaps this is because one hears in them both the specificity of the other's desire and something familiar, what we have already heard within ourselves. My own desire is thus not called into question; it is, in fact, once again reciprocal—our desire. However, Stein does present us with texts beyond those that invite active collaboration, and those that involve what I have termed a pleasurable relaxation of identity occasioned by a willingness to submit to and overhear the other's desire. In these other moments, the loss imposed by our attempt to listen without excluding (to read word by word) does not feel pleasurable since here we confront the discomfort and not the pleasure of our own loss of control. In these moments, we are reminded that the preoedipal space of jouissance and merging with the (m)other is also the space of overpowerment by the (m)other, (ecstasy comes from the Greek meaning "a being put out of its place"). Here, we are pleasured to an unpleasurable point of excess, stuffed and glutted, not collaborating in performing *our* desire, not able to gain the distance that would allow us to enjoy seeing the other perform *her* desire.[43] To read word by word means to reenact this other side of jouissance as well, a side not acknowledged in the feminist reading plots elaborated above.

Almost any Stein text might occasion this response of overpowerment in a reader if she or he reads it for too long. The demand involved in listening this closely, in reading word by word, becomes unbearable after a certain duration; the intimacy required feels claustrophobic, and we put the text down in order to re-gain control. We choose our desire and refuse the other woman's. We do not wish to hear her speak. Our desire is not reciprocal at this point, but prioritized in favor of ourselves. Certainly this refusal must be acknowledged in any discussion of what is involved in listening to (reading) the other woman, in seeking the other in the other. It must stand for the ambiguity and instability of identity itself (including feminist identity), for the terror posed by jouissance: "a permanent threat against identity's mastery and ultimately its stability" according to Julia Kristeva in *Desire in Language*.[44] Our refusal also suggests the gap between ourselves and the other woman, our inability to ever listen fully to her, to know what she wants, to share her struggle completely, to believe that we can speak for her or that she always speaks for us. This gap is painful to acknowledge, ideologically and personally.

In addition to matters of sheer duration, certain Stein texts—often labeled unreadable—pose the demand much more insistently than others. The issue of readability has always troubled critics of Stein. Although few now dismiss her writing as nonsense, her texts do continue to be categorized primarily according to the degree to which they are interpretable. As just one instance of this tendency, Marianne DeKoven writes "It seems to me the most credible defense [of Stein] is one that distinguishes between what deserves admiration and what perhaps does not." Excluded by her are those texts which go "too far" and defy the "sanction of all literature," readability.[45] Having made a commitment to take Stein seriously, and aided by feminist and postmodernist methodologies, we have learned to read many of Stein's works. So prolific was she that many remain to be read. And perhaps some works will remain inaccessible or "unreadable" texts whose demand most readers cannot meet.

But rather than consigning these excluded texts to a category called unreadable, thereby bracketing them from consideration, we might value them precisely for their incomprehensibility since we are thus preserving the possibility that something radically different might speak, or is speaking outside our historical ken of readability (readability being always a complex and historically variable matter—unreadable to whom?). Might it be possible to value these texts as objects of knowledge, a means of displaying or even displacing the limits of what is currently possible, licit, or readable? This is the value Kristeva assigns to poetic language:

Faced with this poetic language that defies knowledge, many of us are rather tempted to leave our shelter to deal with literature only by miming its meanderings, rather than positing it as an object of knowledge. It is probably necessary to be a woman . . . not to renounce theoretical reason but to compel it to increase its power by giving it an object beyond its limits.

The object, or the unreadable text, may reveal to the interpreter "the unknown of his theory and permit the constitution of a new theory."[46] Perhaps it is a perspective on unreadability that might allow us to glimpse a limit to our current theories? Entertaining this possibility rather than consigning some Stein texts to a category called unreadable could give rise to the following questions: what are we refusing when we label a text unreadable? What is the nature of the demand posed by these texts? What limits to our current feminist theories might these unreadable texts allow us to glimpse?

Many Many Women, written in Stein's insistent style, poses such an extreme psychic and perceptual demand on the reader that it verges on unreadability. I quote the following lengthy passage in order to give a sense of the extremity of the demand. In order to really feel the "overload" occasioned by the text one would need to quote several pages of this eighty-page work:

> Each one is one and is mentioning something of some such thing. Each one has been one and is mentioning something of some such thing. Each one is one and is mentioning something of being like any other one. Each one is one and is mentioning having been like any other one. Each one is one. Each one is one and is mentioning having been, is mentioning being that one. Each one is one. Each one is that one, the one that one is. Each one is one, each one is mentioning such a thing. Each one is mentioning something, each one is mentioning having been mentioning something. Each one is one. Each one is mentioning having been that one.
>
> One was one and was mentioning something, mentioning having been that one and in a way that one was that one. That one was one. That one had been one and in a way that one was that one. That one had not been really mentioning quite that thing, had not been quite mentioning having been that one.
>
> That one being that one had been that one. That one being that one was mentioning that thing was mentioning having been that one, was mentioning being that one.
>
> That one being that one was one needing something, was one needing something to have been that one. That one being that one was needing something, was one needing something to be that one. That one was not that one. That one was mentioning

that thing. That one was needing something to be that one. That one was mentioning that thing, was mentioning that that one was something to be that.[47]

Here, insistence becomes "unsuccessful"—may strike us as merely repetition—because we have difficulty sensing the modulations of difference within sameness that the speaker is articulating. We experience only the sameness (or overpowerment by the one); we cannot sufficiently hear the difference, which is to say we have no way to insert ourselves into and construct our difference from the text. The excess here is not the pleasurable abundance of just-one-more, but, rather, an overload that stuns us by a sheer density of language. The perceptual indiscriminacy of the preoedipal state becomes an unpleasurable loss of control. The text is so full (of itself) that it feels completely empty.

Many Many Women is an extended meditation on sameness and difference, a compression of the discourse of self and other. As the above passage suggests, it concerns the ways in which we attempt to speak our differences, our individual identities, by constructing a separate self through language ("in mentioning being one"). Yet here, the saying self is overcome by the voice who describes the saying, collapsing all ones together. Put another way, we as readers have difficulty perceiving the subtle modulations of difference between the "one" who is a singular one and the "one" who is mentioning being like every other one, among the "one" who has been one, "that one" who is *now* one, and the particular way in which that one *is* one in distinction from the way that other ones are ones. We cannot see the distinction between one way of "mentioning being one" and another way of being one, even though this distinction is precisely what we must see in order to retain "one"-ness and not fall into an indiscriminate "oneness." Here, all "ones" (all of the many women described in this text) collapse into the same "one"—the speaker herself. The "something" that we, as readers, "need" in order to "be one" (to maintain our identity) is *not* to be one (with the text, with the other woman), but, rather, to be the other, the second. In this case, we refuse the text's invitation to merge (into oneness), what Schweickart calls the drive to connect; we refuse the other to whom we are in danger of losing ourselves.

Our refusal of the text's demand thus stems from a psychic incapacity based on fear of the loss of identity. Kristeva argues that the desire to give meaning and to gain distance from a text, arises precisely to protect us from such a loss: " . . . to give a political meaning to something is perhaps only the ultimate consequence of the epistemological attitude which consists simply of the desire to give meaning. This attitude is not innocent, but, rather, is rooted in the speaking subject's need to reassure himself of his image and identity faced with an object."[48] Elsewhere, she speaks of a Western cultural obsession with meaning that is evidence of an "unfitness" for jouissance, a psychic incapacity or unwillingness on the reader's part "to shatter his own judging consciousness in order to grant passage through it to [the preoedipal semiotic] drive."[49]

The "unfitness" of which Kristeva speaks may also involve a cognitive or perceptual incapacity (the eye behind the I) that needs to be considered. Using Nietzsche as support, Barthes argues that "we are today incapable of conceiving a true science of becoming. 'We are not subtle enough to perceive that probably absolute flow of becoming. . . . A tree is a new thing at every instant; we affirm the form because we do not seize the subtlety of an absolute moment.'"[50] Stein's project, in part, consists of trying to expand the perceptual faculty in a way that would allow us to "seize the subtlety of an absolute moment," to affirm a flow of becoming rather than a form. The insistent style of *Many Many Women* in particular is premised on a reader's being able to read word by word, (to seize the subtlety of an absolute moment), yet we must acknowledge that there are instances when we cannot cognitively meet the demand; in Nietzsche's terms, "we are not subtle enough."

Finally, Fredric Jameson's description of postmodern "hyperspace" suggests a way to capture the sense of perceptual or cognitive incapacity that prevents a reader from fully encountering Stein's most difficult texts. Following Jean Baudrillard, Jameson uses the term "hyperspace" to refer to "something like a mutation in built space itself which transcends the capacities of the individual human body to locate itself, to organize its immediate surroundings, perceptually and cognitively to map its position in a mappable external world."[51] Hyperspace could also refer to a mutation in textual space of the kind found in *Many Many Women*. In this text, as I've suggested, we lose ourselves, cannot map our coordinates as the eye (I) jumps and does not know where it is. Hyperspace may be viewed as a "mutation in the object unaccompanied as yet by an equivalent mutation in the subject; we do not as yet possess the perceptual equipment to match this new hyperspace."[52] The unreadability of some of Stein's texts suggests this same kind of mutation in the textual object unaccompanied by a corresponding change in our abilities as reading subjects (even if we identify ourselves as feminist reading subjects). Cognitively, even ontologically, we would have to become other than we are in order to comprehend fully this discourse of the other.

Reading Moment 4: Resolute Privacy

The inverse of a text whose demand we must refuse is a text that appears to refuse us. *A Novel of Thank You* is an example of a resolutely private text. Like *Many Many Women*, it has received almost no critical attention, perhaps because it is among Stein's most hermetic works. The tone of the novel is involuted and brooding; the speaker in it appears involved with a private pain, not revolving to encompass a joyous public celebration. One has a sense throughout of a mind continually returning to facets of a painful subject and obsessively wishing to avoid it:

> To be worried whether to be worried about whether whether whether to be worried whether and they went to go. Whether they went to go. Whether they went to go. They went to go whether they went to go and repeat easily whether they went to go.[53]

This passage captures something of the overall tone of the text as well as its stammering rhythm of fitful halts and starts and its nervous indecisiveness (to be worried whether to be worried).

The novel opens with a question, an enigma, "How many more than two are there."[54] In most narratives, an enigma initiates the reader's engagement with the text as a whole and sets up anticipation of a climax and resolution. In *A Novel of Thank You*, however, the enigma is kept in constant suspension. The central "preoccupations" to which the text gravitates—words and phrases suggesting attachment and those relating to separation recur repeatedly as do numbers and naming—are never fully represented or developed. Rather, they are deferred and blurred as the text obsessively slides toward, moves away from, and circles around a missing referent—the answer to the initial question. Significantly, the most consistent stylistic feature in the text is pronouns lacking clear specifiable antecedents, suggesting the speaker's desire to both disclose (it) and to conceal (it). The speaker warns us to "Not ask what is it because it is it," advises us to "consider a novel a novel of it," (a novel of the missing referent,) explains quite clearly that "the difference between a novel and a story" is that in a novel (this novel) "no one said it," suggests that this is "a novel of thank you and not about it," and overtly states that "we can easily be careful it is not by their names that they are called." Numbers are repeated frequently also—especially combinations of one, two, and three—that answer the novel's initial question (how many more than two are there) and at the same time contribute nothing to our understanding, our ability to resolve the enigma.

A reader's expectations of decipherment are nowhere more strongly raised than at the end of a novel. If the speaker has refused to develop, explain, or even to name the enigma that she opens at the outset, she again refuses at the end. In the final two parts of *A Novel of Thank You*, the speaker does not more than suggest a movement away from the central preoccupations that have been raised in the text. Chapter 3, the final chapter in part II, ends with a question "what is it" and in part III, the novel's final section, the speaker suggests that the "subject" of the novel has been concluded already "We are not entirely occupying ourselves with an entirely different matter."

In a resolutely private text such as *A Novel of Thank You*, we are asked to maintain a critical distance that we may desire not to maintain. We are willing, even eager, to listen without excluding, but the text excludes what it is we most want to listen to: the revelation of the enigma with which the text appears to be so involved. However, the speaker insists upon her privacy by withholding the desire or pain, the story we wish she would confess, name, or explain. Our desire in the intimate textual conversation is for greater intimacy, greater self-revelation, a demand that the speaker refuses, thereby frustrating our desire. It appears easier for us to sympathize with the other woman's struggle, to defend her, to collaborate in her celebration, or to take pleasure in her own pleasure, than it does to allow the privacy she wants to establish or maintain.

Both claustrophobic texts, whose demand we refuse, and resolutely private texts, which refuse our demand, involve us in a power imbalance with respect to the other woman. Our desire as readers to structure our experience of the text must necessarily interact with (and in these instances come into conflict with) the power of the text (the other) to structure (or destructure) our experience. In these cases we are not in a relation of perfect reciprocity, engaged in an intimate conversation or celebration as Schweickart's feminist reading model has it. Nor are we united in a joint struggle against the father, with me as a feminist reader testifying on behalf of the woman writer. Indeed, my desire to maintain control in the case of *Many Many Women* or to get at the "truth" of the text, to uncover its enigma, in the case of *A Novel of Thank You*, may well put me in the Oedipal camp.

Desires for Difference(s)

The task of women remains . . . to inscribe not so much difference in itself as a multiplicity of differences [thus] creating the conditions whereby the future of difference will no longer mean a difference of futures.
— Josette Féral, "The Powers of Difference"

In textual instances such as those I have just described, we are negotiating different needs and demands, our different desires. It is a space of difference we should hold open (for now) in order to pursue our differences diligently. *Diligence* means constant careful effort and comes from the root *diligere:* "to esteem highly," "to be apart," "to choose." In choosing to be apart in order to consider our differences, we esteem diversity within and between ourselves and the other woman; we listen carefully without excluding.

By consciously subverting the aesthetic categories, logical structures and cultural norms on which mimetic fiction—in particular the nineteenth-century novel—depends, Stein exposes the degree to which these categories are constructed and not natural. Such an exposure opens room to explore the ways in which the tendency to narrativize imposes itself as a mechanism of coherence—which may silence difference by engaging the subject in specific positions of meaning and desire. In what follows, I claim a specific aesthetic and ideological value for this process of deconstruction. Stein also extends current conceptions of what may be considered appropriately novelistic; like many postmodern writers, she contributes new perspectives to our still-evolving definitions of what novels may be in the twentieth century. My subsequent analyses of Stein's efforts to move beyond mimetic norms and forms in fiction also implicitly promote the value of what Stein adds to the possibilities of the genre. Finally, I would claim that there is a value in demonstrating the limits of what is currently readable (re-writable). It is precisely the value that Kristeva finds in certain avant-garde or "limit" texts: the object may reveal to the subject the unknown of her or his theory and leave open the way for the construction of new theories.

One of Stein's values for feminism arises from the fact that in encountering her works we open a space in which differences—including fear of these differences as well as the joy involved in the play of our differences—might be acknowledged and analyzed. Stein's works remind us of the textual pleasures involved in the "drive to connect," of the dialogic potential of feminist theory. They also stand as a reminder that we cannot always know the other's desire and that we may not always speak for or with the other woman who we seek to explain from a feminist perspective. To confront the other without compromising her difference must remain a goal. To the extent that Stein's most difficult texts serve as a challenge to this goal, they warn us against premature foreclosures of what feminist theory currently is and can do. Stein's "unreadable" or limit texts may help to reveal the "unknown" of our feminist theories, leaving open the way for the construction of new theories.

At the least, they help to suggest the necessity for and the difficulty of moving beyond the oppositions implicit in the feminist narratives of confrontation and escape I have analyzed here. Such a movement is necessary in order to seek more subtle and inclusive theories of reading capable of taking into account nonoppositional differences among women. Such a movement is also difficult, first because narrative is a persistent and powerful mode of structuration that tends to retextualize itself in critical practices and institutional discourses (as my subsequent encounters with Stein's texts sometimes show). Difficult, also, because these feminist narratives of the reading process are enabling narratives that have grown out of real material necessities. In this chapter, I have focused on the questions of what comes before and remains after the position of (feminist) critic has been assumed. This strategy suggests only one place to begin in efforts to propose new feminist models of reading nonmimetic works: with attention to the ways in which narrative as a structure itself may act to obscure differences; to ask within what "plots" are current feminist theories of reading and writing enclosed, in what ways have these "plots" prevented us from understanding the "complexity of our desires in front of works" such as Stein's?

Chapter 2

Curving Thought, Making Nonsense: The Death of Realism in *A Long Gay Book*

As was true of other modernist writers, Gertrude Stein's early narrative innovations developed from a quarrel with the philosophic and aesthetic assumptions of the nineteenth century, assumptions that find their fullest expression in the classic realist novel. "Between birth and fourteen," she writes, "I was there to begin to kill what was not dead, the nineteenth century which was so sure of evolution and prayers and esperanto and their ideas."[1] Couched in the rhetoric of a modernist manifesto, this statement recalls Ezra Pound or D. H. Lawrence's heady pronouncements about the need to shatter the outmoded assumptions of the previous century. Yet in Stein's case, the motivations for and so the nature of this murderous desire differed in important ways from the revisionary impulses of male modernists. For her it was a matter of killing the nineteenth century or being killed by it; her effort to escape nineteenth-century social and literary scripts was not just aesthetically motivated but was personally inspired as well. It grew out of a discovery of and a need to repudiate the ideological agendas and power imbalances replicated within these inherited forms, a discovery that inspired the search for new, more capacious, forms.

Stein's production of enunciative strategies in response to those literary and cultural constraints that make speaking difficult or impossible for women allies her project with those of other women writers whose tactics for confronting, evading, or transcending male authority feminist critics have been mapping for at least a decade. This has involved an effort to uncover the historical, ideological, literary, and social determinants that shape how and why particular events of rewriting occur, an effort arising from the recognition that

representation is implicated in the various relations of power operating within larger cultural systems. Many critics have concluded that
the very specificity of women's writing resides in the fact that it "is
in the business of transforming discursive material that in its untrans-
formed state leaves a woman no place from which to speak, or nothing to say."[2] Yet while Stein's revisionary project may in part emerge
from a similar recognition of women's cultural status and may reflect
a similar desire to escape this cultural positioning, it also differs in
significant ways from those revisions of realism enacted by Virginia
Woolf, or Jean Rhys, or Dorothy Richardson. Not the least of this
difference is the radicalness of the strategies Stein evolved. Hers is
what Luce Irigaray would call an "unparalleled interrogation," one
that not only transforms the categories of realism but, in the process,
displaces and exhausts them and so moves beyond modernist principles as well.

Stein's early years as a writer—her artistic "birth to fourteen"—
were marked by a sustained and systematic investigation of realist
forms. Her first three novels reflect a confrontation and a growing
dissatisfaction with three dominant genres of nineteenth-century fiction. *Things as They Are* is in the tradition of the novel of manners;
Three Lives draws on the naturalist tradition; and *The Making of Americans* shares elements with the family chronicle. As Marianne
DeKoven, Jayne L. Walker, Janice Doane, and Harriet Chessman all
have discussed to varying degrees, during this early period Stein
moved through a gradual displacement of realist principles, writing
within conventional forms—and the ideological agendas they imply—and simultaneously pushing against the limits of these forms
in a search for new literary and social scripts, oscillating between a
position of adherence and a position of critique in each new work.
Janice Doane, for example, demonstrates how Stein begins from a
position of identification with patriarchal certainty in *Things as They
Are*, where, in the figure of Adele, language and rational thought are
considered "infallible instruments for clarifying complex emotional
and moral issues" and moves toward an implicit critique of this position in *Three Lives*, which, in various ways, suggests the limits of
common sense instrumental discourse as a medium for interpersonal
communication.[3] Following Edward Said's observation that "the
novel's beginning premise is paternal," Chessman notes in Stein's
progressive disruption of narrative's linear teleology a growing cri-

tique of the concept of author as parental authority, repressor of female sexuality and autonomy. In "Melanctha"—Stein's "ambiguous farewell to the forms of authority proclaimed by the nineteenth century"—the oscillation between adherence and critique is especially apparent, disturbing the narrative structure of the text as the narrator simultaneously relates and resists relating Melanctha's life story. This struggle eventually leads to a rejection of traditional family forms inspired by the discovery of other configurations of intimacy, configurations based on a nonhierarchic, dialogic, sexual/textual model.[4] Stein's resistance to the linear momentum of realist narrative, a momentum that continued to lead to the same conclusion—death of the female and the interdiction of desire, as Doane succinctly puts it—makes these early texts increasingly circular and self-reflexive, and, thus, increasingly distanced from the tenets of realism. One aspect of this self-reflexive tendency is dramatically demonstrated in *The Making of Americans*, which through its progressive deviation from the conventional expectation that a novel's structure must match the succession of events it narrates, eventually floats free of the readerly expectation that it will narrate a story at all, coming to rest in the continuous present where momentum is short-circuited by a narrative voice that begins again and again, tracing and retracing its own coming into being in language.

Michel Picheux has said that the transformation of dominant discursive formations often is enabled by a process of "dis-identification" in which "ideology does not disappear but operates on and against itself through the overthrow-rearrangement of the complex of ideological formations."[5] Bruce Kawin describes a similar process at work in certain radical literary texts, though he does not link it explicitly to a model of ideology critique. New modes of writing, he says, arise not just when innovative authors become dissatisfied with the limitations imposed on them by existing narrative methods, as Stein clearly was, but when these authors arrive at their new methods by dramatizing the limits of the old form from within existing structures so that the new form appears to create itself out of the exhaustion of the old.[6] Literary change through radical internal disruption is possible because any genre conceals a "principle of contamination or impurity" that the genre—or in this case the discursive formation of realism—must repress in order to constitute itself but that it cannot wholly contain. This "axiom of impossibility" of "participation without membership" inhabits genre as a potential site of disruption for generic or logical limits, that which could confound the sense, order, and reason upon which a given genre depends.[7] The process of foregrounding this principle of "contamination" or nonmembership is perhaps a precondition for the transformation of any ideology; certainly it is a strategy of those who must live within but exist outside of the power structures of a culture.

During this early period of her career Stein worked to transform the discursive formation underlying realism through a process of disidentification with and thus displacement of the enunciative position from which the tenets of realism have been propounded. Each return to and departure from the conventions of realism, each beginning again and again, marks a more extreme interrogation and a progressive waning of realist aesthetics as Stein discovers the limits of realist conventions and increasingly gestures toward what these limits cannot comprehend, causing them to operate on and against themselves. I want to explore more fully the dynamics of this process as they operate in *A Long Gay Book*, a text that has tended to be read as just another example of Stein's transition from the insistent to the lively words style, one that presents ideas and stylistic strategies that find their most complete expression in *Tender Buttons*. I want to argue, however, that *A Long Gay Book* bears sustained attention not only because it is formally interesting in its own right but because it is crucial to an understanding of Stein's artistic evolution during this period. *A Long Gay Book* marks at once Stein's most thorough return to and most radical departure from realist principles, a culmination on structural, logical, and thematic levels of her decade-long process of disidentifying with dominant social and literary scripts. In different terms than *The Making of Americans* it reflects Stein's simultaneous farewell to both realism and modernism, pointing the novel in a direction that is perhaps best understood as postmodernism.

Stein enters this period of her career with a desire to extend the investigation of character she had begun in the early narratives. As she tells us in "The Gradual Making of *The Making of Americans*,"

I always have listened to the way everybody has to tell what they have to say . . . I began to get enormously interested in hearing how everybody said the same thing over and over again . . . until finally if you listened with great intensity you could hear it rise and fall and tell all that there was inside them, not so much by the actual words they said or the thoughts they had but the movement of their thoughts and words endlessly the same and endlessly different.[8]

Her interest in hearing how everybody says the same thing develops into an interest in hearing how everybody says everything, and Stein eventually conceives the plan of "describ[ing] really describ[ing] every kind of human being that ever was or is or would be living." "My idea here was to write the life of every individual that could possibly live on earth . . . to realize absolutely every variety of human experience that it was possible to have every type every style and nuance." "I was sure that in a kind of way the enigma of the universe could be solved."[9] In A Long Gay Book Stein attempts this complete description of "every kind of human being that ever was or is or would be living" by imagining a vast typology of typical human behaviors (thinking, disliking, being angry, etc.) within which someone is placed through elaborate gradations and variations on the same key term. Thus some are angry, some are not angry, some are almost angry, some would be angry if . . . , etc. As is true of other texts from this period, here Stein minimizes many of the conventional features of the classic realist text—in particular those features that contribute most directly to the text's mimetic intentions (a detailed setting, description, plot elaboration, etc.)—in order to focus more completely on others, in this case, the many types of human personalities that exist in the world, which the narrator asserts, "anyone can know by watching."

As far as Stein's intentions in this text then—in certain crucial respects—A Long Gay Book returns to realism with a vengeance, logically extending naturalism's avowal that realism was to be in art what positivism was in philosophy. This impulse perhaps finds its most complete nineteenth-century expression in Flaubert's desire that literature become a quasi-scientific anatomy, a project that Stein might be said to carry forward here. Underlying this program are a number of assumptions that, taken together, constitute the discursive formation of the nineteenth century. These include the belief that a positively determinable world external to the world of fiction exists, that it can be unproblematically represented in language, and that fiction's

business is to record this world "as it is." Since the world is assumed
to be finite, integrated, orderly, sensible, complete, coherent, logically
causal, and hierarchically organized, any obscurity derives only from
its vast diversity and complexity—which science and philosophy are
in the business of mapping. The truthful description of the world
depends on the comprehensiveness and rationality of its description.
Thus Flaubert says, "The leading character of our century is its historical sense. This is why we have to confine ourselves to relating the
facts—but all the facts" or of his method in *Madame Bovary* " . . . aesthetically, I desired . . . to plumb [ordinary existence's] very depths.
Therefore I plunged into it heroically, into the midst of all its minutiae,
accepting everything, telling everything, depicting everything."[10] The
right procedures for accomplishing this exhaustive referentially motivated program are those of mimesis—"the material transcription of
the empirically verifiable data . . . of the physical senses"[11] and the
presentation of this data in such a way as to create the illusion that
the text is a mirror of the material world. Realism does not simply
express the empiricist urge to assemble data exhaustively; it must
assemble this data into a meaningful totality—hence the importance
of closure in realist novels, the point at which all potential contradictions, all challenges to the possibility of constructing this totalized
picture, are resolved. As Christopher Nash puts it in his extremely
valuable book on the antirealist tradition in fiction, "a contribution
distinguishing Realism is its special appearance of presenting the
infinity and complexity of ordinary human life and of still managing
to . . . resolve it all into order. . . . It aims through description to restore
and affirm its readers' sense of the importance of the known and of
its knowability."[12] That is, realism presents not just facts but also a
notion of truth, asserting that interpretation and conceptualization
are proper activities, that it is indeed possible to be truthful and
accurate, to make sense of what is (to solve the enigma of the universe). This then also implies a view of the subject as coherent, rational, and, as Catherine Belsey notes, fixable "as an element in a
given system of differences which is human nature and the world of
human experience [where] all possible action is an endless repetition
of 'normal' familiar action."[13] Realism's interest in the typical (the
normal, the probable) is based on the assumption that the normal is
also typical in the sense that it may be generalized and universalized—
in Stein's terms, formed into a typology of all those who are living

regardless of time, place, material circumstances, etc. Finally, realist texts most often adopt a declarative mode, one purporting to impart objective knowledge impartially and rationally in a tone that is firm, clear, assertive, and detached—in the case of the narrator of *A Long Gay Book*, a perspective from an olympian height.

Stein's initial aspirations in *A Long Gay Book* are to write a declarative text, to order and fix the world (and her place in it) according to a vast typology of human behavior. This, as I said, is an unparalleled interrogation in the sense of its extremity—here realism is pushed to an extreme degree, its philosophical assumptions and totalizing intentions laid bare. In its degree of exaggeration, Stein's identification with the position of authority, certainty, and rationality implied by the realist text has something of the performative about it, suggesting, as it does, a role assumed textually that is unavailable culturally. Stein's interrogation is thus also unparalleled in another way. In attempting to represent the world according to the commonsense logic of realism, she ultimately turns this logic against itself, enacting in the novel a failure of commonsense systems of organization. Her vast logical and genealogical framework begins to buckle—no longer runs parallel to common sense—as forms of paradox, ambiguity, and contradiction emerge from within it, causing it to speak against itself and thus pointing it to another modality of thought. This new "logic," which implies a new speaking position, emerges fully near the end of *A Long Gay Book* where the style, intention, and narrative perspective change dramatically. As Stein matter-of-factly puts it, "every one . . . will see that it changed, it kept on changing, until at last it led to something entirely different. . . ."[14] In this new style, vivid vocabulary is strangely juxtaposed and grows increasingly fragmented, lyrical, incantatory, and markedly less referential. The olympian perspective of the detached realist narrator contracts radically and the focus on universals becomes a focus on "little pieces of everyday." The commonsense logic of classification gives way to a logic in which it is possible to "class an amazing black cap as an hour glass," "class a plain white suit as a fairy turtle."[15]

These radical disruptions of common sense categories are made possible because the discursive formation upon which realism depends, in being ideologically constructed and not "natural," is thus full of the incoherencies, inconsistencies, and gaps of any ideology. Because ideology—always a misrepresentation—is always in danger of betraying its own limitations, it becomes possible to expose the ideological status of what is "obvious," what "goes without saying," through foregrounding these mistakes in logic. In trying to say it all, Stein ends up admitting what should not be said, showing that what goes without saying is built upon a series of exclusions.

A novel is referential when it claims to convey something about the world outside it. Stein's beginning intentions in *A Long Gay Book* are extremely referential since she wishes to relate everything about everyone. Yet the text is not mimetic, since, as I have suggested, it does not represent these claims using the verbal and structural conventions by which this outer world typically is imitated. In the classic realist novel, these two intentions are inseparable. In *A Long Gay Book*, however, the logical categories of common sense are decontextualized, marked off, and detached from the naturalizing conventions that shore up realist illusionism. In the space created by this detachment, Stein opens up the space of a critique. This decontextualized, self-reflexive space is the space of nonsense.

Nonsense according to Susan Stewart is "a failed event, an event without proper consequence . . . that which should not be there, that which is irrelevant to context, that to which context is irrelevant."[16] Like all of logic's "others" nonsense is a category both negative and residual. Because it functions as a place to store any "mysterious gaps" in common sense systems of order, its relation to those systems is contingent and paradoxical, anomalous and taboo—it participates but does not belong. Although nonsense "rescues" common sense by providing a safe category for containing the threat of disorder, it also exposes the constructed and partial nature of classificatory schemes and processes for creating and interpreting hierarchies. Nonsense poses a threat to systems of social and fictional organization by challenging any assertion of tradition as stable and coherent through time:

> Common sense, which throughout everyday life is assumed to be something natural, given and universal and thereby characteristic of a pervasive world view, becomes, when juxtaposed through nonsense with alternative systems of order, an only partial reality, an ideology.[17]

Stewart notes that the effort to fit a set of scientific rationalities such as logic over a set of commonsense rationalities results in an

exaggeration of the senseless quality of the everyday world, the unreal effect of the real. This effort and its results are vividly enacted
in the opening sections of *A Long Gay Book* in which the narrator
asserts that

> everyone of the kinds of them has a fundamental nature common
> to each one of the many millions of that kind of them a fundamen-
> tal nature that has with it a certain way of thinking, a way of
> loving, a way of having or not having pride inside them, a way
> of suffering, a way of eating, a way of drinking, a way of learning,
> a way of working, a way of beginning, a way of ending. There
> are many kinds of them but everywhere in all living any one who
> keeps on looking can find all of the kinds of them. (*LGB*, 16)

This search for "all the kinds of them" starts out well enough as the
narrator applies the most basic logical procedure—affirmation/nega-
tion—to begin this massive categorization effort. Thus, some would
(be sorry, be angry) and some would not; some are and some are
not; some might and some might not. Inevitably, confusion begins
to creep in as finer and finer discriminations become necessary to
distinguish the various ways that people express this fundamental
nature. The urge to categorize and generalize wars with the desire
to particularize; the desire to describe the ways in which all are the
same (how all could be anyone) conflicts with the impulse to show
how all are different (how each is some*one*). The fundamental contradiction of the project—again a contradiction already inherent in the
realist novel—is more and more exposed, leading to various rhetorical convolutions, logical contradictions, negations of context and tau-
tologies, and, finally, leading to a total lack of discrimination as the
narrator asserts variously that "everything is something," "anything
is something," "something is everything and being everything is
something," "something is something," and "everything is everything" (*LGB*, 21–23).

The collision enacted in the novel's opening pages sets up the
nonsensical, impossible context of *A Long Gay Book* and demonstrates
one of the central conclusions of twentieth-century science: that it is
impossible within even a simple system to demonstrate the noncon-
tradictoriness of the system. Both "our powers of empirical observation" and "our powers of pure logical conception"—the two cornerstones of nineteenth-century rationality that Stein wishes to uphold—

are logically incapable by any rational means of ever making total sense of all the facts that make up the "truth." The principles of systematicity and comprehensiveness at the base of realism, when carried to a logical conclusion, impel the novel toward tautology, absolute self-reflexivity, and negation on the one hand, and toward infinite extension, lack of discrimination, and chaos on the other. Each case suggests the potential of an infinitely receding horizon of description: one could go on forever producing distinctions within classes or one could go on producing classes forever.

Hierarchy and direction (causation, chronology) are basic to the construction of a commonsense context, a context basic to fictional organization as well. Nonsense is produced when these two principles of organization are traversed through procedures leading to negation or infinite extension. In the attempt to be comprehensive, the narrator asserts that "anything is something" and "everything is something" thus making one piece of information as important as another, and providing no way to construct a vertical hierarchy of significance that would separate the meaningful from the trivial, an interpretive hierarchy already rigorously encoded in the realist novel. In *A Long Gay Book*, we are overwhelmed by surface, confounded by both excesses and deficiencies of information. At the level of direction and causality (the horizontal level) no principle of causation is easily available; the narrator even overtly states that "beginning and ending have no meaning." Infinitely reversible and invertible, the text short-circuits the possibility that it will develop and "get somewhere"—the imperative of traditional narrative—or that one section will necessarily develop logically from another. Moreover, since the text is written in the continuous present tense, it paradoxically appears to move forward and to remain still at the same time; because origin is unspecified and end perpetually deferred, the text threatens to extend into infinity by moving toward an ever-dissolving parameter. In effect, the text is simultaneously both here and there, both here and not here. Commonsense logic is linear and moves from point to point. *A Long Gay Book*, however, circles around a point the location of which is impossible to determine. The context of this novel—as narrow as the speaking subject in the present moment and as wide as the "millions of them who ever were or will be living"— describes an impossible context, a contrasensible context within which a wide variety of techniques for transgressing common sense come to operate.

Narrative is ideological both in what it says and in what it omits—what it assumes goes without saying. The commonsense logic of realism becomes efficient partly by means of what Stewart calls "metaphorical short-cuts"—the taken-for-granteds of social life, "what everybody knows," the details skipped in order to get "on with the point."[18] In *A Long Gay Book* the details in many ways are the point. And they are not. That is, the text simultaneously is overloaded with an excess of words and paradoxically also deficient in paraphrasable meaning. While it reveals too much—more than is socially adequate—it also doesn't reveal enough, and what it does reveal often seems beside the point.

In passages such as the following one, for example, the narrator, in an effort to be comprehensive, expands the level of description to an extremely literal degree and in the process veers toward rejecting the necessary shortcuts that enable ordinary language to function transparently:

A man in his living has many things inside him. He has in him his being certain that he is being one seeing what he is looking at just then he has in the kind of feeling of seeing what he is looking at just then that makes a kind of them of which a list will be made in making out a list of everyone. This feeling of being certain of seeing what he is looking at just then comes from the being in him that is being then in him, comes from the mixing in him of being one being living and being one then being certain of that thing.

In all of the men being living some are more certain than other ones who are very much like them are more certain of seeing the thing at which they are looking.

In all men in their daily living, in every moment they are living, in all of them, in all the time they are being living in the times they are doing something, in the times they are not doing something, in all of them there is always something in them of being certain of seeing the thing at which they are looking. In all of them in all the millions of men being living there is some feeling of being certain of seeing the thing at which they are looking. Some of the many millions of men being living have stronger the feeling of being certain of seeing the things at which they are looking than others of them.

There are many millions of men being living and many millions are very certain that they are seeing the thing at which they are looking. In many men there is a mixture in them of being strongly certain of seeing the thing at which they are looking and just being certain that they are seeing the thing at which they are looking. In some men there is a mixture in them of being certain of being strongly certain of being quite certain of not being strongly certain of being uncertain that they are seeing the thing at which they are all looking. In all the men who are being living there is something of being certain of seeing the thing at which they are looking. In all the men who are being living there is a kind of feeling about being certain of seeing that at which they are looking. (*LGB*, 20–21)

I quote this passage in its entirety to suggest the extent to which Stein carries her description. From the point of view of the information it conveys, from a commonsense point of view, the entire section might be reduced to the generalization "Everyone feels differently about his or her ability to perceive with certainty." Since no concrete particulars illustrate the generalization, the effect of this extreme degree of specificity is to create an extreme degree of abstraction, an impression reinforced by the vagueness of the pronouns and by the vagueness of the very concept "being certain of seeing." As readers, we remain uncertain of what we are to see; we have trouble seeing through the undifferentiated tangle of words put before us. Yet if we enter into the context Stein attempts to create in *A Long Gay Book*, if we try to see things from this point of view, the passage becomes strangely readable. By repeating variations of the concept of certainty in seeing, she achieves a kind of coherence as well as a remarkably subtle development and amplification of ideas. By extending the description from "a man" to "all men" to "all the millions of men" and by promising that a list will be made of everyone, the narrator gestures toward completing the comprehensive vision of how everyone does everything, which is the aim of the book.

This method of making descriptions too literal by spelling out what ordinarily would remain implicit often fails to produce the kind of "progress" described above. Especially as the book unfolds, passages frequently negate themselves in the process of unfolding as the discourse erases its context, or refers back only to itself. A typical Steinian sentence such as the following one seems to promise a causal connection that will lead to narrative extension, but it folds back upon itself at the last minute. "They are thin things the things that are thin things and some have seen them and have said then that those things are thin things" (*LGB*, 20). The use of "then" suggests a summing up, a generalization, that becomes only a repetition of the original literalization. The nesting of thin-thin(g) suggests a further incorporation of specific into general and emphasizes the correspondences inhering within the materiality of language itself rather than in a relationship between word and world. This procedure is even more extremely demonstrated in assertions such as the following ones that make no sense on the level of logic but that assume the status of "something" on the level of discourse:

> Having not been listening when someone has not come to be talking is something. (*LGB*, 28)

> If they are saying that something is not anything they are then saying that anything is something. (*LGB*, 50)

The following statement, in negating its own context, comes to signify the very essence of negation: "Not having been a baby is something that comes not to be anything and that is a thing that is beginning" (*LGB*, 21). "Not having been a baby is something"; it is a statement in language. Because we all have been babies (as the narrator remarks in the very first sentence of the book), the statement "comes not to be anything"—it literally cannot refer to reality. But this lack of reference is "a thing that is beginning." Babies much have a referent in the real world; language can be born, can begin, within language. In terms of the logic of the book, the statement can also "be something." The narrator takes care to explain how the recognition that they have been "little ones" influences people's capacity to confront themselves. "There are some when they feel it later inside them that they were such [babies] once and that was all there was of them, there are some who have from such a knowing an uncertain curious kind of feeling in them that their having been so little once makes it all a broken world for them . . . kills for them the everlasting feeling" (*LGB*, 13). In order to begin to live, to develop and mature, these people must create a fiction and negate the certainty of once having been a baby.

The text plays with negation of context in another way in the following passage, which provides a good example of what Stewart calls "fiction caught in a stammer of taking itself back." "All who came and said yes said that they said yes and some of them said that they had intended to say no and they would have said no if they had not said yes. Having said yes they said that having said yes they would say yes again if they did not say no" (*LGB*, 60). Here, propositions are framed within the narrowest range of logical possibilities available. At a very basic level, one can either accept (say "yes") or deny (say "no") to something. Every category has a proper not, its exact logical inverse which defines and delimits the category. In conflating and inverting this most basic of categories—(± affirmation)—one cannot decide by the end of the sentence who is saying yes or no and why—the text begins to problematize the very basis of classification by gesturing toward its limits, in this case a nonbinary context in which true and false, yes and no, interpenetrate. This context illustrates the irony of all definitions/classifications, showing them to be constructed in "a relation of intolerance and an avoidance of anomaly, ambiguity and ambivalence."[19] In this same vein, the narrator also uncovers what Stewart calls "the paradox of inclusion and exclusion" apparent in anything that both is and is not by virtue of belonging to two contradictory sets. Sometimes this kind of nonsense play becomes overt as "not nicely having what all are having is to be nicely having what all are having" (*LGB*, 74).

Carried to an extreme, the negation of categories produces utter confusion (the threat of nonsense), an excess of language that floats free of an interpretive context.

If they are all not alike that is enough to arrange being certain that expressing what expressing is expressing is not expressing what expressing is not expressing and any way a pie that each one is putting where each one is putting the pie each one is putting anywhere; in putting the pie where each one putting a pie anywhere is putting a pie each one is not putting the pie where in putting the pie he might be putting the pie and each one is putting the pie where each one putting the pie anywhere might be putting the pie in putting the pie where each one is putting the pie that is anywhere. This is enough to please all and all are not pleased when all are pleased. All are pleased and nicely pleased and completely pleased when all are pleased and all are not pleased not quite pleased when each one doing what each one is doing each one is not seeing that any one doing what each one is doing and a nice house where some have come and a house not so nice where some have come, all of it is what is not annoying and each one has eaten what has left in them all that has come out of them if they face a way which is the other way they were facing when they were facing the way they were facing when they were facing the other way. (*LGB*, 80)

This passage makes it difficult to decide whether we are coming or going. Are we facing a way—pointing in one direction—or facing away—simultaneously turned in the opposite? "Expressing what expressing is expressing" in this manner is, at the same time, "not expressing" anything. It is, in fact, expressing what might be called the negation of expression from a commonsense perspective, the limits of logic where common sense meets what cannot be expressed within it ("what expressing is not expressing").

Stein's effort to enact the aesthetic principles of "beginning again and again" and "using everything" leads to other instances in which commonsense logic is transgressed, specifically the conception of discrete events and causal relations, two cornerstones of realist narrative. Following Derrida, Stewart writes, "At the point of free play, the removal of hierarchical order and privileged significance, there is a gesture toward infinity where the origin and end of things disappear."[20] *A Long Gay Book* gestures toward "infinity" again, on both a horizontal axis—where elements, added to one another, suggest an infinite causality or an unlimited series—and on a vertical level where elements are repeated with potentially infinite variations within a fixed beginning and ending (usually the sentence, but also the fixed but apparently arbitrary boundary of the text itself).

The following statement describes and illustrates both the method of "beginning again and again" and the impossibility of its ever being achieved.

Doing it again is not finishing everything. Doing it again and again is not finishing everything. Doing it again and again and again is not finishing everything. Doing it again and again and again and again is not finishing everything. Doing it again and again and again and again and again is not finishing everything.

Doing it again and again and again is not finishing everything.
Doing it again is not finishing everything. (LGB, 74)

The narrator arbitrarily stops at five repetitions of "again," but even
this relatively small number suggests that the statement could be
infinitely extendable. "Doing it again" + infinity "will never be finishing everything." Moreover, because the passage ends the way it
began—counting backwards toward one—the statement becomes infinitely reversible and perfectly paradoxical.

Among other things, the sort of infinite causality to which the
above passage points contests the commonsense notion that a necessarily contingent causal relationship exists between items or events.
Whether in fiction or in life, causality implies a value, a conception
of life as linear, progressive, purposeful, and filled with meaning.
Patricia Tobin comments, "The realistic novel convinces us not because the contents of its fictional world resemble those of ours, but
because it structures experience in the same way we do; what is
essential to the illusion of reality is not what happens but how it
happens."[21]

The following paragraph, for example, works with the logically
causal structure "if x then y" in the form of chain verse in which the
last word or phrase of a line becomes the beginning of the next line:
"If stumbling is continuing then a side-walk is restoring. If a side-
walk is restoring then eating is satisfying. If eating is satisfying then
undertaking is beguiling. If undertaking is beguiling then shooing is
concentrating. If shooing is concentrating then resounding is destroy-
ing. That is the way to sleep" (LGB, 85). Within the context provided
here, causality is both nonsensical and "logical." Connections between sentences are cryptic, not immediately apparent, yet a context
is hinted at and the language is evocative enough for the reader to
bring the passage into "play." If one stumbles on a walk, then a
sidewalk is restoring (of balance and of general well-being). If one
feels restored, then eating is satisfying, a state of affairs that makes
one well-disposed to continue ("undertaking is beguiling"). The last
lines, more difficult to naturalize, perhaps suggest pestering insects
encountered on a country walk that one has to shoo away and destroy in order to be able to take a postpicnic nap.

This investigation and manipulation of the principles of causation also frequently leads to their exhaustion as the effort to adhere

to logical categories has led to both extension and negation. Negation hollows these categories out; extension pushes them beyond their logical boundaries.

> Any one being one is one. Anything put down is something. Anything put down is something and being that thing it is something and being something it is a thing and being a thing it is not anything and not being anything it is everything and being that thing it is a thing and being that thing it is that thing. Being that thing it is that thing and being that thing it is coming to be a thing having been that thing and coming to be a thing having been that thing it is a thing being a thing it is a thing being that thing. (*LGB*, 48)

Here, a causal sequence is asserted, then frustrated, first by inverting it ("being that thing it is something and being something it is that thing"), then by apparently denying it ("being a thing it is not anything"), expanding it to infinity ("not being anything it is everything"), and, finally, by bringing it back around to the beginning as a tautology ("being that thing it is a thing and being that thing it is that thing").

Manipulating causality threatens to create infinity by the endless addition of elements; an arbitrary "stop rule" and not logical completion puts a halt to the chain. What Stewart calls "arrangement and rearrangement within a closed field" threatens infinity by a potentially infinite combination of elements within a fixed but arbitrary boundary.[22] As Stewart points out, Stein is a master of this latter technique, which occurs throughout *A Long Gay Book* within the "closed field" of individual sentences and paragraphs and between the covers of the text itself. Arrangement and rearrangement forms the essence of Stein's insistent style.

The classic realist text conforms to a declarative modality and intention in which the narrator imparts knowledge to the reader whose position is thereby also stabilized through a discourse that, to a large extent, erases its own status as discourse. As the switches and relays by which nonsense short-circuits common sense become increasingly overt in *A Long Gay Book*, this declarative intention becomes more and more difficult to enact and sustain. The "problem

posed by a text," as Belsey notes, "is not the same as its consciousness of the problem."[23] Here, the "problem" posed by the text—the
contradictions on which it is built—is made increasingly conscious
as the narrator begins to question the project while trying to carry it
forward, acknowledging the contradictions on which it is founded
and trying to evade them. Categories grow increasingly unstable and
ambivalent and the narrator redoubles the effort to assert them, an
effort that leads to further rhetorical convolutions and negations as
this passage from the middle of the text suggests.

> Why if some one is enough that thing to be that one . . . why is
> that one then being one who in being one is being so little that
> one that that one is then being another kind of one. . . . In not
> being the one he is being he is being what he would not be being
> if he were being anything and he being something he is being
> something that would be something if it were anything but not
> being something it is not anything. (*LGB*, 55)

Destruction of the principles of hierarchy and causality—and the consequences of this destruction—are acknowledged and made overt:
"nothing is happening because if anything were happening beginning and ending would be having meaning and if beginning and
ending did have meaning then not anything would be something"
(*LGB*, 56). Confusion alternates with the growing awareness that loss
of these principles means a kind of freedom—at this point "anyone
can say anything" (*LGB*, 74)—and with the acknowledgment that
rigid adherence to the empiricist program—the backbone of Stein's
project in this text—is finally perhaps "not exciting" and even "annoying"—"this can be common, this can be convincing, this can be
perplexing, this can be repeating" (*LGB*, 76).

An oscillation between adherence and critique is most vividly
enacted in the following two paragraphs in which the problem
posed by the text and its solution appear side by side. In this
sequence, Stein announces her movement away from the insistent
style and the project to categorize humanity and her movement into
a new style—what she calls "tropical misuses" of the categories of
common sense—through the surprising emergence of sound and
color: "A tiny violent noise is a yellow happy thing. A yellow happy
thing is a gentle little tinkle that goes in all the way it has every-

thing to say" (*LGB*, 82). These two sentences gain added impact by following directly after one of the novel's most convoluted statements that, like many others, regresses in both structure and content into a negation of its own context: "If in leaving someone is leaving then in having been disappearing some one has been disappearing and has not been saying that he has said what he said he would say if he saw what he would have seen if there had been what there would have been if there was what there was and there was not" (*LGB*, 82).

The final sections of the text are dominated not by minute repetitions of sameness but by difference, a sensuous variety of words—rich, colorful, concrete, musical—yoked together in wildly incongruous ways, and cohering around rhythm and sound rather than through the repetition of key words and structures. As the narrator says, in this section of the book "singing is everything." The universal perspective narrows to focus on humble and domestic subjects—bathing, eating, sewing. And, significantly, abstractions about love and marriage—talk about love—are replaced by love-talk. "Present the time and section the sailing of a coat. Show no theory. Show the satisfaction and see the window. All the gentleness is mixing. There is a dream. . . . Names are mingling" (*LGB*, 105–6). This statement summarizes Stein's method and tone in the latter half of the novel and points to the transformation of her intention from part one. Having begun with the referential intention of the realist novelist writ large—to "cover every possible variety of human type," to "section" humanity—and having attempted to expand logical categories so they might be capacious enough to include "all," Stein ends with a desire to present little pieces of the daily—"all day is all there is to say . . . the necessity the whole necessity is there, there there is material." But this daily space is not simply to be empirically recovered; in this "logical" space "there is no fact," there is no interpretation, only "the time of the pansy [which] is so original." This imaginative space exists between logical categories, in a "dream" or in a time before language acquisition when names mingle and do not point definitively to objects. Rather than showing her theory of how human types may be systematized, she will "show the satisfaction" of life in the sensuous material world.

Often "the satisfaction" is presented quite straightforwardly—as clearly as "see(ing) through a window":

If the potatoe was there and the light were bright then it would
be sweet to be clean and to have the same seat. It is always
necessary to carry the same piece of bread and butter. It is nicely
brown and yellow and prettily sticking together that with what
it is when it is where it is and it is where it is as it is only where
it is. It is the particular attraction by which it is the piece that is
eating and being eaten. It is mentionable. It is not deceptive. It
is the practice of everything. It is what is necessary. (*LGB*, 92)

These simple humble affirmations of everyday pleasures occur repeatedly in the novel's final pages; they are "mentionable" and "necessary." Through an emphasis on rhyme and rhythm they often appear as hymns to the everyday as in this paragraph that shows the
metrical regularity typically associated with lyric poetry:

Little leg of mutton always still and true, little long potatoe is
so like the green, little celery eaten, shows the time of day, little
rhubarb is all red and still there is a last time to discuss a matter,
little piece of pudding is not very red, little piece of fish fried is
the same as bread, little pieces of it are the bread there is, each
one is all happy and there is no time for pears. Pears are often
eaten, figs have such a way, all the time is better and this shows
in that way, all the best is certain and there is that use, when
there is no time to stay there will be no abuse. All the time is
there then, there is time to stay, all the best is mentioned most
and there is more to say, all the length is thickness, all the length
is breadth, talking is a pleasant way and there is not enough,
more is not permitted, there is meaning there, all in that particular time there is the meaning clear. (*LGB*, 103).

Among the simple but remarkable pleasures described are those
involving love including straightforward descriptions of physical interactions: "standing and expressing, open and holding, turning and
meaning, closing and folding, holding and meaning, standing and
fanning, joining and remaining, opening and holding" (*LGB*, 86).
Through the use of active progressive verbs, repetition, and rhyme,
this passage conveys the dynamic coming together of a couple who
embrace, separate to cool off ("standing and fanning"), and open to
enfold and hold again. Hymns of praise for the loved one also appear:

A overly love is sitting and she sits there now she is in bed, she is in bed. A lovely love is cleaner when she is so clean, she is so clean, she is all mine. A overly love does not use any way to say all day she is to say that all the day is all there is to say. A lovely love is something and there is no hand writing, it is that there is no printing. A lovely love is there to be the rest of all there is to put into that which is what there is there. (*LGB*, 101)

The assertions that "she is all mine," "she is there to be the rest of all there is," echo a later affirmation: "Faithful and constant never budge from her side," and foreshadow the passionate coming together of the lovers in the final passages of the book.

These relatively clear descriptions of common objects and activities are interspersed with a final deconstructive move that is Stein's most radical one—an undoing of the very categories by which we structure the world and construct ideas of culture. The following passage, for example, occurs shortly after the tiny violent noise passage cited earlier: "It would sadly distress some powder if looking out was continual and sitting first was happening and leaving first was persisting" (*LGB*, 83). Everything about this sentence is unremarkable except the subject; some person may be sadly distressed; some powder may not be within the realm of common sense. From this simple substitution of inanimate for animate appear scores of examples that play with substitution among classes, including parts of speech: "It would not disappoint a brown or a pink or a golden anticipation" (*LGB*, 83); "Please tell the artichoke to underestimate valor" (*LGB*, 105); "The brown complete has a tall leader" (*LGB*, 103–5), etc. Frequently, both subject and object are at odds (e.g., "The tame coffee is not so stern as the singing of swinging" (*LGB*, 103), or strange combinations of words appear within a recognizable structure, as the structure of definition (e.g., "Pleasure in onions means that gambling has no milk" [*LGB*, 104]) or simile (e.g., "Like no sheep and like a lamb, there is no meat, there is a sheet. Like a church and like a tape, there are circles there, there is a hidden chair" [*LGB*, 105]).

The novel operates increasingly in this realm of the liminal and the taboo, the anomalous (that which stands between existing categories) and the ambiguous (that which has no given category), gesturing toward a space that exists outside culturally sanctioned categories; as the narrator states, "there is no truth to the decision which is

in the center" (*LGB*, 113). The desire becomes "to indicate more wall
flowers than there is paper," to point to the space beyond what is
normally visible, to "indicate more houses than there are houses,"
to suggest a number in excess of the things that are usually counted,
and to "indicate" these spaces and things as the "nothing more," as
newly central. These liminal spaces, objects, feelings, and actions are
proclaimed as "the whole resemblance"—"so keen that [they are] the
not inbetween it is the whole and there is laughing" (*LGB*, 113).
Cultural categories always "stand in relation to what they cannot
stand" or understand. By attempting to inhabit this place of intolerance and misrecognition, Stein reaches a final stage in the deconstruction of realist principles. Having gradually inverted, negated,
and displaced the logic on which they depend—having dis-identified
with them—she begins to operate from the space of nonidentity
opened up by this displacement. Here a new identification is affirmed, a new enunciative position, from which it also becomes possible to affirm the realm of nonsense and paradox, the space that both
is something and is not anything from another (dominant) perspective.

In his study of the antirealist tradition in fiction, Nash suggests
that there are two avenues open to the artist once realism has been
exposed and rejected: to explore the qualities of form itself, the properties of the medium in which the art work is cast, or to elaborate a
"private, non-consensual, perhaps nonprobabilistic vision."[24] Or, in
the case of Stein, one may do both: explore the properties of the
linguistic medium in the name of creating a new enunciative position
and a new discursive reality. "The doctrine which changed language
was this, this is the dentition, the doctrine which changed that language was this, it was the language segregating. . . . Largely additional and then completely exploding is one way to deny authorization" (*LGB*, 109). In the final sections of the novel Stein "denies the
authorization" of common sense and the social scripts allied with it
and questions the ways in which language and reality bear a relation
to one another by "segregating" words from their "proper" relations
to one another, and "exploding" the logical structures on which
meaning is based. In the following passages, repetition is used not
to create a gradual build-up of character types as it was earlier in the
novel but to express the simple joy of repeating, the way a child
repeats sounds to play with them, the way a lover repeats when a

referential use of language is an inadequate vehicle for strong emotion:

> A bird is birdie. A little bird and a little blight and a little balance to a best button. A little bright bitten bucking anything.
>
> (*LGB*, 114)

> Beef yet, beef and beef and beef. Beef yet, beef yet. . . .
> Little beef, little beef sticking, hair please, hair please
> No but no but butter.
> Coo cow, coo, coo, coo.
>
> (*LGB*, 115)

> A lake particular salad
> Wet cress has points in a plant when new sand is a particular.
> Frank, frank quay.
> Set of keys was, was.
> Lead kind in soap, lead kind in soap sew up. Lead kind is so up.
> Leaves a mass so mean. No shows. Leaves a mass cook will.
> Leaves a mass puddle.
> Etching. Etching a chief, none plush. (*LGB*, 116)

In these passages the relationship between word and world has broken down almost completely. Instead of using words to fix the world, words become the world, become objects to play with and embody. Here the narrator plunges "into a vortex of words, burning words, cleansing words, liberating words, feeling words," discovering that "it was enough . . . to play with them; whatever you can play with is yours and this was the beginning of knowing . . . that it could play and play with words and the words were all ours, all ours."[25] As readers, we too are invited to plunge into a vortex of words at the end of *A Long Gay Book*, to burn/bathe orgasmically in language, regressing temporarily to the stage when the letters "b" and "s" were, first of all, something to play with: to bite and balance on our tongues, to repeat and repeat and repeat ("beef and beef and beef"), to sink into deliciously (in a plush puddle). This is at one and the same time an eroticized linguistic space, beyond paradox, and a gesture toward a new social space. The straightforward and upright description of a couple embracing that appears earlier in the text here is transformed into the bright biting and bucking of a couple engaged in actual lovemaking.

That the "couple" described are Stein and Alice Toklas is a conjecture supported by some textual evidence. Toklas formally moved in with Stein during the time *A Long Gay Book* was being written, but Stein had declared her love for Alice some years before this in her portrait of "Ada" (1908). In *A Long Gay Book* she writes "I and y and a d and a letter makes a change. The obligation is mutual" (*LGB*, 106). The addition of a letter, of course, make a d ada, an addition that does change Stein's life and her art, marking her escape from the social, legal, linguistic, and logical categories of the nineteenth century.

The aggressive avant-gardism of modernist writers, their desire to make culture new in the face of a worn-out inheritance, was as much an imperative for female as for male writers. Yet because women's relation to culture and literary tradition differed, their methods of, motivations for, and responses to escaping this tradition also differed. The flip side of modernist celebrations of the new was a (male) modernist terror in the face of a world perceived as having lost all value and certainty, or, put another way, a world in which the hegemony of bourgeois patriarchal ideology was perceived as being at risk. This terror inspired the search for saving forms, for alternative cultural mythologies to shore against the ruin. As Marianne DeKoven has persuasively demonstrated, female modernists also felt ambivalence over the imperative to make it new, but their ambivalence arose from a fear that they would be punished for their newly found freedom from the social scripts of the nineteenth century. "The new order was simultaneously alluring and terrifying, alluring to male modernists in its promise to destroy bankrupt bourgeois culture and to female modernists in its promise, simply, of freedom and autonomy; terrifying to male modernists in its threat to destroy their privileges and to female modernists in its potential for bringing on retribution from a still empowered patriarchy."[26] DeKoven argues that the formal features typically associated with modernist avant-gardism grow out of and reflect this differently gendered ambivalence. Both male and female writers simultaneously use and transform nineteenth-century modes of representation, combining stylistic features that disrupt these modes (e.g., decentered subjectivity, rupture of linearity in plot and temporal structure, foregrounding of preoedipal, presymbolic language, and stylistic indeterminacy, multiplicity, fragmentation) with ones that reinscribe them, though the reasons for this doubleness differ along the lines she describes.

Yet this doubleness, which in part gives the modernist novel its characteristic form, may also, in the end, act in part to reinscribe form and so keep the fundamentals of realism in place. On the whole, modernist fiction continues to be mimetically referential and comprehensive in its depiction of experience, merely shifting focus from external to internal depictions. Stein's avowed project to categorize all of humanity while somewhat shocking in its bluntness could also be compared to Proust's "prodigious embrace" of French society or to Joyce's vision of the novel as a "farraginous allincluding chronicle," as well as to the project of nineteenth-century naturalists. Character as anthropocentric psychology is more rather than less insistently inscribed in the modernist text, "offered without question as an entity to be identified according to thoroughly consistent laws of causality and probability."[27] Modernist efforts to represent the chaos of values, the deluge of external phenomena, the frailty of consciousness, the instability of language mean that form must be struggled over and becomes increasingly plural; but this struggle finally is recontained in terms of realist principles, through various kinds of centering devices (Eliot's objective correlative, Joyce's epiphany or mythic method, Woolf's moment of vision) all of which imply that experience is at base deeply structured, organized, totalizable. In fact as Nash, among many others, points out: "If modernism ever reflects any revolt against the Realist spirit it is to affirm not a more radical but a more metaphysically orthodox credo toward which Realism yearns. . . . Modernism is in some compelling or compulsive way a last ditch effort to trace the figure in the carpet, to make do with, to salvage, some sense of order from the rubble and debris of Realism's own surviving materials."[28] As Jean-François Lyotard puts it, modernist art "allows the unrepresentable to be put forward . . . as the missing contents; but the form, because of its recognizable consistency, continues to offer the reader matter for solace and pleasure."[29]

In the early years of her career, Stein enacted a typically modernist struggle between the chaos of experience and language and the search for saving forms. In *A Long Gay Book* this struggle is writ large. Her simultaneous adherence to and critique of realist modes and the aesthetics of representation on which they depend is a feature she shares with other modernist writers, and vestiges of this struggle remain at the end of the novel. Here the narrator both celebrates a newly found lesbian eroticism and a new relationship to literary language and form, and retains traces of a voice that judges these relationships as "horrid." There is also a sense in which Stein, like other modernist writers, retreats at the end of the novel into a private discursive reality which allows her to value and protect her artistic vocation and her emotional orientation without offering a critique of the larger social structures that make this protection necessary. Yet despite these traces of modernist doubleness, the struggle between "a still ineluctable bourgeois humanism" and "the pressures of a quite different rationality," the text finally comes down on the side of this still newly emergent logic. At the end of *A Long Gay Book* Stein takes up this space at the limits of language, subjectivity, form and proclaims its centrality. She exaggerates the contradictions of realism rather than resolving or holding them in tension, refusing realist and modernist efforts to form totalizing unities by foregrounding the exclusions that these unities cannot admit.

Following Roman Jacobson, Brian McHale defines the "dominant" as a centering component of a work of art, one that governs the remaining components. The evolution of literary genres involves not so much the absolute disappearance of some elements and the emergence of others as it does shifts in the mutual relationships among these elements—shifts in the dominant.[30] In her progressive movement away from those literary elements that act to shore up form and toward techniques that dissolve it (negations, infinite regression, deliberate nonselection, logical impossibility), Stein moves to the limits of a modernist aesthetic and points the novel in a new direction, toward a place where form is in danger of fading completely and a discourse of difference may be heard.

Chapter 3

Metafiction and the Aesthetics of Privacy in *A Novel of Thank You*

What is being modern but the full realization that one cannot begin to write the same works once again.

—Roland Barthes

The form of the traditional novel is a metaphor for a society that no longer exists. . . . Its present function is to sustain a series of comforting illusions, among which one might include the feeling that the individual is the significant focus among the phenomena of "reality" (characterization); the sense that clock, or public time is finally the reigning form of duration for consciousness (historical narration); the notion that the locus of "reality" may be determined by empirical observation (description); the conviction that the world is logical and comprehensible (causal significance, plot).

—Ronald Suckenick

Try to tell what happened without telling stories. . . . Oh do not tell another story.

—Gertrude Stein

A novel is useful for more reasons than one.

—Gertrude Stein

Stein would have applauded Barthes's definition of modernity and Suckenick's assertions about the necessity of advancing beyond the nineteenth-century paradigm for the novel, contemporary assessments that appear belated in light of her early and radical assault on that paradigm. As early as 1912, Stein began to disidentify with and then forcefully to dislocate the logical structures forming the very basis of nineteenth-century novelistic conventions. As I suggested in the previous chapter, *A Long Gay Book* may be considered a work of theoretical transformation because in detaching itself from the ideology of the past, as represented in these conventions, it reveals the past to be ideological and not natural. Suckenick's desire to reject the form of the nineteenth-century novel as "a metaphor for a society that no longer exists," recalls Stein's observation that "the whole business of writing is the question of living . . . contemporariness"[1] and embodying this contemporary sense "imperceptibly" in the form and the content of the work of art. When, in the 1920s, Stein consciously began to reconsider the novel as a literary form, it was with precisely "the full realization" of what could no longer be written and what, therefore, it was necessary to try and write. "Can a novel be of any more appropriateness than it [currently] is and not be expected,"[2] Stein asks. Can the novel tell us anything new?

In a variety of speculations on the subject, Stein makes overt the ways in which the substance and the form of the novel might be altered, giving a rationale for these modifications based on changing conceptions of the production and reception of art in an early-twentieth-century moment. Like many contemporary writers, Stein aimed to reverse the assumption that novels must deliver a declarative content, which the narration merely serves to convey, describing always already there facts or systems of meaning beyond the text. Instead, the writer "must amuse himself . . . and not think to recognize anything beside this thing, beside playing with what he is playing with as he is writing";[3] here, the story of writing replaces the writing of stories. Gone is the centrality of plot as a structure of significance: a series of events cohering to form an overall theme and, in the end, revealing the solution to an enigma or the disclosure of a truth. Stein writes, "The tradition has always been that you may more or less describe the things that happen . . . but nowadays everybody all day long knows what is happening and so what is happening is not really interesting."[4] "The twentieth century gives of itself a feeling of movement and has in its way no feeling for events. To the twentieth century events are not important . . . events are not exciting . . . events have lost their interest for people."[5] Since, in a contemporary moment, the novel is obliged to compete with so many other narratives ("everybody knows so many stories"), "what is the use of telling another story," Stein asks. The new novel must "capture an essence not tell a story,"[6] by embodying the nature of the twentieth century without relying for its existence on a subject matter external to itself as a composition.

If the novel need not be considered a reflection of reality, it might instead be considered an activity, a process, an experience—"about" its own coming into being. Thus a reader's inherited mimetic expectations are simply no longer appropriate. "It almost looks *just like* a bird and therefore [to many people] it is interesting," but, Stein asks, "how can a novel be about resemblances to what is made to look like it to what is really another larger altogether" (*ANOTY*, 172). The novel may add itself to and in part organize the modern composition, but it must do so by refusing to evoke resemblances to external reality—"another larger altogether." Like the writer, the reader "must be at one with the writing must be at one with the recognition must have nothing of knowing anything before or after the recognition—achieving recognition of the thing while the thing was achieving expression."[7]

As she has done before, Stein also deliberately dismisses the linear causal structure that forms the cornerstone of realist fiction:

> When one used to think of narrative one meant a telling of what is happening in successive moments of its happening . . . the important part of telling anything was the conviction that anything that everything was progressively happening. . . . But now we have changed all that. . . . We really now do not really know that anything is progressively happening.[8]

In the contemporary novel "beginning and ending is not really exciting, anything is anything, anything is happening. . . . There is no succession"; instead there is "moving in every and any various direction that may make one thing say itself in a different way."[9] If one proposes to omit story and succession and thus to realign traditional novelistic categories of plot, character, progress through a sequence of events to reach an end and proposes instead to capture "anything and everyone completely moving in every and any various direction," can the novel go on? "Where are we then in narrative writing," Stein asks.[10]

The impasse that Stein points to here is suggestive of the one John Barth later identifies in his influential essay "The Literature of Exhaustion": the situation of the writer when faced with a recognition of the exhaustion of certain literary possibilities—what it is no longer possible to write. Indeed, as my framing of these initial remarks is meant to suggest, Stein's fundamental critique of traditional narrative

categories and her efforts to construct a new form of the novel capable of responding to the modernity of the twentieth century anticipate in striking ways the antirealist programs of postmodern metafic-
tionists such as John Barth, Ronald Suckenick, Raymond Federman,
and Phillipe Sollers. Their experiments in the direction of a radical
linguistic and diegetic reflexivity and even antirepresentationalism
in fiction are summed up in Sollers's pronouncement that "the book
which would be a real book, that is a text, no longer informs, convinces, demonstrates, tells or represents."[11] It must, as Stein suggested, "say itself in a different way."

The relation between Stein's fictional experiments and this particular antirealist strand of postmodern writing practice (which is
sometimes taken for the whole of postmodern writing) has been
noted by a number of contemporary critics. For example, Ihab Hassan
places Stein in his tradition of self-negating literature, a "literature
of silence" in which he also includes Sade, Kafka, Hemingway,
Genet, and Beckett. This uneasy genealogical fit is also evident in
Neil Schmitz's important essay "Gertrude Stein as Postmodernist:
The Rhetoric of *Tender Buttons*." Schmitz evokes a whole tradition in
embryo as he attempts to relate Stein's practice to certain contemporary fictional experiments:

> If only in light of Barth's Beckett-like soliloquies, the agonized
> isolation from which so many contemporary writers speak 'cry-
> ing out for nothing,' as Robbe-Grillet puts it, the feat of Gertrude
> Stein's contented subjectivity, her sense of stylistic liberation in
> *Tender Buttons* deserves close scrutiny. Stein's writing constitutes
> a strenuously experimental canon in which all the vexing ques-
> tions that make contemporary literature so problematic are
> strenuously asked.[12]

Schmitz's placement of Stein in relation to Barth, Beckett, and Robbe-
Grillet both highlights certain formal parallels among them and ob-
scures important differences, differences lurking in the gap between
her "contented subjectivity" and the "agonized isolation" of these
other writers. To claim that Stein's writing prefigures particular
postmodern writing practices is both accurate and, in the end, mis-
leading as such a claim cannot account for the fundamental ways in

which it differs in its aesthetic motivation from writers such as Barth and Robbe-Grillet.

Schmitz's otherwise perceptive analysis of postmodern elements in Stein's work reflects a more general limitation of current efforts to codify a postmodern tradition in writing on the basis of formal similarities alone. Surely the textual disruptions in Toni Morrison's *Beloved*, the alienation in Gayle Jones's *Eva's Man*, or the voice of pained isolation of Kathy Acker's *Blood and Guts in High School* should be distinguished from Barth's dislocations of linear narrative in *Lost in the Funhouse* or Beckett's agonized solipsism in *The Unnameable*. Not all formal dislocations proceed from the same sources. Not all narrative disruptions are equivalent in their motivations or in their effects. Formal comparisons between male and female modernists reveal certain common textual features that allow for the description of a broadly-based modernist aesthetic. However, such comparisons often conceal the difference of female modernism, in particular since the prominent features of the modernist aesthetic, against which these women writers are judged, have been constructed with reference to a privileged group of (male) works and until recently have been promoted as universal. Analogously, most current efforts to map the contours of an emerging postmodern poetics are based on examination of an overwhelmingly male group and thus are in danger of distorting and even excluding alternative practices—repeating the same modernist biases. Jerome Klinkowitz's literature of disruption, Raymond Federman's surfiction, Christopher Nash's antirealist tradition, Brian McHale's ontologically problematic postmodern writing all are advanced as formal descriptions of postmodern textual features that on the whole fail to account for the complex discursive situations within which individual acts of writing are produced—the differently inflected motivations for textual disruptions or self-conscious modes. Specifically, for my purposes here, they fail to consider the influence that psychosexual positioning has had on the development of postmodern aesthetic practices.

A notable exception to this formalist tendency is Patricia Waugh's recent analysis of contemporary fiction that attempts to read gender into the postmodern scene of writing. Influenced by the postmodern critique of representation and subjectivity, as many contemporary male writers have been, contemporary women emphasize in their writing the provisionality and positionality of identity, the

historical and social construction of gender, and the discursive production of knowledge and power. But—and Waugh insists on this
point—women also have an alternate relation to and thus a different
stake in a postmodern critique of culture precisely because they are
differently situated in relation to (discursively produced) power. This
fact suggests the importance of considering the social, ideological,
historical, *and* aesthetic contexts within which postmodern practices
take place in any effort to write the history and locate the specificity
of the postmodern. Indeed, that the aesthetic cannot be detached
from the discursive structures within which it operates is a central
insight of postmodernism.

Both feminist and postmodern theorists have argued that linguistic processes and larger discursive structures parallel relational
processes operating in the external world. As other feminist critics
have done, Waugh builds her theory precisely out of women's relational difference from these external processes. Women's writing,
she argues, exists in a "highly contradictory relationship" both to
"the dominant liberal conception of the subject and writing and the
classic postmodernist deconstruction of this liberal trajectory."[13]
Postmodern male writers have tended to be preoccupied with the
loss of a particular set of historical and moral conditions of which
their concern with a loss of full centered subjectivity is an example—
an extension of a male modernist preoccupation with alienation. Contemporary women's writing, on the other hand, tends to be
grounded in an effort to discover a collective conception of subjectivity that foregrounds the construction of identity in relation:

> It is the gradual recognition of the value of constructing identity
> in these terms rather than as a unitary self-directing isolate ego
> which has fundamentally altered the course of modern and con-
> temporary women's writing and has led it closer to the postmod-
> ern conception of subjectivity.[14]

Although the innovations of modernist and postmodernist writers—
whether male or female—may grow out of a common recognition of
the need for new cultural and aesthetic structures, their responses
to this imperative will differ. Roland Barthes's pronouncement that
"the thing which can no longer be written is the Proper Name,"[15] for
example, will signify differently for men and women as it will be

inflected through two different relations to a socially constructed subjectivity: for the postmodern male writer, an antihumanist rejection of the subject; for the woman writer, a conception of the subject as always already displaced in relation to a subjectivity that takes the male as its norm, but also the subject as decentered because it is constructed in a "relative and shifting positionality" in relation to another.[16]

Waugh's emphasis on the different relational basis of women's artistic productions helps to contextualize the specific aspects of Stein's postmodern practice that I wish to elaborate here: those self-reflexive strategies that act to critique "storiness" and are, therefore, central to her formulation of a new poetics of the novel. Through an examination of one text from the 1920s, in which these issues are confronted with particular directness, *A Novel of Thank You*, I want to suggest: 1) that Stein employs many of the formal strategies commonly associated with postmodern writing practices in her effort to compose a postrealist version of the novel, but, crucially, 2) that these strategies emerge from a complex narrative stance and context of enunciation the elaboration of which is central to a full understanding of her aesthetic practice. Stein's refusal to "tell a story" in *A Novel of Thank You* develops out of a context in which aesthetic, ideological, and interpersonal concerns interact: it emerges from a particular avant-garde stance toward the novel as a genre, a gender-inflected relation to literary tradition and cultural materials, and an individual aesthetic base in which an avant-garde literary response is articulated through and in relation to a specific interpersonal dynamic.

That Stein's aesthetic innovations are intimately linked with larger relational processes in the external world has been a persistent theme in Stein criticism, although until recently this link has been treated in a narrowly causal way. In Richard Bridgman's analysis, for instance, Stein's obscurities and hermeticisms arise primarily from a defensive need to censor lesbian content, and, more generally, to confront and reconcile her psychological difficulties. Recent feminist critics, among them Carolyn Burke and Harriet Chessman, offer more subtle accounts of the interactions between Stein's life and art by identifying the complex ways in which her poetics emerges from changing patterns of connection and disconnection within her interpersonal relations. (These accounts confirm Waugh's insight that women's writing tends to be contextualized in terms of historically situated personal relations often residing at the borders of life and art.) As Burke puts it:

> An entire poetics of gender lies hidden within the apparently formalist concerns of Stein's modern composition which becomes a place to express and interrogate the changing psychosexual modalities operating in the personal life and in larger culture in the very connective tissues of the work.[17]

Chessman also elaborates aspects of these psychosexual modalities in her analysis of Stein's aesthetics of dialogue by which she means a poetics based on "a metaphoric enactment of a relationship between two figures, in a continually shifting exchange that is also an interchange . . ."[18]

Issues of separation, arising from a disruption or even a temporary loss of this intimate relational base, are especially crucial to an understanding of the discursive context and thus the textual dynamics of *A Novel of Thank You*. This text has received almost no critical attention, perhaps because it is among Stein's least accessible works, the more so if one approaches it with expectations of decipherment. An insistently secretive novel that resolutely refuses to reveal its secrets, the text consists of a series of short, apparently disconnected chapters offering speculations on the novel as a form, disembodied dialogue, descriptions of daily life, brief snippets of conventional narrative, and a cast of people "coming and going." Carl van Vechten refers to it simply as "one of [Stein's] most hermetic works," an appropriate designation for a text as involuted, self-obsessed, and full of enigmas as this one.[19] Marianne DeKoven dismisses the novel as "interesting primarily as a stage in the development of Stein's writing,"[20] while Richard Bridgman struggles to read it as narrating the story of "a temporary imbalance in a relationship followed by a return to equilibrium."[21] Bridgman teases a plot from the welter of text by linking the affair he finds portrayed in the novel to the "temporary flurries of infidelity" taking place between Stein and Toklas at the time the novel was composed.

Any reader who has taken the time to struggle through the 267 pages of *A Novel of Thank You* will sympathize with Bridgman's desire to read primarily for a plot, to narrativize, impose a structure, and thus resolve the tension of incompletion evoked by the text. But this attempt to reduce it to a central theme that unfolds even semisystematically in the course of reading fails to account for much of the novel's richness and, even more seriously, deflects attention from the ways in which it deliberately refuses structuration. In *A Novel of Thank You*, Stein frustrates the reader's desire for a metaorder that would dominate and finally account for the text, since she makes it patently impossible to totalize fully the fragments strewn throughout it or to reconstruct a consistently stable point of view, which might center it. The pattern-making enterprise itself is challenged and remains in question; in this way hierarchies, closure, stability, and univocality are contested and give way. Stein undercuts the search for final transcendent structures by a sheer excess of text that refuses to cohere into regular predictable patterns and instead remains in perpetual motion "in every direction." The text is decentered and in it Stein traces the consequences of this impulse on the traditional narrative categories of event, character, and causal structure.

The novel's particular brand of hermeticism—generated from this decentering impulse—is most obviously motivated by a specific avant-garde stance based on Stein's theory of what a revised version of the novel might be and do. Consistent with her critique of story as an outmoded aesthetic assumption, she deliberately manipulates the hermeneutic code (as many postmodern writers do) refusing both the comfortable resolution of nineteenth-century works and the formal commitment to revelation of modernist texts. Realist novels have been characterized as those in a hurry to explain. Stein's antirealist text refuses the comfort of an explanation or even coherent moments of vision by raising permanently unsolved questions and thus deliberately foregrounding absence. This is neither a modernist difficulty nor a coded content that could eventually be deciphered. Rather, it is a permanent refusal to name.

Appropriately enough, the novel begins with a question, an enigma. "How many more than two are there," and keeps this enigma in constant suspension, failing to display even a consistent state of affairs. It critiques the role of events—those actions designed to develop a truth or disclose a character's nature—by teasing us with "events" it never develops or explains. The central episodes or emotional preoccupations to which the novel gravitates—what would ordinarily provide motivation for the entire plot of a traditional novel—are not adequately represented but rather blurred, at times even effaced, in effect, unlocatable, "represented" only by their absence. In this way the novel undercuts the dialectic of presence and absence upon which mimesis depends, "naming" events by speaking its desire not to name them. The novel becomes decentered by this absence at its core, an absence that generates the mobile flux and restlessness of the work as it slides toward, moves away from, and circles around a missing referent, simulating a form of narrative momentum without providing a motivation for it. Significantly, the most consistent stylistic feature in the text is pronouns lacking clearly specifiable referents. Stein plays with lack of reference throughout, admonishing us to "not ask what is it because it is it," advising us to "consider a novel a novel of it" (a novel of the missing referent), and explaining quite clearly that "the difference between a novel and a story" is that in a novel "no one said it" (*ANOTY*, 18).

Stein's insistence on leaving the text's enigma unsolved, her refusal to depict, describe, or tell is ideologically as well as aesthetically motivated, arising from her continuing recognition of the larger implications of particular modes of fictional organization. As I suggested in the previous chapter, Stein's desire to escape the telling of stories arose in part from a realization that narrative involves conquest over its subjects as well as its audience, identified as it is with public and authoritarian discourse and an impulse toward mastery. Her definitive rejection of this position of mastery, her effort to construct a version of the novel that would not depend on it, is made clear when one compares Stein's treatment of the plot of triangulation in her first novel, *Q.E.D.*, with the love triangle "described" in her reconceived version of the genre, *A Novel of Thank You.*

That the texts differ radically in their treatment of this plot indicates how far Stein had come from realist conventions by 1925 and suggests why a strictly thematic approach such as Bridgman adopts is insufficient to account for the working of *A Novel of Thank You.* As Janice Doane has convincingly demonstrated, Stein began her career as a novelist by identifying with a male speaking position. Adele, Stein's surrogate in *Q.E.D.*, renounces the pursuit of a relationship with Helen—gives up the triangle—in order to maintain her own position of integrity and sense of stable identity. The triangular affair in *Q.E.D.*, with all the configurations of the Oedipal drama, reenacts in its development and momentum a search for and acceptance of the father's position of certainty and authority. Yet this position is an uneasy means of survival. As Stein progressively rewrites the plot of this novel in *Fenhurst* and "Melanctha," Doane demonstrates, she does so from a perspective more and more allied with a position that refuses mastery. Doane concludes that Stein "ultimately saw the requirements that secure unity and integrity in both narratives and the life they recount as especially repressive in their formulation of the woman's character."[22]

If, in *A Novel of Thank You*, Stein does recount a temporary imbalance in a love relationship caused by the intrusion of a third party, she decenters this familiar plot by foregrounding the *dynamics* of the imbalance itself rather than the causes, development, or consequences of it, her emphases in the earlier texts. Unlike *Q.E.D.*, the triangular configuration in *A Novel of Thank You* is neither logically developed nor definitely resolved. It is as if the novel is "shot through" with a dynamic of triangulation that nonetheless cannot be said to form the novel's plot. Rather, the dynamic remains a shadowy, though powerful presence in this decentered text, approached obsessively but obliquely and as obsessively avoided.

The first sentence in the text, "How many more than two are there"—what I've called the enigma that initiates the narrative—establishes the preoccupation with numbers and counting carried throughout it. First, numbers occur in the chapter titles, which, significantly, are not ordered in a consistent numerical sequence. Chapter 2, for example, occurs on page fifty-three and consists of the words "chapter two and chapter twenty-two and then to remember chapter twenty-two" (*ANOTY*, 53). Chapter 22 may only be remembered by the narrator since no chapter 22 is provided for the reader. There are, however, two chapter 53s, followed by chapter 79, chapter 70, and chapter 102, evidence of Stein's defiance of the principle of linear sequence. In another sense, numbers function as an abstraction of the principle of narrative development, an answer to one question posed in the text—"how to increase a novel." Literally, the novel is developed by addition in the form of long lists of numbers and invitations to "imagine a thousand imagine three thousand imagine more in between" (*ANOTY*, 62). The reader literally invents the novel by swelling it with a cast of "thousands."

A second more complex and insistent use of numbers involves variations on the number three and the sequence one-two-three. In answer to the novel's initial question ("how many more than two are there") there are thousands more than two in the novel and only one more—a third. Triangles and pairs assume several roles and configurations in the text. Often Stein simply makes statements involving twos and threes that don't appear to "add up" to a declarative content as, for example, "could two syllables make three. All girls call" (*ANOTY*, 119); "There can be two kinds of ladies and cakes two kinds of children and bread two kinds of men and rice. There can be two kinds of birds and weights two kinds of dolls and Simons two kinds of losses and cups" (*ANOTY*, 105). Although these, and many other seemingly random distributions of the number, seem not to form relationships with other segments in the text, they do serve to foreground numbers until, by the end of the novel, ones, twos, and threes have assumed, through sheer repetition at a subtextual level, the force of an obsession. In other instances, the sequence is used in a more directly referential manner, hinting at the "temporary imbalance" to which Bridgman alludes. "Once wait and await. Twice state and understate. Three times ask to be injured in that way" (*ANOTY*, 60). "Can two things be returned and given so that they can be only one?" (*ANOTY*, 108). "After all three times the first a cousin the second an interloper the third an enemy" (*ANOTY*, 75). Finally, perfectly straightforward statements appear to refer directly to the triangle and express the narrator's opinion about being one of three: "Advise now three not as acceptable as two" (*ANOTY*, 68); "Who would prefer one to the other she would the one she had chosen" (*ANOTY*, 26); "Why is it not at all an easy thing to have more than one at a time" (*ANOTY*, 89); "She here they there then where"; "One two three all out but she" (*ANOTY*, 20).

These last statements, which seem to refer explicitly to the pain and confusion of being "one of three," perhaps imply that the love triangle plot is more clearly evident in the novel than it in fact is. Stein's description of how to reveal something and at the same time conceal its identity depicts more accurately the way in which the dynamic operates: "the thing in itself folded up inside like you might fold a thing up to be another thing which is that thing inside in that thing."[23] While the impulse toward concealment—overtly stated here—may reflect Stein's desire to code lesbian content (as Bridgman and others have argued), while it may be considered as part of a larger tradition of concealment in women's writing, I would also suggest that in *A Novel of Thank You* Stein is consciously developing an aesthetics based on assertion of the right to privacy, an author's right to be *anti*autobiographical, rather than on a defensive self-censorship, a willful obscurity, or a necessary self-protection.

In this case, Stein's aesthetics of privacy emerges from a refusal to elaborate the painful loss of connection to another—a loss of the intimate dialogic base that Chessman contends is the primary structure out of which Stein's writing is generated. Here, then, a personal insistence on privacy is articulated in relation to an avant-garde aesthetic, carried forward in Stein's renewed investigation of narrative. With its emphasis on absence and loss, *A Novel of Thank You* shares a similar emotional "ground tone" with works such as Beckett's *The Unnameable* or Barth's *Lost in the Funhouse;* it is not a "contented subjectivity" that Stein describes here. Neither, however, does the novel inscribe an agonized metaphysical isolation as do these male authored texts. If, as Waugh observes, women's writing is often motivated by an effort to discover a collective concept of subjectivity that foregrounds the construction of identity in relation, it might also register the temporary failure of this effort, the tragic disruption of the relational base. This loss and Stein's refusal to speak of it—to turn it into the plot of the text—give rise to the novel's inwardness, its restless circling of a missing referent that "reflects" an absence of intimate connection to another.

The triply motivated context I've elaborated—in which Stein's aesthetic program for the new novel is refracted through the prism of a complex interpersonal dynamic—is articulated within the text through a number of formal strategies. These include methods for disrupting received expectations of what novels should consist of—in particular expectations involving "storiness"—as well as strategies for carrying forward the novel as a genre by refiguring in contemporary terms such things as narrative momentum. As I suggested earlier, both modes of revisioning imply the need for a changed relation of reader to text, a new mode of apprehension—since if one attempts to explicate the novel in a conventional manner one risks reconstructing it as a linear text. It is perhaps necessary to begin with new description terms. It might, for example, be appropriate to speak of a gravitational pull in the text that is not a pull toward the center or of a magnetic attraction/repulsion between certain segments of the text, a drive toward or away from objects that remain in motion. The novel might be considered a map of gathering intensities followed by losses of momentum, or as a nexus of voices, some clear, some muted, some incomprehensible. It *is* possible to identify recurring actions, preoccupations, and motifs in the novel, though again these do not cohere to form a plotted sequence of events, a revealed significance overall, or even a fully logical pattern of internal references. Rather, the manner of their recurrence follows the dynamic model of interaction suggested above. Key terms are distributed throughout the novel rather than developed in it, moving into patterns of relation through the particular ways in which they echo, reverberate, attract, or repel one another within the text rather than in relation to a discursive content outside it.

Centers of relevance shift with each gathering of intensity or promise of significance and then disperse; though not structured by a regular pattern of recurrence, the text is not incoherent. Rather, these centers of relevance are established in the initial twenty pages of the text and recur throughout as leitmotifs operating according to principles of condensation and displacement. In these initial pages, words and phrases suggesting attachment (attraction, attachment, fasten, movement toward, coming toward, staying, union, following, meeting, remaining, uniting, conversation) alternate with those suggesting separation (leaving, parting, moving away, withdrawing, unfastening). The multiple "arrangements" and "changes" among these terms or "tendencies" are explored but motivations as such as not ("He came to Helen. She came to William. In no other ways are reasons stated" [*ANOTY*, 10]). If plot as an abstraction were schematized into forces of relation, it might be presented as just such a configuration: people moving toward or away from some(one) (thing) based on a principle of attraction or repulsion that could be called motivation. Stein comments early on that she is writing the "story of a preparation for and because of a disturbance" (*ANOTY*, 9), a word whose etymology—to drive asunder—suggests disruption of something once united such as a close couple. This disturbance "makes them wish and leave and afterwards" (*ANOTY*, 9). In terms of an exploration of the nature of the novelistic, then, a novel is the form that explores and explains desire (wishes) and disequilibrium (disturbances), perhaps the basic reasons for movement, narrative or otherwise. Significantly, the result of the wishing and the consequences of the leaving—what comes afterwards—is kept vague and unstated, just as preparations for and because of the disturbance are highlighted rather than the nature or consequences of the disruption itself. This is, after all, a novel of irresolution that refuses to link events causally. The terms suggested above therefore function as numbers have: to evoke in an abstract way and self-reflexively comment upon a feature of narrative, again, in the context of a particular interpersonal dynamic that is gestured toward here.

As this early example suggests, key terms float through the text and at various points converge, creating what I have called centers of relevance or emphasis, although they do not function to develop plot, motivation, or character. Instead, the motion of dispersion (forward movement) followed by points of accumulation (climax) simulates the progressive movement normally associated with narrative without actually progressing toward anything. For example, the initial pages of the novel establish that "We have decided to leave for the country at once . . . very likely she said she would stay" (*ANOTY*, 3). The leaving/staying opposition becomes, in the next few pages, a losing/having dynamic: "It is easier to have, to have and to directly and indirectly fasten and unfasten and liberate and inclined to be inclined to take it . . . she said united and reunited" (*ANOTY*, 4–5). Union is replaced by separation in the sentences "so much makes willingness to go . . ." (*ANOTY*, 9) and "it is very satisfactory to engage to go" (*ANOTY*, 15); "I think it is very likely that she is going out this evening" (*ANOTY*, 15); "All the left, left, left I had a good job and I left" (*ANOTY*, 16). The text moves as these passages suggest "forward and back and back to back to back to back to back further back" (*ANOTY*, 11). This rhythm of attachment-separation-attachment promotes coherence and a textual momentum or "pull" that substitutes rhythm for causation. Yet the pattern created by this rhythm is only momentary—made and unmade, "fastened" and "unfastened" almost in the same breath.

One point of coherence or rest for this movement to and fro of key textual items occurs in chapter 42:

Union
A conversation between them.
They came every day.
They came every other day. They came every other day.
Virtually.
And now extra merriment and meant.

This is introducing and this is arranging and this is
returning
and this is resembling this is resembling too.
He was immensely interested. (*ANOTY*, 48)

A number of terms unite here—coming to visit, returning, resembling (and reassembling). Union is the subject of the passage also as the first line indicates. The earlier terms echoed here help to convey a sense of coherence and consistency of preoccupation as well as a sense of the liveliness of a conversation with its dynamic of introducing and arranging and returning (the form of the novel as a whole). It thus signifies in both substance and form the process of intensification and dissipation of textual energy that serves in lieu of significant events to "structure" and move the novel. This passage, like many others throughout the text, expresses union without unification, convergence without synthesis, movement-toward without teleology. Whatever is asserted—for example, "They came every day"—is quickly undone—"They came every other day. Virtually."

The following passage further elaborates the process of condensation operating in the text as a whole and provides a good example of the way in which the triangulation "theme"—coded and private— intersects with Stein's specification in the novel of a new narrative technique.

Everything that will be said in connection with porters will also have the same meaning in connection with carriers and subjects and animals and advancing and returning and going and coming and returning and collecting. Everything that will be said will have a connection with paper and amethysts with writing and silver with buttons and books. In this way she knows what I mean and he knows what I mean and I know what I mean. (*ANOTY*, 114)

As in the previous example, here the textual movement of going and coming, advancing and returning, halts, is collected and connected through a process of infolding or heightening of intensity where one thing becomes another (union) and a suggestion of climax or significance is generated. The passage, in fact, is saturated with suggestions of significance and submerged double meanings: porters are carriers of luggage, as subjects are the carriers of names and content in novels, as animals can be carriers when they are beasts of burden, as human subjects are also animals. This sentence is more easily accessible than the final one where these multiple meanings directly point to private significations—not named.

The passage also indicates another major emphasis in the novel: naming/meaning vs. concealing the name of something. On one level, names function, as numbers do, to suggest narrative development in an abstract way. Long lists of proper names occur throughout, suggesting a deranged Russian novel or a surreal roman à clef (Carl Van Vechten tells us in the introduction to *A Novel of Thank You* the real personages to whom many of these names refer). Lists of names substitute for character development, as numbers and counting have substituted for causal sequence and plot development. Typically proper names unify and identify characters by signifying a coherent collection of specifiable traits, a separate, recognizable identity. Stein undercuts this process of constructing identity by refusing to assign traits to her "characters" or even to allow a single name to refer to a single character. The emphasis falls not on identi(ty)fication, but on a process of transformation that dislocates unitary notions of identity:

> Everybody can change a name they can change the name Helen to Harry they can change the name Edith to Edward they can change the name Harriet to Howard and they can change the name Ivy to Adela. This makes it impossible for all of them to say what they mean. (*ANOTY*, 38)

It is impossible because identity and representation depend on the construction of difference, a principle disrupted here.

As key terms become conflated and condensed, collapsed into "events," so "everybody is named Etienne, everybody is named Charles. Everybody is named Alice. Everybody is named everybody" (*ANOTY*, 43). All characters become Alice; the thousands become one plus the one who names. At the same time, no "one" can be singled out and named since everybody is everybody else, a process that foregrounds the naming of names and conceals identities at the same time, Stein's most elaborate working through of the insistence on privacy, an insistence that at times becomes deliberate and overt. "I will not use her name," the narrator flatly tells us early in the novel and later rather slyly comments that "we can easily be careful. It is not by their names that they are called" (*ANOTY*, 24, 161). This refusal may seem mysterious unless it is contextualized by an elaboration of Stein's multiple reasons for refusing to tell.

Conflating identities in this way signals Stein's rejection of one of the fundamental principles upon which the novel typically depends: the construction of a hierarchy of significance by which particular textual details are marked as more important than others. *A Novel of Thank You* also fails to provide a stable center of orientation in the form of a narrative persona, a fixed psychological center that, in the absence of other kinds of orienting devices—a comprehensible structuration of events or coherently structured characters, for example—might serve as a center of thematic coherence and narrative authority. As events in the novel are abstracted and indeterminate, so the narrative voice is both present and not clearly locatable. The text unfolds in language—someone is speaking—but the narrative "I" does not remain at a stable point or level of enunciation, nor does it cohere long enough to allow for clear construction of a persona to which it might be said to refer. A shifting marker, "I" does not name a location, a perspective, a site of structuration; instead it indicates a force of dislocation, the site of structure's dissolution and dispersion.

A Novel of Thank You lacks the climactic teleological structure of traditional fiction in which events are ordered into a temporal sequence and developed progressively toward resolution. In place of an explanation or motivation, the novel displays shifting incomplete centers of relevance. It also lacks a coherently structured central consciousness. Finally, the novel dismantles an ontological hierarchy in fiction by which textual levels (the real, the remembered, the imagined, for example) are ordered and kept distinct. One level, in effect, obsessively haunts another, making it difficult to construct a stable context of narration from which to distinguish authorial commentary on the plot from the "plot" itself, or metafictive statements about the novel from the actual novel under construction. Real, fictive, and metafictive interpenetrate—in an ontological flickering or oscillation—and context shifts so frequently and unsystematically that no satisfactory means is available to definitively place such shifts. Instead the shifting of the text itself predominates—the movement that occurs before the impulse toward structuration, textual flux unmediated by a stable narrative form.

As it is possible to describe points of condensation, several levels of enunciation also emerge in the novel however thoroughly these intermingle and however difficult it is to specify the relations among levels. The novel's key terms are thus also displaced across textual levels, and in this way, the text becomes intratextually reflexive. At one level of enunciation, a subconversational or peripheral reality, a narrative voice self-reflexively mumbles in a region on the edge of full consciousness, a subject turning around and around in language—perhaps one indication of a disruption of the dialogic base.

> To be worried about whether to be worried about whether whether to be worried whether to be worried whether and they went to go. Whether they went to go. They went to go whether they went to go and repeat easily whether they went to go.
> Around a mound and mind and kind. To like that kind and remind remind and reminded, have it and ashamed and nicely to be placed where they can be. Be can be changed to see.
> Finally fed fairly well.
> To-day to lay and obey exchanged for Sunday.
> To let and to let them and to imagine to let them and to manage to arrange to manage to exchange and to let them. Should cousins marry.
> They had said one another they had said their mother they had said their brother they had said their cousins and their mother. They had said one another they had said more than that and then one and two make it easily arranged that they were not easily believed to be as soon as they were named. (*ANOTY*, 47)

As others in the novel do, this passage indicates many of the novel's recurrent preoccupations—going, arranging, naming, transforming. It also captures the involuted obsessed tone of much of the work, its stammering rhythm of fitful halts and starts. ("Whether whether to be worried whether to be worried . . .") and its nervous indecisiveness ("whether to be worried whether . . . they went to go") as if the emotional residue of disruption suffuses the text.

At another textual level appear perfectly straightforward passages of conventional description. Since the bulk of the novel is not conventionally coherent or declarative, these passages stand out in sharp relief, as when in chapter 186 a speaker breaks into lyricism:

> It was early in the spring and a yellow butterfly which had flown was observed. Also it was to be noted that the trees which had put forth their buds and mistletoe in them which also was putting forth blossoms and berries. All this made the morning and the afternoon most delightful. (*ANOTY*, 158)

This passage might be called pure description, save for the interpretive comment at the end of the paragraph. Paradoxically, however, this type of passage does not shore up a sense of "reality" by providing a stable location or perspective from which to judge other levels of the text. Rather, passages such as this highlight the constructed dimension of the real, embedded as they are in a text where discontinuity, flux, and fragmentation predominate rather than coherence, consistency, and easy comprehensibility.

At this level also are snippets of realistic dialogue (as opposed to subconversational mumblings). These range from abstract and disembodied conversations that suggest disruption ("Hear me out. Why. Hear me out. Why. Hear her out. Why." [*ANOTY*, 57], "He said she said and he said she said . . ." [*ANOTY*, 77]), to statements that more directly suggest the love triangle plot ("Come and kiss me when you want to . . . Dear Dearest. Come and eat. Very well come and eat"), to frankly autobiographical comments ("Miss Alice Toklas wishes to engage someone who will be reliable courteous and efficient" [*ANOTY*, 15]). However tempting it is to accord greater importance to statements such as these, autobiography in fact has no greater narrative authority in the text (it is no less "fictive") than the narrator's subconversational mumblings or the lists of numbers, since *A Novel of Thank You* is a story of arrangements and not of discursive hierarchies. Thus these statements also highlight a strategy of saying and unsaying—they are suggestive but refuse to deliberately point, tantalizing us with the impulse to interpret the text autobiographically (to make this plot predominate) and undercutting this impulse.

Finally, the text contains both overt metafictive statements on the novel as a form and short sequences of what might be called conventional narrative, in which family relations are the central preoccupations. As we might expect, these embedded speculations on the novel do not cohere into a consistent theory of the genre, but in their diversity they do serve to suggest the flexibility of the novel as a form. "It is very easy to change a novel"; "a novel is useful for more reasons than one," as my argument about the triply motivated context out of which the text emerges is meant to suggest (*ANOTY*, 112, 18). It may even have contradictory qualities. Thus "a novel is usual" (*ANOTY*, 93) and "a novel is news" (*ANOTY*, 81); "a novel is once in a while necessary" ("he needed a novel") (*ANOTY*, 152) and "no longer necessary" (*ANOTY*, 188). A novel may be indistinguishable from reality ("a novel can tell everything that is true . . . it can tell everything that comes out not fancifully but really" [*ANOTY*, 134]); it may be "changed into a story of adventure" (*ANOTY*, 112); and it may be about only its own coming into being as writing ("a novel of thank you and not about it. It might be allowed" [*ANOTY*, 180]). *A Novel of Thank You* embodies and contains these contradictions; it is both commonplace and remarkable, mundane and exciting, about reality and about itself. The identity of the novel genre may be transformed, Stein seems to suggest, as easily as "everybody can change a name" (*ANOTY*, 38).

This emphasis on transformation extends to the sequences of "conventional" narrative scattered throughout the text that enact thematically the rhythm of dispersal/separation, at play in the "structure" of the text as a whole. In most cases these passages focus on family relations in a state of metamorphosis or disruption as in the following "tale":

Suppose a man in Portugal had a wife a son and a daughter and another daughter and he came to live in a place where there had been plenty of water would he want to would he be ready to place his wife in another place which he had bought for her where he would not sit with her or with either daughter or with the son he would not mind the son he might not have another daughter would he mind leaving altogether leaving his wife or one daughter or the other daughter would he mind altogether altogether leaving his wife altogether leaving his wife not with this daughter or with that daughter would he mind leaving his wife altogether in the place which he had bought her with or without either daughter. As the daughters were both young they would naturally stay with their Portuguese nurse which they did. In this way there would never be any reason for one who was older to be as it were older every reason and the one who was a little younger to be as much as a little younger. (*ANOTY*, 66)

The two daughters are named several pages later as the tale of confused family relations continues:

Theodosia was ten and Hilda seven and their brother seventeen or older and their father and their mother and the Portuguese nurse another and if the brother had another brother and if the father had a mother the family did have a mother and if the mother did not have it either and she meant them to stay and they did for a little while. (*ANOTY*, 67)

This passage progresses in a fairly straightforward descriptive manner until the end at which point the identity of the children's mother and of the father's mother grows undistinguishable—is there one mother or are there two? Finally, the family disperses totally into an utter confusion of relations reminiscent of the assertion that in this novel everybody is (named) everybody else.

They were never altogether. They never saw one another or had seen one another all together. . . . having lost a father and a mother they had one son and a daughter the son was older and another father and they had one daughter the daughter looked older and one mother the mother was as old as ever and one mother she was another mother and so much. Every time a family is another, three sons and a daughter and they were as richer and richer than their father and their mother and the father and the mother were as richer and richer than their father and their mother and they used everything over and over. To separate them now. (*ANOTY*, 67–68)

Here, in a replication of the process of condensation described earlier, the family is both dispersed ("They were never altogether." "They never saw one another . . . altogether," "To separate them now") and mingled in confusing ways. One mother is another mother; lost fathers are replaced by other fathers. Similarly, the genealogy described in the penultimate sentence, with each generation richer than the one before, is disrupted summarily in the final sentence. If family members are confused and separated in the way depicted here, then the family can no longer function as a unit; it becomes simply a collection of individuals. If the family is too unified, relations become "inappropriate" and the hierarchy constitutive of the family itself also disintegrates: "He married her she married him how very often it is true that her father married his mother or the other her mother married his father" (*ANOTY*, 80). While this passage points to the commonplace theme of a woman marrying the image of her father in the man she chooses for her spouse, the emphasis also falls on what is fundamentally an incestuous marriage; "he" and "she" in effect are brother and sister if their parents, previously unrelated, marry.

These "scrambled family" passages function in several ways in the novel. First, if we take seriously Bridgman's reading, they might reflect the confusion and flux in the Stein-Toklas "family" at the time the novel was composed; the intrusion of a third party disrupts, disperses, and distorts the previously happy couple. More generally, the passages could refer to the nature of any lesbian relationship when measured in conventional terms against a standard heterosexual family. A lesbian couple "distorts" and "disrupts" this norm; they are "cousins who marry" to paraphrase an earlier question.

Finally, then, these passages also disrupt the genealogical imperative of patriarchy replicated in the structure of traditional realistic fiction. Patricia Tobin, among others, makes clear the connection between patrilineal authority, on which the traditional nuclear family is based, and the causal structure of realist narrative, a connection that Stein, once again, appears to have anticipated:

> Within the extended family, the individual member is guaranteed both identity and legitimacy through the tracing of his lineage back to the founding father, the family's origin and first cause . . . By an analogy of function, events in time come to be seen as begetting other events within a line of causality similar to the line of generations, with the prior event earning a special prestige as it is seen to originate, control and predict future events. The same lineal decorum pervades the structure of realis-

tic narrative: all possibly random events and gratuitous details are brought into an alignment of relevance, so that at the point of conclusion all possibility has been converted into necessity within a line of kinship—the subsequent having been referred to the prior, the end to the beginning, the progeny to the father.[24]

When the genealogical imperative of the realistic novel is contested (decentered) and gives way as it does in *A Novel of Thank You*, so do traditional notions of coherence, succession, motivation, and narrative hierarchy. In their place appear motion, discontinuity, free-floating parts, transformations, proliferations of possibilities: in short, a breakdown of realist form in favor of the textual flux that defines Stein's new novel.

Stein refuses to develop, explain or even explicitly to name the enigma that is raised at the outset of *A Novel of Thank You*. Instead, she advances a theory of textual sliding or movement in every direction to replace the conventional novelistic technique of development through the causal connection of discrete events. This genealogical imperative, as Tobin reminds us, accords to prior events a "special prestige" to the degree that they "originate, control and predict future events." Expectations of decipherment and significance are nowhere more strongly raised than at the end of a novel. In the final two sections of *A Novel of Thank You* (labeled part 2 and part 3 and consisting of only several pages), Stein refuses to bring the mobile textual fragments into an alignment of relevance and does no more than to suggest a moving away from the central preoccupations that have been raised previously. Chapter 1 of part 2 opens with the word "Christening," suggestive of new beginnings, and ends with the phrase "We have left the pagoda behind us" (*ANOTY*, 237). This emphasis on starting anew is reinforced by the second chapter in which openness operates as a key term (doors are opened, gates are opened). Yet Stein reminds us that she will no more explain the reason for this rebirth than she has explained the development of the disturbance. Chapter 3, the final chapter in part 2, ends with a question—"What is it" (*ANOTY*, 238)—rather than with any definitive resolution. And, in part 3—the novel's final chapter—Stein suggests that the subject of the novel has been concluded already: "We are now entirely occupying ourselves with an entirely different matter"

(*ANOTY*, 239). Far from using the conclusion to convert possibility into necessity, to refer "the progeny to the father" as Tobin suggests the realist novel must do, and as Stein herself had done earlier in *Q.E.D.*, she concludes *A Novel of Thank You* by suggesting that the father has been dispensed with entirely: "A man may not be there at the time. This is the difference between this [the novel we are reading, the current state of affairs] and that [the realist novel, as well as the previous disturbance]" (*ANOTY*, 240).

In "The Ends of Man," Jacques Derrida suggests two potential strategies for deconstructing logocentric systematics; first, deconstruction can attempt its work without changing ground and by repeating the original problematics, use against the system its own resources; second, it can attempt to change ground and abruptly step aside, affirming total discontinuity and difference.[25] In *A Long Gay Book*, Stein employs the former strategy by dismantling the comprehensive genealogy she struggles to erect even as she is constructing it. In *A Novel of Thank You* Stein works toward the second strategy, and, in the effort to change ground, opens new textual spaces within the novel. Neither the static linear plot of realist fiction, nor the mobile and fragmented but ultimately recombinable (centered) space of the modernist novel, this is a postmodern space of flux and resolute indeterminacy. Put another way, *A Novel of Thank You* anticipates a contemporary problematic in that it is among the first literary works to manifest fully a rupture in the traditional concept of centered structure that Derrida identifies as one of the defining features of our postmodern era. Yet it does so through a context of enunciation that differs in significant ways from the narrative stance of many modern and postmodern male writers. Thus the novel also illustrates the importance of redefining the cultural emergence of this decentering impulse in terms that take into account gender positioning.

Chapter 4

Per(form)ance in *Lucy Church Amiably*

The great obsession of the nineteenth century was, as we know, history. . . . Space was treated as the dead, the fixed, the undialectical, the immobile. Time, on the contrary, was richness, fecundity, life, dialectic. . . . The present epoch will perhaps be above all the epoch of space. We are in the epoch of simultaneity: we are in the epoch of juxtaposition, the epoch of the near and far, of the side-by-side, of the dispersed. We are at a moment, I believe, when our experience of the world is less that of a long life developing through time than that of a network that connects points and intersects with its own skein. . . .
—Michel Foucault, "Of Other Spaces"

It is scarcely any longer possible to tell a straight story sequentially unfolding in time. And this is because we are too aware of what is continually traversing the story laterally. That is to say, instead of being aware of a point as an infinitely small part of a straight line, we are aware of it as an infinitely small part of an infinite number of lines, as the center of a star of lines. Such awareness is the result of our constantly having to take into account the simultaneity and extension of events and possibilities. . . . Prophesy now involves a geographical rather than historical projection; it is space not time that hides consequences from us.
—John Berger, *The Look of Things*

There is not much conversation in abundance. . . . There is a widening of reverberation of accompanying pleases with pleases.
—Gertrude Stein, *Lucy Church Amiably*

In his useful essay on the emergence of a postmodern worldview, Hans Bertens describes two aesthetic modes or tendencies operating within much contemporary fiction, each premised on a desire to go beyond the aesthetic principles of a mimetic tradition and to invent new fictional responses for a contemporary moment.[1] In the first, a self-conscious or metafictive mode, fiction reflects on its own coming into being, its own linguistic status and form. The role or goal traditionally claimed by fiction—producing knowledge about the world— here is replaced by an impulse to explore the world of/as signification and to chart, through these movements of the signifier, the nature and meaning of writing in a contemporary moment. Such fiction is implosive in its impulse, turning back on itself—sometimes in entropic frigid isolation, sometimes in an anarchic spray of self-generating permutations. In the second mode, fiction expands outward, based on an awareness that, as Raymond Federman puts it, "everything can be said now."[2] Collapsing traditional narrative hierarchies and subject/object distinctions, this postmodern mode is impelled by a desire to incorporate the world, become deliriously involved with it. This impulse may take the form of a vitalistic, ritualistic, even a mystic postmodernism that overtly rejects the values of Western rationalism in favor of a preliterate, prerational "all-embracing acceptance of the here-and-how . . . characterized by a certain reverence, a certain awe."[3] Ihab Hassan names this tendency "Immanances" by which he means "the capacity of mind to generalize itself in the world, to act upon both self and world, and so become more and more immediately, its own environment."[4]

These two postmodern tendencies, while perhaps overly schematized or not as easily separable as my summary of Bertens suggests, nonetheless provide a useful point of departure for situating in general terms Stein's responses to one of her major aesthetic preoccupations in the 1920s: how to reanimate the novel as a contemporary genre without relying on outmoded realist assumptions and principles. In *A Novel of Thank You*, an introverted text, Stein operates largely within the first mode, inventing self-reflexive strategies that critique "storiness" but also allow the novel to "go on." In *Lucy Church Amiably*, her second major novel of the decade, she works within the terrain of the second, moving toward a delirious involvement with, even incorporation of, the world.

Begun in 1927 at Stein and Toklas's summer home in the Rhone valley near Belinguin, *Lucy Church Amiably* may be read as Stein's effort to refigure the novel as a "bright filled space . . . of silence, stillness, and quick movement," what she refers to as "landscape."[5] "Landscape" is Stein's metaphor for a paradoxical textual dynamic composed of intense nonpredictable and nonteleological movement along with moments of simultaneity and stasis, an endlessly changing textual space that, as such, escapes the rigid hierarchies of realist fiction and the imperative toward formal coherence of modernist texts. More specifically, landscape writing reorders the hierarchy traditionally erected between a textual momentum based on plot—that which moves horizontally through narrative space on its way to completion—and what, in a realist conception, is the "dead," fixed immobility of narrative space itself, that which is "continually traversing the story laterally," in Berger's words, impeding the forward momentum of linear narrative.

In upsetting this traditional hierarchy of narrative significance Stein disrupts a fundamental generative principle of mimetic fiction. Its disruption also has implications for the social hierarchies such fiction reflects, specifically, for my purposes, those gender hierarchies inscribed within the very morphology of narrative and with which it is thus complicit. If, structurally, realist narrative assigns activity and agency to a masculine subject position, then, within a realist paradigm, the feminine occupies the position of obstacle, the mute space of delay in which narrative movement occurs, or the object of desire that represents the end of questing. As Teresa de Lauretis comments:

> In its making sense of the world, narrative endlessly reconstructs it as a two-character drama in which the human person creates and recreates *himself* out of an abstract or purely symbolic other— the womb, earth grave, woman . . . [6]

Throughout the history of metaphysics, nature/space has been spoken—given a narrative, an origin, and a telos—through the arts of mimesis. Traditional social and narrative scripts also mandate that the female body must bear meaning (as the material aspect of language must bear meaning) "a discourse which speaks for her and to which she has no access."[7]

In *Lucy Church Amiably* Stein takes these traditional scripts out of the hierarchical relation through which they have operated, enacting in the novel the consequences of a radical breakdown of them: desire for affiliation replaces desire for the end; sexual differences collapse; the boundary between subject and object as well as among human, animal, and nonanimate, blurs and remains in flux. In this novel, Stein wishes to "bring them back to an appreciation of natural beauty or the beauty of nature hills valleys fields and birds. They say it is beautiful but will they sit in it."[8] In order to appreciate natural beauty, one must "sit in it"; in other words, one may no longer construct the natural world as an object viewed from the perspective of a subject, one may no longer make nature speak and speak as a narrative. The notion of an "environment" that depends for its construction on an empirical belief in separation of subject and object, mental and physical, inner and outer, is refigured in *Lucy Church Amiably*. Nature and culture, self and other, no longer in contradiction, instead interpenetrate and begin to move together assuming new, unpredictable configurations.

Similarly, the "two-character drama" that de Lauretis suggests is central to the functioning of narrative, depends for its existence on construction of a stable and consistent subject position as well as a secure opposition between (an active) subject and (a mute) object. As de Lauretis, Luce Irigaray, and others have shown, the subject counts on the silence of the other—she is that "eternal elsewhere from which the 'subject' continues to draw his reserves,"[9] for without a stable subject/object opposition, identity itself becomes radically unsettled. Thus to give voice to the desire of the other is potentially catastrophic; it is to signify what is untenable in the symbolic, nominal, paternal function.

In *S/Z*, Roland Barthes elaborates the dangers—for the structure of realist fiction and for patriarchal capitalist society in general—of collapsing the subject/object dualism that forms the basis of Western culture.

> . . . it is fatal ["Sarrasine"] says to remove the dividing line, the paradigmatic slash mark which permits meaning to function, . . . life to reproduce (the opposition of the sexes), property to be protected. . . . In short, the story *represents* . . . a generalized collapse of economies . . . This catastrophic collapse always takes the same form: that of unrestrained metonymy. By abolishing the paradigmatic barriers, this metonymy abolishes the power of *legal substitution* on which meaning is based: it is then no longer possible regularly to contrast opposites, sexes, possessions; it is no longer possible to safeguard an order of just equivalence; in a word, it is no longer possible to *represent*, to make things *representative*, individuated, separate, assigned. "Sarrasine" represents the very confusion of representation, the unbridled (pandemic) circulation of signs, of sexes, of fortunes.[10]

The form of realist fiction is premised on the development of strategies for containing the threat that Barthes describes (containment strategies that operate within modernist texts as well). "Unrestrained metonymy" disrupts the form of mimetic fiction with its underlying genealogical authority; it short-circuits narrative order and processes of representation; it subverts bourgeois social order and the clear construction of social and gender identity. This is so because unrestrained metonymy prevents the construction of stable hierarchies of difference, clear dualisms, or patterns of metaphoric equivalence upon which these orders depend for their smooth functioning.

For Stein, however, this "generalized collapse of economies" is not "Catastrophic"; she seeks no saving forms. Rather, in *Lucy Church Amiably* she celebrates the "unbridled circulation of signs" that mimetic fiction must suppress and revels in the merging of economies that "proves fatal" to narrative order and individual identity. Subject and object are set in motion and remain in irresolvable oscillation throughout the text. Individual identity, property, and sexual difference become scrambled through interaction with an economy in which eros, transformations, union, affiliation, generosity, abundance, and pleasure predominate. The preoedipal fantasy liberated at the end of *A Long Gay Book* returns full-blown in *Lucy Church Amiably* as a generative principle, creating a space elsewhere in which "everybody is rich quietly," where the desire is to "let it make a cause to celebrate," where "it is a disappointment to have all in order" (*LCA*, 21).

This leaking or dissolving of generic, cultural, psychic, even ontological boundaries is one defining feature of Stein's new form of the novel (and much postmodern art); ultimately she came to see it as an important characteristic of her work as a whole, as this passage from *Narration* (1935) suggests:

> The inside and the outside, the outside which is outside and inside which is inside are not when they are inside outside are not inside in short they are not existing that is inside. The more a novel is a novel the more a play is a play the more a writing is a writing the more no outside is outside outside is inside is inside.[11]

Stein's description of a textuality generated by the kinetic interplay of inner and outer, subject and object anticipates in many ways con-

temporary efforts—in particular by feminist writers—to move beyond
the limitations of conventional narrative form. Two important theoretical examples here are Luce Irigaray's concept of anamorphic
movement, part of her theory of the mechanics of fluids, and Alice
Jardine's notion of gynesis. Like Stein (though with somewhat different motivations), Irigaray and Jardine wish to map the emergence of
a repressed dynamic that eludes and disrupts cultural and textual
forms, moving through (as the *ana* prefix suggests) but not fully containable by them. As Jardine explains it (drawing on the work of
Jean-François Lyotard), this dynamic traverses and is at odds with
the master narratives of Western culture: those discourses through
which power-knowledge historically has legitimated itself and, more
generally, the narrative function itself as a structure of explanation
and mastery. The emergency of gynesis into/as a postmodern discursive space is thus part of that crisis in legitimation—the "catastrophic" collapse of these Western metanarratives and paternal fictions—that gives rise, at least in part, to the postmodern condition.
Jardine explains this process as "the collapsing of certain structures
into, within, and through new spaces . . . which refuse to stay silent
[to be spoken for] within [their] frame of representation." More specifically, gynesis is "a space . . . coded as 'feminine' [hypothetical and
unmeasurable] . . . over which the narrative has lost control."[12] In
terms similar to Jardine's, Irigaray views anamorphosis as a history-
transcendent (anti) form, equated directly with the female libidinal
economy, and more generally as a figure for the cultural and textual
repression of the "feminine." As such it refers to a "vacancy or gap
in form," a dynamic existing invisibly (potentially catastrophically)
within form as an internal disruption and consisting of "in(de)finite
transformations, metamorphoses with no completion, transmutation
with no telos."[13]

These theories, sketched all too briefly here, are significant efforts to identify and, in Irigaray's case, to enact a dynamic not animated by an Oedipal scenario with its commitment to structure and
telos, a spatialized dynamic still largely invisible—or incomprehensible—through the lens of inherited aesthetic and social categories
as Irigaray stresses. Among other things, such theories help to place
in a larger historical context the cultural functioning of the "feminine," to illuminate new "feminized" dynamics operating within a
contemporary postmodernity, and, crucially, to specify relations be-

tween the two. In proposing and valuing models of textual productivity not based on a demand that form and mimetic intent be the defining features of fiction, they also point to the need for a revision of traditional aesthetic principles—the application of which continue to obscure the nature of these fictional experiments—and a need for the development of a new spatial and kinetic hermeneutic, one suitable for what Foucault calls the epoch of simultaneity.

The specific aesthetic implications of this shift from a temporal modality emphasizing form, teleology, and, above all, mimesis to a kinetic spatial mode emphasizing simultaneity, indeterminacy, and nonmimetic strategies are worth elaborating briefly before turning to a fuller discussion of *Lucy Church Amiably*. The spatial features described thus far in relation to Stein's work are significant aspects of a postmodern performative mode, considered by many to be a genuinely distinct aesthetic that, in part, foregrounds and revalues suppressed or devalued aspects of the aesthetic process itself. As a feature of contemporary visual art, dance, theater, music, and literature in widespread evidence, performance has been called "the unifying mode of the postmodern,"[14] a root metaphor or model that finds parallel expression in a variety of art forms and in the breaking of boundaries between forms. Though broadly used and variously defined (like the postmodern itself) performance, in a general sense, may be considered 1) a cultural orientation that "defines reality in terms of process, flow, interaction, play, and participation,"[15] evident also in philosophy, science, and social thought; 2) a critical approach to texts as when Barthes animates and performs Balzac's "Sarrasine"; and 3) a specific aesthetic activity—in this case a type of writing practice—whose assumptions, values, and strategies depart in definable ways from realist and modernist modes.

Performance engages artist and audience in processes whose goals are fundamentally different from those of a mimetic tradition with its commitment to formal coherence and "truthful" representations of reality based on ordering principles such as causation or chronology. Performative works, by contrast, are not primarily committed to rendering accurate representations or carefully patterned aesthetic wholes, whether of the world or the human psyche. Rather, they are involved in generating strategies for engaging the reader in dynamic (non-re-)presentations, for creating experiences not reproducing them, often with "no sense of direction or time or goal beyond [their] own happening."[16] In place of accuracy, comprehensiveness, or uniqueness, performative works promote the values of immediacy (as in Stein's desire to make the reader "sit in" nature), spontaneity, nonteleological movement, incessant change, openness, partiality, transitoriness. As Richard Poirier comments, "a performance in any medium is made up of thousands of tiny movements"[17] to be experienced primarily for their own sake, ones not necessarily ordered into aesthetic wholes or comprehensible patterns of meaning through the prism of interpretation. Thus within the spatialized performance framework, the novel provides neither an occasion for interpretation nor a source of information; it is not a formalism. Rather it is redefined as a generating environment, an open-ended field of action, offering readers multiple occasions for experience and promoting the intrinsic value of these improvisatory performative moments.

Within the performative text, space no longer encloses and passively supports action but itself becomes activated, mobilized, inhabited in its tiniest nooks and crannies, perhaps even "emptied and carved up" in Josette Féral's words.[18] Neither the public spaces or domestic interiors of the nineteenth-century novel nor the intimate psychological spaces of the modernist, these new performative spaces arise from an unstable mixture between the two, existing in what Féral calls a shifting "infrasymbolic zone," simultaneously physical and imaginary. The writer "traverses, explores, and measures [these spaces] effecting displacements and minute variations within them," becoming "the point of passage for energy flows that traverse him [sic] without ever standing still in a fixed meaning or representation [anamorphic movement]."[19] The writer as performer plays at putting these flows to work, seizing networks, "charting accumulations and connections of signifiers that have been organized neither in a code . . . nor in structures permitting signification," working with "pieces of bodies, pieces of meaning . . . libidinal flows, bits of objects. All without narrativity."[20]

Such radical reconceptions of content and form as are characteristic of a postmodern performance-based art thoroughly undermine (at least) two of the central assumptions of mimetic fiction: that form is the foundation of fiction and that the constitution of the subject as character is the heart of its matter. In *Lucy Church Amiably*, Stein dispenses with these values summarily—she calls it "letting alone names" (164)—thereby deconstructing what Barthes considers the essence of narrative: "not the action but character as Proper Name."[21] Proper names in realist fiction have a purely referential function, being nominal units designed to fix a collection of traits and position an individual within a particular genealogy. As Alain Robbe-Grillet comments:

> A character must have a proper name, two if possible: a surname and a first name. He must have parents and a heredity. He must have a profession. If he has property, all the better. Finally, he has to have a "character," a face which expresses it, a past which has molded them both. His character dictates his actions, makes him react in a predetermined way on every occasion. His character allows the reader to judge him, hate him. It is thanks to this character that one day he will *bequeath his name to a human type* which was, as it were, awaiting the consecration of this baptism.[22]

As Robbe-Grillet indicates, the proper name supports construction of character as a consistent and coherent structure positioned in relation to a social, economic, and psychic hierarchy with which the reader is asked to identify. Such a positioning reflects an ideology of the self as fundamentally intelligible, rendered so in part by the ways in which that self reproduces the same genealogical imperative that structures bourgeois patriarchal society as a whole.

Stein emphasizes this naming function throughout *Lucy Church Amiably*—proper names are the text's most consistently recurring stylistic feature—as if to acknowledge its primacy in establishing social and narrative intelligibility. But "Lucy Church," the person or place or concept that gives the novel its title, refuses to remain consistent or predictable as the proper name in realist fiction is obliged to do. Unpredictability is the novel's only constant; "Lucy Church" and other "characters" in the text "could be, were and can be erased" (*LCA*, 123) as easily as they are written into "being."

The signifier "Lucy Church" refers throughout the novel to—variously—a person, Lucy (who is an old woman, a modest girl, the sister of Frances Church, and her own mother); a building, Lucy church (which is also "a pagoda"); a geographical location ("there is a church and it is in Lucy" [*LCA*, 7]); the spirit of a place ("Lucy Church felt as an illumination" [*LCA*, 82]); space itself ("Lucy Church intermediary intermediary between at a distance in between" [LCA, 107]); a large embracing natural force, transformative in its impulse ("Lucy Church can change mushrooms to daisies and daisies to oxen and oxen to church" [LCA, 218]); "Lucy Church is one and indivisible" (LCA, 230), "Lucy Church an authority" (LCA, 85); a spirit of fecundity ("Lucy Church is to be here if there are to be any births or marriages" [LCA, 166]); and a spirit of pure pleasure ("Lucy Church is very impressed by having been very much and very pleasantly surrounded by what she feels and felt to be very much what is desirable and that is pleasantly" [LCA, 69]).

The novel comes down to "a question of who is who" (LCA, 208) and renders the question itself irrelevant. Through multiple displacements of the term, all identities and differences collapse since no one meaning coheres long enough or consistently enough for anything like a subject to be created. "Lucy Church may be anyone" (LCA, 132) or anything when a novel is not committed to the construction of personalities but instead is "a novel instance of what is the difference what they are like" (LCA, 340).

Stein's technique here recalls Féral's account of the stance adopted by the postmodern performance artist where, as she puts it, "the subject's being [in this case the potential "subject" Lucy Church but also Stein's narrative persona] is simultaneously exploded into part objects and condensed in each of those objects which have themselves become independent entities, each being simultaneously a margin and a center."[23] In the metonymic principle operating here, parts of an association are displayed without any whole being invoked as Lucy Church is not fully any one of the above people, places, or abstract concepts, but the signifier that names them all. Not a process of metaphorization in which Lucy Church represents, say, the spirit of the French countryside or a female creative principle, the term instead moves anamorphically throughout these categories: the space of passage and space as passage-of-energy-flows and partial significations that never stand still in fixed representations.

As the unnamed "event" in A Novel of Thank You does, Lucy Church's presence pervades the novel, but does not center or fix the text. Instead, Lucy Church migrates wildly and unpredictably across the range of registers suggested above as other proper names in the text do. The term names, scatters, reenters the signifying space of the novel, and is again displaced, shifting along the entire spectrum of person, place, thing, spirit within a page or two, or sometimes within a single sentence: "Lucy Church came to know Helen that is Helen drank pansies" (*LCA*, 163); "Lucy Church in meadows and very well remembering Lily Lilian very well remembering mauve lilies with a short stem" (*LCA*, 136); "Lucy Church might have been rain Lucy Church might have been going and hearing in the rain. Lucy Church did not sing it is not the habit of the country to sing" (*LCA*, 128). Human and organic interpenetrate associatively without warning and without explanation. Lucy Church "may be a church," and on the next page may "go to church," and several pages later may be an "admirable meadow where clover is found," since "Lucy Church was the one who when she came to ask never came at all by left and right and so they may be what ever they wish..." (*LCA*, 92–95). Recurring frequently but not predictably, refusing to behave according to any standard pattern of recurrence, Lucy Church "never came at all by left and right." Each repetition of the term "Lucy Church" generates new possibilities and new contradictions rather than any resolution; each return only further expands, proliferates, and confuses the "meaning" of *Lucy Church Amiably*.

This semantic dispersion or displacement of the "part object" Lucy Church, its seemingly infinite semantic horizon, generates textual momentum and creates a spatialized signifying network that forms the "landscape" of the novel. Each return of the term echoes but does not develop previous ones, as if all exist simultaneously in different discursive spaces. Thus the term generates around itself an indefinite space that consists simply of the projective possibility of its going on to recur elsewhere, a tendency reinforced by the structure of speculation—"Lucy Church might be x..."—that appears throughout the text. The possibility of infinite semantic extension (unrestrained metonymy) is, of course, central to the functioning of language; in a most dramatic way *Lucy Church Amiably* performs the signifying process itself in which determinate meaning (presence) is constantly displaced and deferred in an endless web of signification.[24] "Away from the demand that it name, language plays," as Edward Said puts it, "it is a trace bringing together an economy of the here and there, of inscription and effacement, or of continuation and recognition as aspects of the play of differences."[25]

The ludic possibilities that arise when language is viewed as a material presence animates much of the text (as they do other Stein

works and performative texts generally) as the following example—
one of many—suggests:

> Miche is not Michel. It is ed i belle. This is all well. Says my very
> famous Belle not Belley. This is to introduce Lamartine to a
> queen. This is to introduce Lamartine as seen. This is to intro-
> duce Claudel as well. This is to introduce Severine in between.
> Feeding nettles to ducks and chickens makes graduation and
> raspberries and strawberries in autumn change Bertha to Barbara
> to Belle to William Tell. (*LCA*, 21)

A strong pattern of internal rhyme ("Michel," "ed i belle," "Belle,"
"Belley," "Claudel," "William Tell," "as well") and alliteration (especially the liquid "l" sound) predominates in this passage and collapses differences by promoting semiotic connections rather than semantic distinctions. The passage is full of proper names, but again
these names do not act to secure individual identity. Rather, here and
throughout, Stein exploits the ludic potential of the proper name as
a sound to be played with materially—sung, "let it be louder than
allowed," Stein says elsewhere (*LCA*, 35)—tasted (people become
edible [ed i belle] in the first half of the passage; foods become people
in the second half) and digested in our "Belleys."

Stein also disrupts the traditional naming function in other ways
throughout the text, sometimes overtly reinforcing the link between
naming and patriarchal genealogical authority. Ulla Dydo suggests
that Stein's return to an overt critique of this authority—located most
directly in the family—may have been inspired by her and Toklas's
confrontation with the legal system as they made out their wills pre-
paratory to buying a house. A system based in heterosexual privilege
and "regular living," as Stein was fond of calling it, could find no
way of representing a lesbian couple, and the overall transformative
impulse of the novel, its commitment to a fluid open nonhierarchical
dynamic, may well have been motivated in part by a desire to escape
the tyranny of these social and legal strictures.[26]

The novel opens with an account of confused family relations
much like those described in portions of *A Novel of Thank You:*

> The husband had been in England. The wife had been brought
> up by a family that had had her mother there and this gave such

a gracious pair an additional restoration of their share. Having a
daughter she had married a man who because of wounds or
because of character made it inevitable that she should falter and
so having left it more than a mother two children for this and
that brought to her. (*LCA,* 9)

Here, the husband/father is separated from the family and the emphasis falls on the wife, the mother of the wife, and the daughters
of the wife, almost a matrilineal descent. Several pages later, the
narrator asserts that "he does not believe that a family is necessary
necessarily a family" (*LCA,* 10). Finally, the hierarchy of differential
relations by which families operate collapses entirely in an incestuous
heap in which "there is no difference between fathers daughters sons
sisters brothers mothers . . ." (*LCA,* 38). The imploding of family relations and gender distinctions initiated by the absence of the father,
mirrors the generalized collapse of economies and the rise of principles of affiliation (unrestrained metonymy) that, as I have suggested,
operate throughout the novel to efface differences.

    While "Lucy Church" dominates the text as the locus of affiliation
(by which I mean conjoined in relationship, though not in a "legal"
or "sanctioned" one as would occur in families or logical systems),
she/it is joined by two other "characters," Simon Therese and John
Mary who/that operate in the same wildly transformative manner.
As Lucy Church is a name, person, place, and abstract concept, so
the latter two terms most notably combine genders—showing gender
itself to be performative. Stein delineates the consequences of this
gender instability throughout the novel as, for example, in the following passage:

Simon Therese is always married to Mrs. Moffett and she has
taken very good care of him she is not married to him because
perhaps she has another husband living and after all if he were
to be sure to be sure to be go she would be very well after all as
it is did her say who is a member of the family anyway. This can
make Simon Therese not a not a mother his mother was blonder
with blue eyes and blonder and now not blonder how can anyone tell from white what white is. How can anyone tell from
white what white is. (*LCA,* 235)

Surrounded in this passage by wife (Mrs. Moffett) and mother, Simon Therese appears to be gendered male. Yet the categories of wife, mother, husband, and the genders male/female are by no means fixed and stable. Simon Therese is both married and not married to Mrs. Moffett (who "perhaps has another husband living"); moreover, he is not a mother, a fact that in its apparent obviousness raises questions about his gender in the first place. Whether or not Mrs. Moffett is married or Simon Therese is a mother appears to be of no concern to Simon Therese who apparently does not care to definitely fix and assign position by asking "who is a member of the family anyway." Significantly, the passage ends by reasserting the principle of affiliation that collapses differences (including gender): one needs a contrasting color to distinguish "what white is"; one needs difference in order to fix and name people, places, concepts. In this novel, however, differences, family, individual identity cease to matter; as Stein reiterates everywhere in the text: "what is the difference what they are like."

The "themes" of affiliation (the collapse of difference) and transformation are also reiterated in explicit statements throughout the novel, as in "It does not make any difference when the difference between a poplar and a fig tree is ascertained" (LCA, 62); and "There is no difference whether he looks like Simon or whether he does not" (LCA, 56). The phrase "there is no difference" recurs nearly as frequently as proper names do, as the following passage demonstrates:

> There is no difference between younger and older between told and told her between him and between him. There is no difference hurriedly. When this is said said said said. . . .
> There is no difference at all whether it is he or having him or his or held or Brillat Savarin or their laudation or by the time or with a window and respect or in respect to losses losses of wild pansies which can be used as an infusion none of these make any difference permanently as they are all rich. (LCA, 23–24)

The first paragraph collapses differences based on age, on the distinction between subject ("told") and object ("told her"), on individual identity ("him" and "him"—the pronouns functioning here to minimize difference as well), and on the differentiating function of language. This emphasis on effacing individual identity (viewed as a private possession) is developed further in the second paragraph: "There is no difference at all whether it is he or having him or his or held. . . ." In the landscape of *Lucy Church Amiably* identities become fused together ("infused"), and private property (including, again, subjectivity as a form of private property) does not matter "as they are all rich."

Suggestions of richness, abundance, and transformation appear in the following passage also, which illustrates well the principles of affiliation and exfoliation at the heart of the novel:

> All gold is put into water and all water is put into butter and all butter is put into apples and all apples are put into trees and all trees are put into flourishing and all flourishing is put into welcome and all welcome is put into translation and all translation is resisting to their having felt that it was most and best and called called it at the time that it was actually reunited in spite of their addition of which and whether it is mine. (*LCA*, 12–13)

The processes of flourishing and translation by which gold becomes water becomes butter becomes apples become trees (a kind of alchemy in reverse) opposes ("resists") the impulse to draw distinctions and separations: to fix by naming, to establish hierarchies ("most" and "best"), to place in time, to fix something as a possession.

The passage also suggests that the writer's task of translating these values into language must employ principles appropriate to a topographical and not a historiotemporal aesthetic. "In every instance," Stein states elsewhere in the text, "there is a difference between history and geography" (*LCA*, 15). The geographical impulse behind landscape writing conveys not events moving through time but things "being always in relation the trees to the hills the hills to the fields the trees to each other any piece of it to any sky and then any detail to any other detail, the story is only of importance if you like to tell or hear a story but the relation is there anyway."[27] Landscape writing subordinates the transmission of story/content to the exposure of associations created through spatial relations such as juxtaposition or contiguity; in this it shares features with the "spatial form" of many modernist texts. However, within the landscape aesthetic, individual elements move in and out of relation to other details that are themselves also moving in relation to other details (etc.) rather than in relation to a unifying pattern of images or a fixed center. Created through this process is a decentered network of kinetic relations or spatial functions in which, theoretically, no one detail assumes greater viability or authority than another, and in which combinations of details are, as I have suggested, potentially infinite. This is a model appropriate to the epoch of space . . . of simultaneity, of juxtaposition, of the near and far, of the side-by-side, of the dispersed, relationships that permeate *Lucy Church Amiably* at its most basic level and that are reinforced by overt spatial and kinetic references throughout (e.g., opening and closing, going and coming, moving in and out, back and forth, up and down, near and far). Again, this model is to be distinguished from the modernist spatial turn that, as Fredric Jameson suggests, serves to reinscribe the authority of form and subordinate space to existential time, deep memory, experience, and expression, values that "are altogether not of place in and anachronistic in a postmodern age." In retrospect, spatial form in the modernist sense has "more in common with the mnemonic unifying emblems of Frances Yates's memory palaces than with the discontinuous spatial experience and confusions of the postmodern. . . ."[28]

Lucy Church Amiably is subtitled "A Novel of Romantic Beauty," and "Romance," Stein tells us, "is there but it does not continue it has no time it is neither past nor present nor future it is there because it is something with which you cannot come into contact as it exists of itself and by itself and looks as it does when it is. . . ."[29] Like romance or like sound in John Cage's formulation, landscape is occupied with the performance of its characteristics. It "does not continue" through time but neither is it static; it "exists by itself" but consists of dynamized parts moving in relation to each other. It is "something with which you cannot come into contact" so it cannot be known as an object of speculation, but if one enters into its rhythm and moves with it one may learn appreciation. In *Lucy Church Amiably*, Stein displays the landscape of/as Lucy Church and she does so, as the etymology of the word suggests, (from *plier*—to fold or bend but also to deploy) by unfolding its multiple contradictory characteristics and deploying them across textual space. They are "inhabited" in their shifting displacements and minute variations, in their thousands of tiny movements and partial significations. In displaying them Stein also plays them—like wind or waves or flames play, ir-regularly, intermittently—and offers new imaginative spaces to in-habit actively, receptively, amiably.

Suggestions appear throughout the novel that Stein considers the generative transformative force, Lucy Church, to be emblematic of her own creative powers. Like Stein, "Lucy Church made master-pieces readily and excitedly" and often is "in hyperbole" (*LCA*, 59), "Lucy Church does not introduce subjects" (*LCA*, 66), as "there is not much conversation in abundance" (*LCA*, 71). Stein acknowledges the demand that an author "put into a book what is to be read in a book, bits of information and tender feeling," but also makes overt her (ongoing) intention to undercut this expectation. "You can tell yes," she says, but "you can [also] tell less and less" (*LCA*, 128) and wryly asks the reader at the end of the novel "how do you like your two percent bits of information and tender feeling?" (*LCA*, 174). From the point of view of the information it conveys, *Lucy Church Amiably* is a two-bit novel.

How then are we to value a text that conveys little content, preferring to chart "accumulations of signifiers," that displays the "realities of the imaginary" rather than the life stories of characters, that appears structurally chaotic, and inhabits shifting indeterminate spaces? Obviously it is important not to judge such a text by criteria developed to explain another tradition, in particular when there is a "fundamental irreconcilability" between these two traditions such as exists between performance theories and the classic theory of art as mimesis.[30] I suggested at the outset that *Lucy Church Amiably* might be profitably considered within a postmodern incorporative mode in which fiction becomes deliriously involved with (and in so doing reconstructs) the world, a process initiated by the collapse of privi-leged centrisms and Western dualisms. Within this mode, often seen as an outgrowth of the earlier (performance-based) surrealist and dadist avant-garde, art rejects social and psychological limitations in favor of celebrations of the irrational, the ritualistic, the ceremonial, the communal, the vitalistic, or what Victor Turner calls the liminal.

In Turner's account, the liminal refers to a threshold state or process that, like nonsense, exists "betwixt-and-between the normal, day-to-day cultural and social states and processes of getting and spending, preserving law and order, and registering structural status." Liminality describes a time and place of contradictions, open possibilities, experimentation, and play when "anything might, even should, happen."[31] Within folklore traditions or certain tribal initiation rites, the liminal stands between the process of separating from daily life and the final return to it. As this transitory space within which transformations occur, the liminal functions structurally like the middle ground of plot that, occurring between beginning (initiation) and ending (resolution), complicates, delays, confuses, and threatens the return home.

The carnivalesque, most extensively theorized by Mikhail Bakhtin, is perhaps the most well-known description of the cultural function of this liminal state. According to Bakhtin, the carnivalesque describes a space and time in which secular, political, and legal hierarchies are inverted in a temporary (and licensed) transgression after which structures of authority are reinstated. Less purely ceremonial than critical in intent, as Natalie Davis points out, the carnivalesque is frequently associated with the eruption of "female unruliness" or a "carnivalized female principle" that functions culturally as a "mark of the ultra liminal or the perilous realm of possibility, of 'anything may go.'"[32] According to Davis this "ultra liminal" female principle doubly threatens any social order since, within culture, women function as the permanently or "quintessentially liminal" being always positioned as the marginalized and other, always in danger of losing control.[33] Because it exposes experiences or states of mind outside the customary or proper, the liminal space of the carnival, particularly as enacted through this female principle, may propose and legitimate within the performance itself "new paradigms that invert or subvert the old" by bringing forward what remains unthought within them. In this regard, Davis's analysis of the role of the feminine within the liminal shares features with and functions culturally in a manner similar to Jardine's gynesis. It is important to note however that female unruliness may have had very little to do with the lives of actual women as it was used most often to refer to men who cross-dressed during carnival time, using cultural stereotypes about female behavior to signal their inversion of dominant social hierarchies as a whole (a fact that recalls Jardine's caveat about the danger of assuming that gynesis as a cultural process is necessarily liberating for women).

According to Turner, contemporary performance-based art (and perhaps avant-garde art in general, I'd argue) is a liminal-like or "liminoid" genre that emerges historically from ritual and carnival, and shares features with them. These include escape from the everyday world and inversion of conventional social hierarchies such as gender and class distinctions. However, liminoid genres function less as public rituals than as private expressions developed in the margins and unofficial spaces of central political, economic, and cultural processes. Plural, fragmentary, experimental, they are often "more idiosyncratic and quirky, more spare, original, and strange"[34] than ritual proper or the carnival. In addition, liminoid genres quite often have as their expressed intention full-blown subversion rather than simply temporary inversion of the status quo; the liminoid does not or would not necessarily reinvoke the socially normal by framing liminality with a return to the official spaces of dominant social reality. The effect of this is to destabilize these dominant categories and, potentially, to offer the space of the liminal as an alternative to them.

This is Stein's strategy in *Lucy Church Amiably*—a liminoid text—which is not to say that in it she offers a full-blown social critique; she does not, although, as I have suggested, within the novel values are implied that stand against culturally dominant value systems (e.g., abundance, sensuousness, celebration, the end of oppositions and hierarchies). Rather, Stein frames the novel as a space of open possibilities, preferring not to visualize and elaborate fully an alternative model—a utopia. Instead, she chooses simply and dramatically to mark off a space of indeterminacy, and radical changeability, a realm that eludes current signifying systems. Such a (hypothetical) space is valuable, as I suggested in chapter 1, as a means of preserving a (potential) realm of difference, doubt, and nonknowledge. These spaces of difference might rejuvenate the rigid coding of inherited discourses whose demand that they "be named, or even connoted— as poor copies, for example—" has historically eliminated "any value they may have as truth."[35]

In the previous chapter, I argued that it is vital to take into account the motivations that might inspire an author to transgress the limits of realism and move toward a vision of the novel as other than mimetic—in this case, as performative. Otherwise we risk subsuming, uncritically, all formal deviations from a mimetic norm under a generalized—ungendered—postmodernism that, in effect, still takes the work of white male writers as its norm. In this regard, Ulla Dydo's account of Stein's renewed desire during the late 1920s to disrupt the stability and authority of social conventions, especially as figured in the bourgeois family, is important to consider. Equally important in sketching the motivating context for Stein's composition of the novel are Marianne DeKoven's insights regarding Stein's movement toward a greater acceptance of her femaleness during this period. These insights help to suggest the importance of considering how gender, as a relation to cultural power and privilege, shapes an artistic vision or self-conception, and lend additional support to my earlier suggestion that Stein considers the indeterminate and constantly changing force "Lucy Church" to be emblematic of her own creative powers.

However, in suggesting that "Lucy Church" in part embodies Stein's own attitude toward her writing and the conditions best suited to express it, I don't mean to suggest that *Lucy Church Amiably* be reduced to this meaning. That would simply reinscribe the authority of mimetic categories by pinning the text to a stable signification.

It is also tempting to value the novel as a "female text" since it does celebrate an almost stereotypical picture of (mother) nature over culture, of matrilineal affiliation over patriarchal descent. But the novel also takes these terms out of opposition, performing in and through their dissolution a movement that makes it impossible to determine who is who, what is what, and which is which. The anamorphic textual dynamic of the novel may also be viewed as emerging from a preoedipal desire associated by Irigaray and others with the female libidinal economy and an imaginative preoedipal (re)union with the mother. But it becomes problematic to speak of a fully female vision in a text where the stability, even the existence of gender is so thoroughly questioned. And it would be difficult to use the term gyno- or femino-centric to describe this text that refuses a center. "Lucy Church" is not fixable as nature or culture, as animal or human, as spirit or matter; she/it refuses to be the point of departure or reference that would center the text. Instead, insofar as it is possible, "Lucy Church," that "center" is ontological undecidability itself. In this, Stein's practice is consistent with Julia Kristeva's call for an art of permanent negativity that "dissolves identity—even sexual identity—in the name of a feminist practice at odds with what already exists"[36]—a "negativity" that, in the case of this novel, points to a signifying space, an affirmative, desiring space of potential—held open, in motion—elsewhere.

Chapter 5

History and the Everyday in
Mrs. Reynolds

The future is not a single path so we must renounce the linear.
Fernand Braudel, *On History*

In the following excerpt from *Everybody's Autobiography*, Gertrude Stein analyzes the international situation preceding World War II with characteristic directness—and insight:

> There is too much fathering going on just now and there is no doubt about it fathers are depressing. Everybody nowadays is a father, there is father Mussolini and father Hitler and father Lewis and father Blum and Franco is just commencing now and there are ever so many more ready to be one. . . . The periods of the world's history that have always been the most dismal ones are the ones where fathers were looming and filling up every-thing. . . . [F]athers come up and fathers go down . . . just now everybody has a father, perhaps the twenty-first century . . . will be a nice time when everybody forgets to be a father or to have one.[1]

"Fathering" in Stein's framework refers to a specific set of cultural values and operations, which includes the need to form hierarchical power relations, to impose control and authority on others with an aim toward mastering them, and, as a corollary, the desire to "fill up everything," dominating so as to exclude other voices and other representations of lived experience. "Fathers" are those with the power to define and enforce such a cultural order, and history, within this framework, has "fathering" at its center. The rise and fall of fathers form the rhythms of "history," which, according to Stein,

"happens from time to time" and means "living with a sense of time."
Depressed by the dominance of fathers and/in history, Stein expresses a desire to escape patricentric orderings of experience, in this
instance by projecting a future time in which "everybody forgets to
be a father or to have one." Literature actualizes this future imaginative possibility in the present, according to Stein, since, as she defines
it, "literature" operates out or alongside the temporality of fathers.
Unlike "history," literature "happens all the time" in an ongoing but
not necessarily progressive rhythm at odds with conventional notions of historical teleology and continuity, at odds with the impulse
to master experience. Connected to the everyday, "literature" borrows from the local, the temporary, the limited, the provisional, the
habitual; as such it escapes a regular narrative trajectory and continuous narrative form encompassing and enduring through the times
when fathers erupt into/as history.

Stein's deliberate separation of "history" and "literature" undoubtedly is meant in part to dramatize and critique the unquestioned assumption of an automatic relation between the two, in particular the presumed relation between history and the novel. As
David Carroll emphasizes, in the nineteenth century the novel explicitly modeled itself after history, acquiring value to the extent that it
was considered to be a form *of* history.[2] What this means, of course,
is that a certain form or mode of the novel (realist) and a particular
structuration of history (what Michel Foucault has called continuous
history) were privileged as definitive, united around specific assumptions concerning the historical nature of the world and the narrative
form best suited to represent and interpret it. Whether in the writing
of history or the writing of fiction, realism is premised on belief in a
closed universe and a continuous world ordered according to a generative, progressive, linear, causal temporality and in which the individual subject is the vital force. But a realist narrative ordering, which
imposes coherence and continuity for the purposes of making history
intelligible, in effect also reduces its complexity since such an order
conceals gaps, discontinuities or interruptions in the progressive
movement of time or in the coherence of the subject as agent of
history. Thus the form and the frame of traditional continuous history are not neutral having as they do ideological effects on the production and sense of history, on what and who will count as historically significant. History functions through construction of a set of

normative concepts that interpret and fix available cultural meanings and may repress alternative constructions. As a discourse of authority, legitimation, and prohibition, narrative history—in the way it structures and orders meaning for culture—accrues to itself the power to define and legislate "what happened." As it can be said to replicate and reinforce existing social and legal codes, narrative history may also act to justify and perpetuate unequal power relations (such as the cultural dominance of patriarchy) that are the legacy and effect of these cultural arrangements.

Stein's recognition that certain kinds of exclusions result from the imposition of particular orders on lived experience, her growing awareness that some stories resist being known in the terms set out by narrative history, inspired her first radical break with the form of realism. As Janice Doane and others have shown, Stein's first three novels, written more or less according to the principles of realism, and her first fragments of *The Making of Americans* (subtitled *History of a Family's Progress*),

> seemed to yield an implacable momentum toward the conclusion, a conclusion contingent upon death and the interdiction of desire, a conclusion that left those standing in the place of the father in a position of authority, ownership, and control and those in the position of the other immobile, passive or dead.[3]

Stein's growing dissatisfaction with the conclusions held out by realist modes, conclusions that seemed to replicate the power relations created by sexual difference, directly led to her invention of the continuous present tense, according to Doane: "if locating oneself in history seemed the necessary, unhappy return to the father, Stein refused narrative momentum toward the conclusion by beginning again and again."[4] Harriet Chessman uncovers a similar trajectory in Stein's career, over the course of which she rejects those "monologic and authoritarian" literary forms allied to historical and narrative linearity and embraces alternative forms of creativity, "not identified with public and patriarchal discourse," and thus not "antagonistic to the lyric female impulse associated with freedom from narrative command." These new dialogic modes embrace the realm of "literature," diffusing narrative authority, disrupting linear sequence, and thus admitting possibilities grounded in nondominant social and erotic relations,[5] what conventional history must repress as a condition for its intelligibility.

But Stein's early (modernist) solution to the problem of the incommensurability between patriarchal orderings of reality and the representation of female experience and desire—the invention of an aesthetic realm apart from the workings of traditional history— proved problematic in the face of that period of "fathering" known as World War II. In 1935 Stein remarks that, for her, history is "the state of confusion between anyone doing anything and something happening," and she concludes that she would "rather not know that know anything of the confusion between anyone doing anything and something happening."[6] Eventually, of course, she did "know" and live through the "confusion" of this period; in the face of the pressing political, social, and economic crises of the thirties and forties in Europe, one was forced to recognize the effects of history. This knowledge forms the basis of *Mrs. Reynolds* (1940), a novel written in "an effort to show the way anybody could feel these [war] years."[7] It is Stein's first novel about a "father's" rise and fall since *The Making of Americans* and her most explicit critique of the ideology of linear narrative. The patriarch in this case is depressing indeed, and the link between linear narrative and authoritarian control depressingly literal. The novel charts the career of Angel Harper, a dictator, by describing his impact on the daily life of common people and his eventual undoing. Stein complicates the rigid temporal order of Harper's march through time, complicates the narrative momentum of continuous history, not by attempting to escape it to live in a continuously present moment—her solution in *The Making of Americans*. Rather, in *Mrs. Reynolds*, she confronts "father-time" directly and brings it into dialogue with other temporal orders, other representations of lived experience. In so doing, she both demonstrates the weight of public or official history and dislocates its unitary authority, showing it to be an unstable ideological construction whose ideology includes its appearance of being coherent and self-contained.

Traditionally, the production of continuous history "arises out of a desire to have real events display the coherence, integrity, fullness, and closure of an image of life that is and can only be . . . imaginary."[8] Every historical account, however complete, is constructed on the basis of a set of elements that might have been included but were left out, an exclusion that Fernand Braudel calls the historicist

error—to narrate all history in terms of the same récit. Braudel proposes at least three types of temporal series in opposition to this
assumed temporal unity of traditional history. The first is "a history
that is almost changeless, the history of man [sic] in relation to his
[sic] surroundings. It is a history which unfolds slowly and is slow
to alter, often repeating itself and working itself out in cycles which
are endlessly renewed, . . . which exist almost out of time."[9] This series is related to what Julia Kristeva calls cyclic or repetitive time—
which she links explicitly with female subjectivity, more closely in
tune, she says, with "the eternal recurrence of a biological rhythm,"
and with a "monumental" or mystic (cosmic) time.[10] Braudel's second
series is a "history of gentle rhythms, of groups and groupings," a
social time that does not flow at one even rate but that "goes on at a
thousand different paces swift or slow, which bear almost no relation
to the day-to-day [regular] rhythm of a chronicle or of traditional
history." Braudel's third stratum is the time of traditional linear or
continuous history—"history so to speak on the scale not so much
of man [sic] in general as of men [sic] in particular . . . the history of
events."[11] Here, as I suggested, time is structured in the form of a
teleology, measured as a narrative of departure, progression, and
arrival, the beginning, middle, and end that structures realist fiction
as well. Linked by Kristeva (and of course others) to the cogito, to the
paternal function, to representation, sign, syntax, and narration, this
mode "renders explicit a rupture, an expectation, or an anguish
which other temporalities work to conceal,"[12] those other temporalities that are themselves concealed, inexplicable, or simply unavailable within the telos of linear history. Braudel's third stratum is the
time when, as Stein would put it, fathers erupt into/as history.

This decomposition or decentering of history into temporalities
that unfold at different rates, according to different logics, provides
a useful paradigm for describing the temporal rhythms interacting in
Mrs. Reynolds. In the novel, Stein complicates the form of temporality
and the mode of structuration usually projected onto history to ensure its unity and progression precisely by including elements that
ordinarily would be omitted. History in the traditional sense is relativized through interaction with the temporal rhythms of the everyday; its claim to be the only authoritative and legitimate account of
what happened is contested through interaction with other "illegitimate" modes of explanation—chief among them prophecy. In this

way history as a coherent and continuous narrative is replaced by an emphasis on "the temporal discontinuity and the conflictual plurality of the various orders constituting it."[13] As a result, the possibility of constructing a coherent, unified, and complete account of lived experience is called into question and potentially new accounts of experience are foregrounded.

In this respect, Stein anticipates an aspect of the postmodern critique of totality whose link with totalitarianism has been stressed repeatedly in this era—totalizing systems being those that unify with an aim to power. This critique proceeds through what Jean-François Lyotard calls "a decomposition of the great stories (History, Science, Religion, Philosophy) and the manifold emergence of simpler, smaller, local 'recits'"—historically repressed within these totalizing metanarratives.[14] Unmasking as incomplete continuities that have been assumed as stable within a Western (narrative) tradition, exposing those "forms and forces which reduce, simplify, and attempt to transcend the contradictions at the heart of history,"[15] and mapping the multiple alternative orders of this tradition's exclusions have been major aspects of a postmodern revision of history, evident in the work of Michel Foucault, Michel DeCerteau, and Hayden White among others. Such an emphasis has not only led to fuller, more complete descriptions—the motivation behind accounts such as Braudel's—but by uncovering new strategies and sites of contestation and resistance within official history, by exposing alternative logics that have operated unseen in the margins of these official modes of rationality, the postmodern critique has also encouraged the development of new knowledges. Among these have been new understandings of what counts as political intervention or struggle—tactics not recognizable as such within the old master narratives of liberation.

In what follows, I want to explore Stein's problematization of her own earlier modernist aesthetic through an analysis of her efforts to pluralize history in *Mrs. Reynolds*. This approach will also allow me to reframe as politically significant particular imaginative strategies employed by Stein in the novel, strategies that, I argue, function as tactical interventions into the forward progress of official history and thus ones that on an imaginative level operate as discourses of resistance to it. In taking this approach I wish in part also to contest early assessments of Stein that regarded her as the quintessential hermetic modernist, a high priestess of art whose elitist experiments with language excluded engagement with larger political or social concerns.[16]

As many recent accounts of Stein have suggested, much of her work in fact articulates a sophisticated (if sometimes coded) set of perceptions concerning the relations among gender, power, and cultural production,[17] perceptions that, again, in many ways prefigure the insights of postmodern theorists who seek to expose discourses of resistance and sites of new prefigurative social formations within what were previously regarded as neutral literary and linguistic structures.

Mrs. Reynolds, Stein's reluctant return to history, redefines the perspective from which history is traditionally recorded. Much of the novel is preoccupied with the rhythms of daily living or daily habit. Interspersed with the narrative of Angel Harper's rise and fall, Mr. and Mrs. Reynolds wake up, eat, talk of trivial matters such as the weather or their neighbors. They go out; they come in. They are "pleased to stay at home," "pleased to go to bed early." The tempo of life appears to remain consistent here; time moves in a slow, steady, monotonous rhythm, and the Reynolds's actions are repetitive, habitual, seemingly inconsequential. This is Braudel's "almost changeless" temporality or what Maurice Blanchot (following Henri Lefebvre) calls "the everyday." The everyday is a region of experience or level of discourse where "nothing happens," where there is nothing to know "insofar as it has always already been said, even while remaining unformulated that is to say not yet information." Banal, platitudinous, "inexhaustible," "irrescuable," the everyday is always unfinished. It is a residue resisting analysis, that which exceeds "every speculative formulation, perhaps all coherence, all regularity." At the furthest remove from the gaze of official history, the everyday "escapes"; it is regular (customary, habitual) but not as such "regularable"—governable according to a fixed rule or procedure (i.e., narrativizable).[18] This is its limitation and its power.

Stein evokes the dailiness of the Reynolds's life through repetition of key terms, most notably "going to bed early." Repeated on nearly every page, this phrase functions to evoke an orientation to living. Agreeing to go to bed early stands for a range of feelings and behaviors: the comfort, habit, security and mutual compatibility of the Reynolds's relationship. Descriptions such as the following ones from the beginning, middle, and end of the novel are typical:

> Mrs. Reynolds and her husband did not mind wind and rain, they did not mind heat, they did not like snow very much, it

made Mr. Reynolds stay in the house and it kept Mrs. Reynolds from going very far, they often talked about dates in cakes and they often talked about bread in soup, they also often talked about eggs and butter but most often of all they talked about guinea hens and geese. They liked that best of any subject of conversation. Of course they listened to the news, they had well not exactly an adopted son but one who could never become one and his name was Roger. (*MR*, 2)

It was a rainy day and the evening came to be dark early and some friends telephoned and then they sat quite quietly and they heard Angela Haynes come home and Mrs. Reynolds said and what of it and Mr. Reynolds laughed and he said what of it and he said it is bedtime and they both went to bed. And what of it. (*MR*, 103)

It [the war] is finished said Mrs. Reynolds, it is not ended yet but it is finished . . . and she went home and said it to Mr. Reynolds. Yes said Mr. Reynolds. And now if we have money well not now but later when it is ended as well as finished said Mrs. Reynolds and we can buy and they can want to sell well then said Mrs. Reynolds after the first excitement is over will we like it as well. I suppose so said Mr. Reynolds and it was not cold but it was quite cold enough and there was not much heat and he was beginning to be very sleepy. I suppose so said Mr. Reynolds and then Mrs. Reynolds said she would quiet down and then they would go to bed and so she read a detective story that did not interest her and she did not quiet down and then they went to bed. (*MR*, 265)

In the traditional novel, as in linear history, time passing or duration is always given a meaningful orientation; each moment further reveals both the author's intention and a character's destiny. As these passages in *Mrs. Reynolds* suggest, by contrast, each moment tends to repeat a previous one with minute variations; little is developed or revealed but the inexorableness of the daily, which undermines the sequential movement of narrative and its convention of finality; like the continuous present tense, dailiness begins again and again. Little if any narrative progress occurs at this level of the text, nor do the characters change in any significant way (indeed, Mrs. Reynolds is called Mrs. Reynolds from the day of her birth, and appears to be always the same Mrs. Reynolds from first page to last). The Reynolds do comment on Angel Harper's progress more frequently and with more emotional intensity as the novel unfolds. Various references to the war's impact on them appear as well (food shortages, neighbors evacuating the area or disappearing, emotional upset), and, at one point, Mrs. Reynolds "almost forgot that there was day to day" (*MR*, 148), so preoccupied is she with Angel Harper's actions. The novel makes clear that the war is impossible to ignore, but the Reynolds's daily interactions remain largely unchanged by either the calamitous events occurring around them or by the cessation of these events. The recurring rhythms of the daily— unremarkable and commonplace though they may be—bind the Reynolds together and, in effect, allow them to endure the war by sustaining a sense of the ongoingness of life. As Mrs. Reynolds comments: "Just every day and going to bed every night seemed too good to be true" (*MR*, 131). The everyday functions as a means by which despair is refused; it is that which endures and survives beyond the unpredictable rise and fall of fathers, and in this it becomes the means to invent a tactic of resistance.

Stein reinforces the peculiar temporality of the everyday, suggesting its immediacy, its continuity, its all-encompassing nature, through a carefully chosen temporal confusion. Although the novel is written in the past tense throughout, it conveys, in Lloyd Frankenberg's words, "the sensation of being an immediate past, of being a present moment continuously becoming the past" (a historical present tense?) (Intro. to *MR*, ix). Stein conjoins the past-present-future also in the text, especially in the early pages of the novel. For example, she begins to describe Mrs. Reynolds's birth and childhood (distant past), but in the next paragraph switches to a description of Mr. Reynolds's adopted son, Roger (immediate past), who disappears one day (future) never to be seen again. Next we are back in childhood where Mrs. Reynolds begins to make predictions about men of war coming (reference to the future, which is the becoming present of the novel). The effect of this temporal confusion is to suggest a realm where past-present-future coexist simultaneously in an almost timeless realm, an ongoing but not progressive temporal rhythm consistent with the rhythm of dailiness: as a child one must get up, eat, go to sleep; as an adult one must do the same. The habitual both roots us in the present moment and confers a sense of timelessness on us all, a paradoxical temporality, one that escapes notice and remains irreducible to any unilinear narrative sequence.

Braudel's second level of historical temporality—"a history of gentle rhythms . . . a social history of groups and groupings"—corresponds to the ordinary life stories of community members and the gentle rhythms of their interconnections, which appear throughout the novel, most especially in part I. These too are rooted in the space and temporality of the everyday. For instance, we learn in great detail about the genealogies of the Reynolds's relations: "Mrs. Reynolds grandfather's cousin was a lawyer"; we are told, "he was a lawyer but he knew a lot about eating and cooking and he wrote a book about it, and he had a daughter-in-law and a grandson and the grandson married a widow with five children. The grandson never had a child of his own" (*MR*, 13). There is a cousin whose mother was charitable but whose children made unhappy marriages; a cousin whose uncle was a doctor and married an Egyptian whose sister married an engineer; a cousin who specialized in "Oriental" diseases and married a "well-to-do and rather stout Greek woman," and so on (*MR*, 13–16).

Whereas in previous Stein novels, families tend to break down, here family convergences and connections, however distant and oblique, are stressed excessively. A person gains identity through his/her complicated position in the genealogy and/or by reference to a single memorable trait, a method of characterization that reflects the informal way in which relatives are remembered to one another (my uncle the lawyer). However, this emphasis on genealogies does not serve to reenthrone the authority of the father. It is not the patriarch as origin and first cause that is stressed here but rather the possibility of interconnection that the extended family structure helps to guarantee. The narrator prefers to say Mr. Reynolds's brother's sister's daughter, for example, rather than Mr. Reynolds's niece, a technique that both emphasizes these relationships and makes it difficult to trace the connection to determine who is related to whom. What emerges instead is a kind of decentered communal "we" that de-emphasizes a focus on the individual as a discrete subject or agent in/of history. Traced through these communal ties is a space in which social relations are produced, in which an incoherent, often contradictory plurality of relational determinations interact, a focus that offers the promise (and the threat) of the disappearance of the subject as such.

This "focus" is reinforced by the similarly exhaustive descriptions of the connections between the Reynolds and their neighbors and of people in the community who intersect through friendship or proximity. Very little explanation is given for why people meet or what the impact of their meeting is since these meetings do not function to advance the narrative or to reenthrone the subject as agent. *That* relations can be formed seems more important than how and why they occur. Like the brief segments of the text in which they are described, people move into relation with one another through contiguity rather than logical causation, a loose associative movement with lines of intersection moving in every direction. This perhaps is the "structure" of the everyday (if it can be said to have one), the "thousand difference paces" of Braudel's social time, a structure that may appear incoherent or random in that it is not mappable but one that nonetheless moves in a harmonious fashion.

For example, Mr. Reynolds's brother, who lives next door, has a best friend who is "the widow of a tea-king, and she liked to wander in the rain in wooden shoes and carry an umbrella. She felt she was a Chinese heroine" (*MR*, 19). Predictably,

> The widow of the tea-king had a friend, he was a librarian of a legislative assembly. He and his wife had been married many years and had no children and then they had a little girl an unusually pretty one . . . He knew another librarian of a legislative family and he also had been married for twenty years and they never had had a child and then they had one, a little boy, he was not very good looking, his mother was Swedish, and he did not look like her . . . He and his wife and the little boy went away and they could be met once in a while as it would happen. (*MR*, 20)

The widow of the tea-king, the librarian, the Greek wife, or the Swedish mother do not appear again in *Mrs. Reynolds*, as is true of most of the characters mentioned in the novel, this because Stein intends not so much to elaborate the nature of these affiliations or the individual identities involved in creating them as to value the possibility and the pervasiveness of their existence. In characteristic fashion, Stein also dispenses with physical details of setting, the carefully rendered sense of place typical of the historical novel. Nevertheless, the first section of the novel does effectively convey a sense of human connection and affiliation, a vast interlocking web of people who transcend national identities and who are all somehow related through friendship, genealogy, or simply by virtue of proximity—living in a small community where "nothing much does happen and every day is a pleasant day."

As the novel proceeds (parts 2–10), this emphasis on the rhythms of the everyday is sharply disrupted by the community's preoccupation with and response to Angel Harper. Direct references to Harper do appear in the first section of the novel, but by the final sections, discussing his progress has become an obsession that threatens to overtake the importance given to the daily. Here the everyday is invaded by history; what is depicted is the "rupture" of daily life, the "anguish" of the father erupting into history, looming and filling up everything. The "natural" incoherence of the structure of everyday life here becomes the chaos brought about by excessive fathering.

With the growing dominance of Angel Harper comes an emphasis on disruption, and "unnatural acts," violations of the human ties and gentle rhythms stressed in part 1, which reflect on both literal and symbolic levels the impact of the war. References are made throughout to families passing by the Reynolds's house ("a great many people coming who did not come to stay they were passing that way and [Mrs. Reynolds] did not say anything when she saw them because there was nothing to say" [MR, 145]); to the fact that there are no weddings, few births, and no houses built (MR, 139); to the change in preoccupation ("in the spring a young man's fancy lightly turns to spring offensives" [MR, 178]). Episodes also appear in which the theme of unnaturalness is played out, as in the following one:

> Some one perhaps it was a cousin told Mrs. Reynolds about two sisters they were daughters of a farmer and they had both had children, that is to say the oldest had a baby in secret and the younger sister helped her to kill it, yes kill it, and then the younger sister had a baby in secret and the older helped her

younger sister to kill it. And then somebody found it out and the police came and they took both sisters to prison and the oldest began to cry and tell everything and the younger did not cry but she told everything and when everything had been told she said and now you know everything let us go home so we can milk the cows, cows have to be milked and she could not see why they did not let her. Cows have to be milked when milking time comes. Cows do. (*MR*, 114)

Certainly the action of killing one's children can be judged as unnatural. How do the sisters become pregnant? Do they kill the babies because they are unable to care for them during the war and not because they are uncaring (as evidenced by their willingness to "care" for the cows), or have they killed what would interrupt their everyday? Is Stein suggesting that cows have become more valuable than human life and so it is natural to kill children but unnatural to make cows suffer? Certainly the reaction of the civil authorities—confinement for the crime—must be weighed in relation to the millions of children being killed during the war for unnatural causes, for as little reason. How can law even operate under these circumstances? As Mrs. Reynolds puts it in response to this episode, "Everything is puzzling if it is not troubling" (*MR*, 114).

Significantly, narrative indeterminacy, so much a hallmark of Stein's style for so long, takes on a menacing, threatening quality in this episode. Gone is the tone of playful celebration over the dizzying proliferation of textual possibilities evident in works such as *A Long Gay Book*, *Tender Buttons*, or *Lucy Church Amiably*. Here the "puzzling" is "troubling" and the desire is for the certainty of a causal explanation, for some way to account for the disruptions caused by the war. However, Stein resists returning to notions of logical causation; she refuses to reerect a realist mode of explanation. Instead, she reinforces the unnatural effects of Harper's influence through symbolic statements in which the natural world is seen as reflecting the disorder of the social world, a powerful method of conveying in terms of the everyday the emotional experience of living through war time.

As Harper rises in prominence, it rains for twenty-eight days in a row (*MR*, 60); the weather in general grows more changeable during the war (*MR*, 71); it grows colder in response to Angel Harper (*MR*, 74); when "Angel Harper was forty-nine the sun did not shine when [he] was fifty all eggs broke" (*MR*, 148). James Mellow explains that during the war years Stein read and reread English classics— Dickens, Byron, Shakespearean plays—and that "the present with its violence and emotionalism seemed Shakespearean to her."[19] As Shakespeare would have it, during World War II the "times are out of joint." In positing correspondences between natural and social, the novel reflects an archaic (Shakespearean) notion of causality, appropriate to explain an era in which, according to Stein, there is "no realism," in which "life is not real it is not earnest it is strange."[20] As I will discuss in greater detail below, illogical conceptions of causality such as natural omens, dreams, and predictions form a major motif in the novel and function as alternative explanations to the traditional (logical) notions of historical causation that we typically encounter in novels.

Statements also appear that both depict a facet of wartime behavior and, importantly, obliquely comment upon Stein's own earlier stylistic experiments, which the novel suggests are themselves relativized by history. At one point, for example, the narrator states that "his name used to be William but now it was Henry and it used to be Vandermeulen and now it was Anderson" (*MR*, 147). This familiar Steinian device of changing names so as to dislocate unitary notions of identity, especially prevalent in *A Novel of Thank You* and *Lucy Church Amiably*, assumes a new significance in *Mrs. Reynolds*.[21] As Stein would be well aware, name changing for Jews in particular was a matter of survival and not an aesthetic statement about the construction of character in novels. One recalls this passage when, several pages later, Mrs. Reynolds has a dream in which she decides that "nobody had a name," a dream of annihilation and not a vision of a productive loss of individual ego within a communal "we." She tells Mr. Reynolds her dream and "he said perhaps it will come to that that nobody will have a name and Mrs. Reynolds said she would not like that at all, and Mr. Reynolds said her liking it or not would not stop it. And she knew he was right it would not" (*MR*, 150). On literal and figurative levels, dictators are those with the power to name and, crucially, to forceably un-name.

The subject matter of *Mrs. Reynolds*—the effects of fascist power on the daily life of a small community—poses additional challenges to Stein's antirealist aesthetics. In realist novels, narrative intrusion conventionally acts to clarify the overall design of the plot or the motivations of the characters, the narrator pointing out the significance of particular episodes or drawing connections that allow the reader to interpret them more fully. In *Mrs. Reynolds*, the narrator both asserts an impulse to do more than report wartime events by offering some explanation for them from a position of knowledge greater than that of the characters and admits her inability to do so: "it made everybody [including the narrator] just a little nervous to know that there was no reason" (*MR*, 106). Similarly, Mrs. Reynolds's poignant statement offered as the war nears its end—"I like to know that it has not been useless" (*MR*, 261)—speaks to the emotional need for a cause to explain the devastating effects of the war. But, as Stein herself puts it elsewhere in referring to the times: "the meaningless of why makes all the nothingness so real."[22]

Hayden White has argued that the demand for closure in a narrative is a demand for moral meaning, a demand that sequences of events be assessed in terms of their significance as elements of a moral drama.[23] Stein's earlier refusal to offer logically causal connections and explanations in her novels stems from an aesthetic principle that "in the twentieth century we don't know for certain that anything is successively happening,"[24] and as I suggested earlier, from a refusal to return to the position of authority and certainty associated with fathers. However, the narrator's and Mrs. Reynolds's statements in the novel itself and Stein's own comments on the war also suggest that the demand for narrative significance, for the moral meaning of which White speaks, may well be a human emotional need, made particularly acute in the face of the knowledge that meaninglessness, lack of cause, is terrifyingly reflective of a larger political reality. In *Mrs. Reynolds*, Stein does not so much abandon her earlier aesthetic principles as place them in a specific historical context—the war—one in which the demand for a clear explanation of events becomes psychologically apparent and understandable. Throughout the novel, the desire for rational explanations, for statements of moral value and meaning, is held in tension with the recognition that such an explanation is impossible to construct with any certainty at all—not just ontologically, but because of the material history of war itself that especially defies these frames of certainty—and with the recognition that authoritative explanations are themselves part of the thinking that leads to war.[25]

This tension between a desire to narrate—to report the world—

and a desire to narrativize—in White's terms, "to make the world speak itself as a story" that "terminates by summing up the meaning of a chain of events"—becomes more apparent in the description of Angel Harper's rise and fall. This level of the text roughly corresponds to Braudel's traditional (linear) history—"on the scale not so much of man in general as of men in particular." The repetitive rhythms of dailiness and the fluid movement in every direction of people in relation intersect with chronology, a linear teleological movement that leaves no doubt that Angel Harper's career *is* successively and continuously happening. The novel conveys the inexorableness of Harper's influence through repetition of the phrases "Angel Harper is [x] years old . . ." or "When Angel Harper was [x] he . . ." linking his chronological development, measured with exact regularity, with the development of his impact on the community. The novel follows him from a birth of mysterious origins ("Was he born in a church, was he born in a town, was he born brown. He did not know and nobody else knew" [*MR*, 38]) to his death at fifty-five with the emphasis on chronology growing more insistent as he gains in power and influence, the extremely rigid teleological movement being linked with exercise of power. Unlike earlier sections, the Harper sections also strike the reader as tedious in their repetitiveness. Harper literally *does* fill up everything, reducing the complexity of daily living through imposition of a rigid order—a comment on the desire of fathers/fascists to impose order and law and one of the means by which Mrs. Reynolds exposes the ideological implications of the way "life" is ordered by history.

Although Harper's story unfolds teleologically, the progressive accumulative movement of narrative (of Harper himself) is disrupted through interaction with two other temporal orders: prophecy and memory. Through prophecies that predict his defeat, Harper in essence has already fallen even as he is rising; through childhood memories, he is pulled back in time even as time also pushes him forward. Prophecy and memory complicate the time of history by relativizing the authority of its linear movement. They also operate in place of other, more conventionally logical reasons as tactics to evade the promotion of explanations. Angel Harper ends because a seventh-century prophet predicted that he would, as good an explanation as any for the meaningless unpredictable events of World War II, Stein seems to suggest. Finally, the discourses of prophecy and memory function as acts of imaginative resistance on Stein's part to the power of fascism, prophetically announcing in 1940 the certainty of Harper's/Hitler's demise. The novel as a whole might be thought of as an incantation to Harper's mortality, a (death) wish that it fulfills on an imaginative level.

The predictions of St. Godfrey of the nineteenth century and St. Odile of the seventh century are the most obvious prophecies appearing in the novel and are predictions in the conventional sense of the word if you will—statements supposedly made under the influence of divine guidance that foretell the future. Interestingly, these prophecies, which from a conventional viewpoint would be considered spurious or illegitimate forms of history, contain the only conventionally historical discourse in the novel, couched in terms of specific geographical locations, specific times, and specific dates. They function as alternative histories, operating in an excluded archaic or monumental realm in which World War II is pictured not as a struggle between nations, but as a struggle between St. Odile and Angel Harper, a struggle between two kinds of truth, two ways of knowing, two value-systems. Conventional historical truth, associated with the father, and with the values of autonomy and mastery, comes into dialogue with prophetic truth, associated most directly with women, St. Odile and Mrs. Reynolds herself who "liked to prophesy."

What is typically thought of as prophecy is also deliberately linked with and thus redefined through association with the cyclic rhythms of nature and the level of dailiness which are, of course, predictable. "Everybody believed in prophecies," the narrator tell us "and everybody was right because the prophecies prophesied what was going to happen," and, like the everyday, "what was going to happen did happen. . . . Yes said Mrs. Reynolds one knows that there is going to be a spring and summer and fall and winter, yes everybody is right about that" (*MR*, 57). Everybody *does* believe in prophecy in *Mrs. Reynolds*, and many of the characters dream, read signs, hear voices foretelling in equal measure and with little real distinction ordinary and extraordinary occurrences, trivial and historically significant events thus reflecting the balance of life itself. In one sequence, for instance, Mrs. Reynolds hears a voice predicting the coming of men of war (*MR*, 6), predicts that she will have a bed of strawberries (*MR*, 7), dreams that Angel Harper will be a dictator (*MR*, 17), and dreams of five artichokes and a piece of meat (*MR*, 17).

Prophecy thus is both an extraordinary ability, a divine inspiration, and an ordinary one, within the grasp of people such as Mrs. Reynolds, a perfectly extraordinary ordinary woman.

The final paragraph of the novel ends not with the father's truth but with confirmation of another vision: "Beginning again was to believe to really believe to have no doubt that St. Odile was right. Mrs. Reynolds was not mistaken in believing in St. Odile because St. Odile had not been mistaken. Angel Harper was not fifty-five alive." But as I have been suggesting, the novel does not erect prophecy as a final explanation—a metaorder that would account for all the events of the novel. Instead Mrs. Reynolds's final triumph is simply that she has been able to hold on to belief, that she refuses to despair, accepting and asserting the validity of St. Odile's prophecies as an article of faith, a means of sustaining hope, much like reliance on the daily. As simple as this action is, however, I also would argue that prophecy and artistry (Stein's writing of the novel)—both acts of invention—are important tactics of intervention, political acts by which the everyday registers resistance to authoritarian structures.[26]

Unlike Mrs. Reynolds, Angel Harper operates as a subject in control of history, as an agent of will and power. Yet on an individual psychological level, his chronological movement forward is halted and pulled back in time—his progress undone—through juxtaposition with childhood memory. This is a second tactical resistance on Stein's part, one by which she minimizes Harper's power in refusing to frame him within a mythological discourse of immortality and greatness that might typically be associated with a powerful man. Instead these childhood memories become an incantation to Harper's mortality. Incidents from Harper's childhood are rendered in much greater detail than any incident in his present career; what he *does* in this novel is remember, returning to the fragments and debris of the past that escape official history and, the novel suggests, undermine it. Completely self-absorbed Harper lives with a constant awareness of identity and the passage of time. Unlike Mrs. Reynolds, Harper cannot live in time, in the day to day, nor does he participate in the gentle rhythm of being in relation, facts that are accorded an almost ethical value in the novel. Harper is a father who seeks to master time, a hero—"he who fears the everyday," in Blanchot's words, "fears it not because he is afraid of living in it with too much ease, but because he dreads meeting in it what is most fearful: a power of dissolution."[27]

While Harper's childhood memories are too fragmentary to allow the construction of a coherent picture of his youth, the recurrence of key motifs, most of which concern fear and isolation, help to sketch Angel Harper's psychological state as both a child and an adult. In some cases, the link is not logically apparent and seems trivial, incomplete, or nonsensical as "when Angel Harper was forty-three he remembered that when he was thirteen he would sit by a drain and whisper in it to someone on the other side of it" (*MR*, 85); "when Angel Harper was forty-three . . . Angel Harper remembered that when he was twelve he liked to sit and swing a string and on the string was a swing and in the swing suspended from the string were two dolls and he liked to sit and swing the string which made the swing swing and in the swing were two dolls and Angel Harper liked to sit and swing the string that swung the swing" (*MR*, 87). Examples such as these, inconsequential by themselves, accumulate in the novel to produce a vague but pervasive sense of menace and psychic disturbance; (Harper "plays" with dolls as he will later play with people's fates).

In other instances, the memory appears to offer the outlines of an actual psychological cause for Angel Harper's later damaging effects:

> When Angel Harper was fifty-three, he remembered that when he had been nine he asked the others to build him a little room that would be like a prison and in that he sat and he knew that it was true, that he was too old to cry and too young to feel excited and so he would rather be there even if he did care he would rather be there. And when he was fifty-three he remembered that when he was fifteen he asked them to make a very small inclosure of stone and in that in a chair he sat alone and sometimes he let another boy sit in there with him and near him and he let a little girl make a little park with flowers and when he was fifty-three he remembered all that. (*MR*, 221)

This passage stresses Angel Harper's desire for isolation and self-protection, a solitude that in fact imprisons him. The image of the small boy, alone in an "inclosure of stone," foreshadows the later adult, also alone, and as the narrator repeatedly reminds us, afraid. Comments appear as well that suggest more explicitly that although Angel Harper progresses chronologically, he never develops emotionally beyond childhood:

> Angel Harper remembered, he was so afraid of fifty-two as afraid of fifty-two as anybody had ever been of sixteen, he remembered that really he had been too old to play being a driver and having other children harnessed in front of him as horses far too old and still yes he had been far too old to do it and still he had been doing it when he was too old to do it and suddenly well not suddenly but underneath, he was afraid that that was what made him afraid of being fifty-two, it was frightening, fifty-two being fifty-two was frightening and he was afraid. (*MR*, 189)

As Angel Harper is too old to play horse cart at sixteen (significantly, he is the driver, with the other children "harnessed in front of him"), so he is too old to "play" at being dictator at fifty-two ("having been in a war he thought another war would be fun" [*MR*, 136]).

In the following incident Angel Harper's present becomes the exact inverse of his past, a past he attempts to undo by forcing everybody else to actualize it, the novel seems to suggest.

> Angel Harper when he was fifty-three he remembered that when he had been fourteen he had been thin and tired, tired and thin and now he was fifty-three he was not thin and he was fifty-three and he was not tired and everybody else was tired and everybody else was thin . . . when he was fifty-three he remembered that when he had been eleven he had felt that he was undersized, he really had not been but he felt he was undersized and he liked to play with water. . . . (*MR*, 237)

Again, no strictly logical causality exists here. Literally people are thin because of food shortages during the war and not because Angel Harper was once thin, yet on a symbolic level, in terms of the logic of the text itself, the link between Angel Harper's past and everybody else's present state is directly causal.

References to Harper's childhood and especially to the fact of his isolation grow more numerous as the novel progresses and he comes closer to being "all over." These range from quite straightforward assertions of his solitude ("how is it to be well at forty-six—no one asked him and nobody answered him" [*MR*, 101]) to descriptions of his own attitude toward being alone: "as he slept he knew that he was blue, blue with care and white with hair and afraid at night which was his share" (*MR*, 74). The motifs of being alone at night and having difficulty sleeping appear again in the following passage, a good example of the ways in which levels of the text interpenetrate and comment upon one another:

> I wish said Mrs. Reynolds and she did not finish her sentence. It was late that night and Mr. and Mrs. Reynolds were tired and were going to bed and it was late and they were tired and they did go to bed.
>
> Angel Harper was still fifty-three dear me dear me he better had be fifty-three, and nevertheless he saw it was like a picture book, he saw a door, and in the door, well not in the door, but in the doorway, it was not a light and it was not clear but he was there and it was not queer that he was there but was he there well anyway a boy of ten was there and he had a neighbor and he was not born there, he was left there, the wife of the soldier was dead, the soldier was not dead the boy knew how to draw, and he was left, he went to the grave of his mother and he sent a flower that he had plucked on the grave of his mother to his father but his father never answered from anywhere, and the boy was left there, and believe it or not it was true he was there.
>
> Angel Harper closed his eyes and he opened them again and he knew he never had been married and he never had any children, and, he knew that if he lost a wedding ring and an engagement ring in his sleep that is if he dreamed that he had lost them it did not make any difference. Angel Harper sometimes cried when he slept, not always but quite often. He was and is fifty-three. (*MR*, 239)

Here, Stein juxtaposes the Reynolds going to bed with Harper's going to bed. Like them he must engage with the level of the daily— even a dictator must sleep; unlike them he is alone and does not sleep well. Framing this simple ritual is the middle paragraph that could be their dream of him but is more likely his own dream/memory. Most of the memories reported emerge clearly, but this one appears shadowy and uncertain, suggesting perhaps that it has been more deeply repressed. Certainly the events of the dream are the stuff of which traumas are made: death of a mother, abandonment by or death of a father, an isolation stressed by repetition of the word "left." Are we to take this as an explanation for Angel Harper's isolation and insomnia reported in the above paragraph, where, alone with the recognition of his aloneness the powerful father is a small child crying in his sleep, fatherless and father to no one?

Stein only obliquely suggests a cause for Harper's rise and fall, yet passages such as the one above accumulate steadily throughout the novel. They combine to produce a remarkably complex and vivid impression of a fearful, isolated, and vulnerable child behind the facade of the powerful dictator. While *Mrs. Reynolds* is neither a full-fledged psychobiography of a tyrant nor a conventionally historical account of a "great man's" ascendency and decline, the repeated references to Harper's impact on the daily life of the community do emphasize the destructive and depressing effects of this particular father. Here, the father's power is acknowledged—definitively; it is pervasive and impossible to ignore. Yet that power is also contained and relativized: "Angel Harper was not fifty-five alive"; the father's story ends.

Angel Harper rises and falls, his career following the trajectory marked out by conventional narrative history, but the rhythms of daily living go on—insistently, unremarkably, much as they always have. These are the rhythms of what Stein calls "master-pieces," which she distinguishes from works produced with the recognition of time and identity. Obsessed with his past and with himself, Harper forces everybody else to confront his obsession. But, says Stein, "Governing has nothing to do with master-pieces it has completely to do with identity [by which she seems to mean the assertion of ego] but it has nothing to do with master-pieces."[28] By encircling linear history within the temporal dimensions of other orders of experience—the repetitive, ongoing rhythms of the daily and the natural, and the archaic or mythic time of prophecy—Stein shatters patriarchal claims to sole mastery over what happened. In *Mrs. Reynolds*, she uncovers and claims authority for other measures of lived experience. In so doing, Stein creates a masterpiece, one that leaves the father's attempt to master experience in pieces.

In her analysis of "Mildred Aldrich Saturday," which Stein wrote during World War I, Chessman argues that Stein, recognizing the relation between narrative plots and national plots leading to war, prevents further narrative production (in an imaginative sense prevents the production of war) by rooting her portrait in the continuous present. The continuous present "disrupts the narrative arc of history," rendering it "irrelevant."[29] In *Mrs. Reynolds*, the narrative arc of official history is not refused (a modernist gesture); there is no way to evade this particular moment of "fathering" the novel suggests. Neither is the text a counternarrative of confrontation with the father's power that might simply serve to reensconce another authority. Instead, Stein deflects that power and on an imaginative level erodes it, by multiplying the ways in which lived experience and the social field might be described—joining the narrative arc of history with the complex temporality of the everyday and with the monumental time of prophecy. Prophecy might be thought of as a kind of continuous future tense, what will have been, or as the future perfect temporality Julia Kristeva discusses in "Women's Time." As Thomas Foster describes it in his article on this essay, the future perfect "installs a radical historicity within the present moment" that is thereby "no longer the moment of a presence [of a father filling up everything] but is instead hollowed out by its relation both to a different past [the rewriting of official history through prophecy] and a potentially different future, a future . . . defined in terms entirely external to existing discourses"[30] and at odds with them. *Mrs. Reynolds* describes neither a passive retreat from history, nor a formal resistance to it. Instead, the novel as a whole functions as a tactical intervention into the workings of power itself from the perspective of what those in power have excluded. Stein's novel does not inhabit a space outside or at the end of history. Rather, it names some places where alternative social forms might be organized, inscribing within the workings of official history the possibility of a future time "when everybody forgets to be a father or to have one."

Chapter 6

Modernism/Mass Culture/ Postmodernism: The Case of Gertrude Stein

> It is the people who generally smell of the museums who are accepted and it is the new who are not accepted. You have to accept a complete differ-
> ence. . . . [A]nd in my work the newness and difference is fundamental. . . . It is hard to accept that, it is much easier to have one hand in the past.
> —Gertrude Stein, *Everybody's Autobiography*

Stein's distinction between an art of the museums—tied to the past and to official culture—and her own fundamentally different art of the present, until quite recently has seemed merely an apology for her own quirky experiments. But as the aesthetics and the ideology of modernism are reassessed from a contemporary postmodern perspective, this air of apology begins to seem more like real prescience. Increasingly, many of Stein's texts *do* appear distinct from other works of High Modernism, having more in common with our own dispersed and heterogeneous postmodern textuality/reality.[1]

As part of my continuing project to analyze those ways in which Stein differed from a dominant modernist aesthetic and, in so doing, to map some of the historical precedents of our own postmodern moment, I want to focus in this chapter on an important and heretofore overlooked aspect of Stein's aesthetic practice, one toward which she gestures in the statement above: her ideas concerning the relationship between an emerging mass culture and avant-garde art. Through this exploration, I want also to suggest that postmodernism be understood in relation to an earlier cultural moment, one in which mass culture and high modernist culture emerged simultaneously and in an adversarial relationship.

Unlike many modernist writers, Stein did not participate in the modernist repudiation of mass culture, did not insist on a rigid dis-

133

tinction between those two cultural spheres. Rather, in much of her work she embraced postmodern assumptions about art and culture, an aesthetic orientation growing out of her recognition that an early-twentieth-century moment represented a rapidly changing cultural situation, one in which an emerging mass culture played a central role. Recognizing the inescapability of mass culture in any effort to account for contemporary reality, and fascinated by it, Stein attempted to merge high art with certain forms and genres of mass culture and the culture of everyday life, self-consciously mixing these popular modes with avant-garde discourses in order to undermine the premises of realism. Thus Stein's texts not only anticipate many of the forms and logics widely evident in postmodern cultural practices; they also represent one of the first attempts to articulate the modern *through* the popular rather than in reaction to it. Stein refused the rigid dividing line erected by many modernists between high and low art, a barrier that also marks the great divide between modernism and our own cultural postmodernity.

The modernist idea of culture was generated out of a specific sense of cultural hierarchy that divided cultural spaces and products into highbrow (true culture) and lowbrow (popular culture). As Andreas Huyssen, Lawrence Levine, and others have shown, this cultural separation developed at least partially in reaction to the growth of the culture industry in the early years of this century. Through various strategies of containment and exclusion, modernist artists sought to preserve the autonomy and integrity of institution art against the encroachments of technological modernization by defining art as a privileged site of creativity, imagination, and subjectivity. Not surprisingly, therefore, one of the characteristic features of the modernist aesthetic is a gesture of "warding off" the threat of a developing mass culture, viewed as trivial and banal on the one hand, monstrous and devouring on the other.[2] Moreover, within the political, psychological, and aesthetic discourses of the early twentieth century, mass culture and the masses were persistently gendered as female.[3] Thus the modernist effort to "make it new" also concealed the fear of losing cultural authority to women artists and to what Henry James called "the ethnic apparition" as well as the "nightmare of being devoured by mass culture through cooptation, commodification, and the 'wrong' kind of success."[4] Cooptation was the constant fear of the

modernist artist who tried to stake out a secure territory by fortifying
the boundaries between genuine art and inauthentic mass culture,
between high culture and the signifying systems of everyday life.
Defining culture in these hierarchical terms enabled the construction
of cultural spaces "free of intrusion, free of dilution, free of the insistent demands of the marketplace," spaces that made it possible to
"identify, distinguish, and order this new universe of strangers" by
defining the worthy and the beautiful as existing apart from ordinary
society.[5] Mass culture acted both as a complex symbol of this perceived threat to cultural hegemony and an overdetermined cause of
what the modernists saw as an overall decline in culture—Ezra
Pound's "botched civilization."

Ezra Pound and T. S. Eliot were perhaps the most vocal of the
American modernists in their desire to construct a firm opposition
between the complex and difficult skills demanded by high art and
the "seductive" pleasures of mass culture. They argued in favor of
the specialized status of the aesthetic, privileging in the values of
uniqueness and organic wholeness a discourse of authenticity that
certified the original while repressing notions of repetition and imitation operative in an age of mechanical reproduction. They advocated
an art separated from the realm of everyday life, foregrounding
through a quasi-private language the importance of personal style
and individual genius. They self-consciously appealed to an intellec-
tual elite educated in the master works of Western culture as when
Pound confessed that he wished to write "not the popular language
of any country but an international tongue common to the excessively
cultivated."[6]

While accounts such as Allan Bloom's *The Closing of the American
Mind* attempt to maintain a modernist vision of cultural hierarchy,
this vision has become increasingly untenable in a postmodern condition in which the cultural decentering that modernism sought to
evade has become widely acknowledged. Within a contemporary culture of mass information, knowledge must no longer be considered
monumental or monolithic but is dispersed and nomadic, and high
culture becomes "just one more subculture," one more option in a
mosaic of competing cultural styles.[7] Here, as Fredric Jameson rue-
fully notes "[high] culture is eclipsed as an autonomous space or
sphere; culture itself falls into the world." With this shift comes the
emergence of new kinds of texts "infused with the forms, categories,

and contents of that very Culture Industry so passionately de-
nounced by all the ideologies of the modern from Leavis and the
American New Critics, . . . to Adorno and the Frankfurt School."[8]
Postmodern art more and more frequently incorporates popular and
vernacular forms, and mass culture itself increasingly reflects a discontinuity generally attributed only to experimental art, evidence of
a postmodern eclecticism and hybridization that reflects the fragmented and conflictual nature of contemporary culture.

As older hierarchical models of culture give way to notions of
culture as "a tension-filled semiotic environment,"[9] formerly simple
distinctions between mainstream and avant-garde, between good and
bad taste, between the profound and the trivial are increasingly difficult to discern. And the high modernist values of originality, organic
wholeness, aesthetic autonomy, and authenticity are contextualized
by a postmodern set of assumptions regarding artistic production.
Chief among them is a model of the text (of culture itself) as composed
of an unstable network of previous codings and representations, or
in Roland Barthes's famous formulation, as "a vast stereophony . . . of
the already read" of "quotations without quotation marks."[10] If, as
Walter Benjamin argued in his influential essay "The Work of Art in
the Age of Mechanical Reproduction," the modern era also marked
the beginning of an age of mechanical reproducibility and thus the
waning of an aesthetics based on the unique and irreplaceable, then
postmodernism represents a further dissolution of these aesthetic
assumptions in favor of a full-blown aesthetics of reproducibility, an
aesthetics of the previously written and the already said.

In *The Political Unconscious*, Jameson speaks of the structural breakdown of the older realisms at the turn of the century from which
emerged "not modernism alone, but rather two distinct literary and
cultural structures, dialectically interrelated and *necessarily* presup-
posing each other": mass culture and high culture [emphasis added].[11]
Jameson's view of this early-twentieth-century moment in essence
predicts his later assessments of postmodernism where—in his equation—culture is debased because it is no longer possible to keep high
culture separated from a commodified mass culture. He maps this
historical emergence in such a way that a decentered postmodern
culture can *only* be seen as a falling off from a modernist cultural ideal
where the oppositional version of the best that has been thought and

said was easily determinable and easily championed. Among other things, what Jameson's model excludes is the possibility of alternate responses to the emergence of mass culture in this early-twentieth-century moment, an exclusion that prevents a historical understanding of the potentially various interactions between high and mass culture throughout the century. This suggests a need for the construction of multiple histories of multiple avant-garde responses within modernism—especially those made by women and ethnic writers.[12]

I want to explore one such instance through Stein's case whose response to mass culture differed significantly from those of other modernist writers. Many of these writers, as I have suggested, attempted to sharply differentiate high and mass culture as a precondition for the development of a modernist aesthetic. Stein, however, tried to express the modern *in relation to* them both. Far from pathologizing an "inauthentic" mass culture and fearing its intrusion into the realm of high art, she developed aspects of her aesthetic practice in dialogue with popular forms and idioms, in many cases taking her ideas for textual innovations directly from them. For her, the new forms of an emerging mass culture were not morally, psychologically, and aesthetically regressive but were tied to the very essence of the modern—"where the twentieth century was."[13] Unlike writers who insisted that serious art be kept pure, aligned with a mythic past, a great tradition, an autonomous realm elsewhere, Stein situated the contemporary composition—her term for the avant-garde text—within the everyday.

For Stein, writers who deny their connection to the popular and the daily remain frozen in the literary compositions of previous generations, whereas she believed that "the whole business of writing is the question of living in . . . contemporariness":

Nothing changes from generation to generation except the composition in which we live and the composition in which we live makes the art which we see and hear. . . . The composition is the thing seen by every one living in the living that they are doing, they are the composing of the composition that at the time they are living is the composition of the time in which they are living.[14]

Each generation has to do with daily life . . . any sort of creative artist . . . can't live in the past, because it is gone. He can't live

in the future because no one knows what it is. He can only live
in the present of his daily life . . . everybody lives a contemporary
daily life. The writer lives it, too, and expresses it imperceptibly.[15]

If the writer is to reflect "what the world in which he lives is doing,"
if the writer is to "make it new" in Stein's sense, art can no longer
borrow from the forms and the aesthetic practices of the past. Rather,
a contemporary art must merge with the "art" of contemporary life
as simultaneous embodiments of a changed twentieth-century composition, an interaction that may also lead to new art forms capable
of reflecting this change.

Of course other modernist writers had recognized fundamental
shifts in the nature of contemporary lived experience. Virginia
Woolf's oft-quoted observation, "On or about December 1910 human nature changed," or D. H. Lawrence's pronouncement, "It
was in 1915 that the old world ended," suggest that the modern
stylistic revolution arose at least in part from a historical opportunity for change in human relationships and human subjectivity. Like Stein, Woolf, Lawrence, and many others also attempted
to move beyond what were perceived as the constraints and the
outmoded aesthetic assumptions of nineteenth-century realism.
What is significant for our purposes, however, is that unlike Woolf
and Lawrence, Stein recognized and attempted to respond to the
ways in which mass media forms also contributed to these changed
human relations.

The cinema, the motor car, the radio, the mass circulation newspaper, Stein realized, had not simply entered culture in the early
twentieth century; they also were helping to transform it by altering
the ways in which lived experience was perceived or "composed."
These new mass technologies not only reflected experience in new
ways but mediated and in a complex sense helped to revise the very
nature of this experience, a point made by Benjamin also, who notes
that:

the mode of human sense perception changes with humanity's
entire mode of existence. The manner in which human sense
perception is organized, the mediums in which it is accom-
plished, is determined not only by nature but by historical circumstances as well.[16]

Among other things the new forms of mass media created in this historical moment were acting to transform the conditions for producing, distributing, evaluating, and, especially, receiving art. Given these changes in cultural production, then, "culture" in Stein's terms could not be considered part of an autonomous realm apart from lived experience, something located in the museums. Instead it involved what Raymond Williams calls a "whole way of life," "a complex lived in structure of feeling."[17]

Stein reflects aspects of this new "way of life" in her textual practice and defines features of the twentieth-century composition in scattered places throughout her theoretical essays, although these speculations do not cohere into what might be called a systematic cultural or aesthetic theory. As I have been suggesting, they are persistently drawn with reference to or metaphorically linked with mass cultural forms, and, in part because of this, their similarity to many contemporary forms and logics is often striking.

In some instances, Stein attempts to create a prose equivalent of a mass culture form as in the case of her insistent style, which she began developing as early as 1906 and which she compares with the cinema. Looking back at the evolution of her method from the perspective of the 1930s Stein comments:

> it was like a cinema picture made up of succession and each moment having its own emphasis and its own existence and so there was the moving and the existence of each moment . . . I of course did not think of [the insistent style] in terms of the cinema, in fact I doubt whether at that time I had ever seen a cinema but, I cannot repeat this too often, everyone is of one's period and this our period was undoubtedly the period of the cinema.[18]

On an analogy with the individual frames of a film, each syntactic unit in the insistent style differs slightly from the previous one suggesting a series of fluid continuously present moments that gradually build toward an image as in this passage from Stein's *Many Many Women* (1910):

> In coming and going she was being one expressing enthusiasm and in expressing enthusiasm she was expressing needing enjoying and in expressing needing enjoying she was expressing

feeling everything and in expressing feeling everything she was expressing being one coming. In expressing being one coming she was being one who in being coming was continuing enthusiasm. In continuing enthusiasm she was one being loving. In being loving she was being one being feeling. In being feeling she was one coming and going. In being feeling she was one coming. In being feeling and going she was one being feeling. In being feeling she was coming, in being feeling she was going.[19]

Stein's style in effect locates us inside the camera, asking us to perceive each discrete "frame" as we progress through the "film." It might be thought of as a prose equivalent of unsutured cinema—cinema with the seams showing rather than cinema as seamless narrative, Stein's exposure in textual form of the essence of the new medium.

The mode of reception demanded by the insistent style—which depends on shifts in surface rather than development in time—departs in striking ways from nineteenth-century modes, reflecting the changed perceptual skills required by the cinema and by the twentieth-century composition that endeavors to reproduce these changes. Obviously this mode requires a level of attention and intimacy perhaps unprecedented in fiction as I suggested in chapter 1. As Stein puts it, in referring to the insistent style: "reading word by word makes the writing that is not anything [from one point of view] be something [from a twentieth-century perspective]."[20] It also exposes regions of experience not normally represented in fiction, as the cinema itself expanded the field of representation by making visible what Benjamin calls "an unconscious optics." The cinematic close-up, for example, expands space, as slow motion extends movement—revealing in the process "entirely new structural formations of the subject" and the object, according to Benjamin.[21]

In other instances, Stein uses new technological forms less literally, as a metaphoric means to explain the fundamental difference of and a rationale for the new textuality she is attempting to create. A case in point is her notion of "twentieth century movement," which maps "the rhythm of the twentieth century" and in so doing decenters and replaces the outmoded linear narrative ordering of the nineteenth. As Stein puts it, when one used to think of narrative one meant a progressive telling of things that were progressively happening ... the important part of telling anything was the conviction that anything that everything was progressively happening. But now we do not really know that anything is progressively happening instead there is movement in every direction.[22]

Stein clarifies the nature of this movement in another striking image: "A motor goes inside and the car goes on but my business my ultimate business as an artist was not with where the car goes as it goes but with the movement inside that is the essence of its going."[23] Here, as in the previous statement, Stein gestures beyond an older narrative logic—where the car goes—and toward a new discontinuous experience of spatiality and temporality appropriate to the modern. Stein's twentieth-century text—"a space of time that is filled with moving"—replaces an older textual model in which events are chronologically connected in linear fashion and lead to closure, as she herself literally replaces older habits of composition with new modern ones that might be called composition in a state of distraction: "Gertrude Stein worked a great deal not as in the old days, night after night [the logically consistent habits of the nineteenth-century author], but anywhere, in between visits, in the automobile. ... She was much influenced by the sounds of the streets and the movement of the automobiles."[24]

The speed of the automobile, like the movement of the frames in a film, exposed early-twentieth-century spectators to a new flux of imagery—a new fluid universe—and made this imagery navigable. It created alternate perceptual values, in effect a qualitatively new experience, that extended and perhaps transformed the social reception of the image. In many of her texts, Stein recreates in textual form an experience similar to that of navigating this new perceptual field. Texts such as *A Novel of Thank You* situate the reader within a shifting landscape of discourses moving into focus and fading, without clear transition, into other conversations or moving from public observations to private conversations to individual speculations and back again, as this passage suggests:

Yet and Henriette and where are they placed they are placed before and next to two, one steady and stayed the other easy and jointed and all all three just as you see excellently used to be here. Here here.

Rosy rhymes with cosy and posy rhymes with rosy and rosy rhymes with rosy and posy rhymes with posy and cosy with rosy and with an effort. It is easy to say knitted.

Everything I need to-day is here. Have it here.

Everything one thing.

She began. What did she begin. She began eating. What did she begin eating she began eating what she began eating. . . . They have it. At once. Twice at once. Better four.

He makes a finer wider hat than she. Does he.

She said not to say.[25]

A Novel of Thank You shifts between its brief individual chapters as dramatically as it does within these chapters. In negotiating the text we must remain alert to these modulations of context and flexible enough to listen for echoes among them, to hold several perspectives nearly simultaneously. In "rapid transit" texts[26] such as this (*Ida* is another example, which I discuss at length in the following chapter), one moves forward but does not necessarily progress toward a goal—"it moves but it also stays," Stein says, proclaiming the equivalence of all destinations. The reading stance required here in essence mimes the "distracted reception" of driving in a car, a mode of reception that Benjamin argues increased noticeably in all fields of art in the age of the cinema and thus one symptomatic of the profound changes in apperception occasioned by mass technological changes.

As I have been suggesting, in the early twentieth century, the codes, texts, and images of mass culture were helping to alter the expectations and competencies of a reading and viewing public; new mediums such as the cinema and the radio were in fact helping to constitute new structural formations of the subject. Stein recognized that the culture of mass information had affected the ontological status of high art in modern society, and high print culture must respond to this change. But again rather than repudiating or pathologizing, she sought to understand and incorporate. Thus she comments: "The tradition has always been that you may more or less describe the things that happen . . . but nowadays everybody all day long knows what is happening . . . one knows it by radios, cinema, newspapers . . . until what is happening does not really thrill anyone."[27] In an age of the mass transmission of information, the nineteenth-century novel is no longer new; literally it is no longer news. "So much happens everyday and . . . anybody can read or hear about it the day it happens . . . as it happens." Lacking this immediacy, events, as typically described in the novel, are no longer "important" or "exciting." "The Twentieth Century gives of itself a feeling of movement and has no feeling for events . . . events have lost their interest for people . . . everyone knows so many stories what is the use of telling another story."[28] Similarly, characters have lost their interest for people:

> The characters in the novels of the Nineteenth century lived a queer kind of way. That is to say people lived and died by these characters. They took a violent interest in them. . . . can you imagine anyone today weeping over a character. . . . Today no one is interested in personalities enough to dream about personalities.[29]

Character as unique personality is replaced by the immediacy and transitory appeal of the public icon, an image created by mass media such as the cinema, widely available to a heterogeneous audience and capable of unlimited reproducibility. Given these changes in the public reception of texts, Stein asks "where are we then in narrative writing?"

What she develops as a response in works such as *Ida, Lucy Church Amiably,* and, as I will discuss later in the chapter, in her detective novel *Blood on the Dining Room Floor,* is a complex twentieth-century art of textual wandering, the dynamics and features of which I have only suggested here: immediacy in a continuous present vs. conventional narrative chronology; a discontinuous surface movement of images or textual moments vs. deep description and logically causal development; spectacle or sheer happening vs. events moving forward in a plot. Like "crime stories, newspapers, radios, and funny papers," this new textuality does not focus on "succeeding or failing"—the fate of a character developing through time. Instead, it attempts to capture the sheer "excitement" of "moment to moment happening,"[30] a continuing process of becoming with no intrinsic purpose or direction. Stein's efforts to construct new formal features and aesthetic values for the novel, ones capable of responding to cultural changes occasioned in part by the development of new technologies, recalls Benjamin's observation on generic change. "The history of every art form," he says, "shows critical epochs in which a certain art form aspires to effects which could be fully obtained only with a changed technological standard, that is to say, *in a new art form*" [emphasis added].[31]

In addition to Benjamin's insights—upon which I have partly drawn to analyze Stein's method—two recent attempts to theorize aspects of the complex structure of our contemporary mass culture—Dana Polan's analysis of spectacular form and Raymond Williams's concept of televisual flow—provide suggestive analogies to Stein's textual method and help to clarify it. Polan defines spectacular form with reference to Hollywood musicals, noting their opposition to more traditional narrative form. Like the most radical of avant-garde texts (and this is Polan's point), spectacular form is a nonnarrative, "non-signifying notion of art as endless . . . display" that demonstrates the irrelevance of narrative "to an art that wishes to celebrate an endless, de-sublimated spectacle cut off from all narrative ends . . . an endless performance."[32] Spectacular form, like the performative mode enacted in *Lucy Church Amiably*, exceeds the realm of narrative and representation, avoiding consideration of narrative regularity or significant theme in favor of pure visual and aural display. This spectacle of movements and sounds that "ceases to be about anything but [its] own kinesis"[33] is reminiscent of Stein's observation that the twentieth century has conceived an intensity of movement so great "that it does not have to move against anything [be put in narrative terms] to be known."[34] Posited in both descriptions is a form based on seriality in which one element follows another in rapid succession with no necessarily meaningful linkage between them.

For Polan, the texts of postmodern mass culture, like certain avant-garde texts, work through a montage of moments of coherence and incoherence, moments that "engage in contradiction, undercut[ting] every sense by a subsequent or coincident nonsense."[35] The effect of the whole comes from the "incongruous confrontation" be-

tween each moment or bit that creates an ongoing but nonprogressive "flow" that forces each scene to give way to the next. Polan
borrows this term from Raymond Williams's analysis of the operations of commercial television where the continuity of the signal—in
that it is always on(going)—becomes a flow. In a much more complex
and extreme sense than Stein's car metaphor or its textual equivalent,
television flow exposes the viewer to a continuous stream of images,
pieces in an ongoing montage that robs each individual scene or
show of any specificity, any enduring sense of discrete value. Each
moment or show or indeed each individual work of mass culture
becomes part of an intertextual panorama of "gestures, images,
styles, and cultures in a perpetual collage of disintegration and rein-
tegration,"[36] a model of postmodern culture itself. The permanent
present of contemporary mass culture is a much more complex nexus
than Stein could have anticipated in her attempt to inhabit the "complete actual present" of early-twentieth-century culture. Yet, like the
flow and the spectacle of these popular forms, a Stein text invites the
reader to "not solve it [unravel the text to reach a truth] but be in it,"
immersed in textuality rather than contemplating the text, coextensive with the speed and spectacle of "a space of time that is filled
always with moving."[37]

Stein's injunction to "not solve it but be in it" is particularly apt advice
for the reader of her playful (anti)detective novel, *Blood on the Dining
Room Floor* (hereafter cited in text as *Blood*). Here, again, she juxtaposes avant-garde strategies and popular forms within a single text,
using the mixture to redefine the form and, in so doing, to critique
the premises of, in this case, the typical detective novel. *Blood* teases
the reader with the expectation of a solution, but suspends it indefinitely. We wander among proliferating "clues," promises of a significance to be revealed, an enigma to be solved, but we remain as
mystified as the narrator, who also fails to find a unifying system or
explanation that would make the clues cohere. By all accounts, Stein
was an avid reader of detective stories (sometimes two or three a
week she tells us in "Why I Like Detective Stories") and claimed for
them a particular contemporariness: " . . . the detective story which
is you might say the only really modern form of writing that has
come into existence gets rid of the hero to begin with . . . the man is

dead to begin with so you have so to speak got rid of the event before the book begins."[38] Because it erases character and event, the detective novel—in Stein's redefined sense—becomes "interesting," unlike the typical nineteenth-century novel where the reader "lived and died by" the fates of the characters. Those motivations that drive the plot forward to solution—what we often take to be a defining feature of the form—fail to interest Stein ("crime if you know the reason if you know the motive if you can understand the character is not interesting"[39]). And the other "hero" of the genre is dispensed with as well: the detective as logical force who, in solving the crime, tames the confusion unleashed by the mystery and therefore restores order and rationality. Stein's transformed version of the detective genre destabilizes a view of the world and the subject as coherent and solvable. As many postmodern texts are, it is characterized by an absence of finality, by openness and permanent indeterminacy.

The detective novel seems a particularly appropriate genre for Stein's transformation of a nineteenth-century work into a twentieth-century text since—despite her assertions—it is, in its typical form, an extreme version of the narrative impulse. Stylized, ritualized, indifferent to deep characterization or significant theme, the genre apparently exists solely to answer the question "what happened," to fulfill the reader's expectation that an enigma will be solved. It thus approaches "pure" narrative. Seymour Chatman's definition of the predominant form of the nineteenth-century novel—what he calls narratives of resolution—in fact reads very much like the plot of a detective story. These novels develop "through a sense of problem solving, of things being worked out in some way, of a kind of ratiocinative or emotional teleology."[40] A mystery is proposed, delayed, and finally solved at the moment of climax by giving the reader a solution, previously withheld, that completes the text. Roland Barthes goes even further in claiming that all narrative engages a desire "to denude, to know, to learn the origin and the end. . . . Narrative is a delayed truth and the truth is that which is delayed."[41] By delaying truth indefinitely, refusing to posit an origin or an end to the mystery, Stein exhausts the defining feature of detective fiction. *Blood* thus cannot be considered a continuation of the detective genre or a further development of its potential. Instead, it is a highly creative mutation of its underlying rationale.

This is not to say that *Blood* retains no connections to the conventions of detective fiction; indeed, the interplay between the reader's conventional expectations of the genre and the frustration of those expectations is crucial to the workings of the text. As is the case in much of Stein's writing, the "story" here draws on autobiographical details, recounting a "strange" summer full of mysterious incidents, among them the difficulty of retaining servants in the Stein-Toklas household, the death of Mme. Perlott, a hotelkeeper, and the romantic escapades of a young horticulturalist, Alexander (who "may be a witness" to the Perlott death). Stein inflects these incidents with an aura of mystery, as the opening of the text—full of the stock devices of a detective thriller—suggests. There is a country house, cars that won't start because they have been tampered with, dead telephones, hair and dust that are "no accident," and the "tragical event" of Mme. Perlott's unfortunate fall from the hotel balcony. These opening incidents recur repeatedly throughout the text, miming a logic of progression—in which events steadily accumulate toward significance—while at the same time not getting anywhere. Each reconfiguration of the incidents is merely a repetition of a promise-of-significance, as these passages from the beginning and end of the text suggest:

> Has everybody got it straight. So far we have two families and besides
>   a country house.
> We have three times crime.
> Remember there was a country house where everything happened one day
>   and other things happened other days.
> Then there was a funeral. . . .
> Then there was a hotel where something happened and everybody went,
>   . . . It was wonderful the way they covered it up and went on. . . . (*Blood*, 25–26)

So now you see. We have the triple theme, servants, yes of course servants, hotel, why there is always a hotel in every town by which you know who comes. . . . Then also there are three young very young married women . . . And then there is the ho-

tel. Oh there he is never seen, nor has he been nor been ever
seen. Nowhere Alexander has never no never never been seen.
(*Blood,* 65–66)

Because these incidents are juxtaposed and flagged, as it were, they
seem charged with significance. However, they remain mysterious,
failing to lead to an interpretation, as the narrator wavers between
promoting a connection between the events and being unable to
make them cohere. This process is perhaps most economically symbolized by the pun on "cover-up" that suggests both a concealment
of the true facts and a literal cover-up in the burial of Mme. Perlott's
body. Literally, the "triple themes" *do* cohere around the notions of
betrayal and victimization (the plot of many detective stories). The
servants betray their employers; the three young women, Alexander's lovers, are unfaithful to their husbands; Mme. Perlott has been
the victim of her husband's infidelity (which indirectly may be responsible for her death).

One could claim a coincidence in the events, since all are domestic tragedies—metaphorically leaving blood on the dining room floor.
In this case, however, coincidences do not fall together to solve a
mystery since the events are merely coterminous and are not causally
related. The narrator comments: "A fact is not a surprise, a coincidence is a surprise. There is always coincidence in crime. There are
so many ways in which there is no crime. Coincidence is not succession" (*Blood,* 42). Mysterious coincidences do exist in crime, as the
narrator points out, coincidences being surprising but accidental co-
occurrences of events that appear to suggest a causal relationship.
They form an intermediate step in the logic of detection, a boundary
between sheer random events and facts meaningfully connected to
produce an explanation, a solution. In order for coincidences to be
productive in a detective story, they must be proven to succeed one
another causally—they must be narratable. Although the narrator
seems to have found these incidents surprising coincidences, they are
not meaningful enough to be constructed into a crime; thus, there are
so many ways in which "there is no crime" (*Blood,* 42).

By both unifying incidents thematically and refusing to posit any
definite causal links among them or between them, the narrator
keeps us poised on a logical boundary, simultaneously advancing
and unravelling a narrative trajectory. As the above passages sug-

gest, this oscillation is reflected in the positioning of the narrator who both takes responsibility as a detective and refuses this role. On the one hand we are reassuringly told "Everybody proposes that nobody knows even if everybody knows. . . . Remember that I wish to tell you in every way what they do not say" (*Blood*, 39). This reassurance is not at all helpful, however, since we never find out what "they do not say" nor do we know what everybody else knows. When the narrator does attempt to fill in the blanks, the information is hyper-significant. We are overwhelmed by details that don't add up as when we are given a complicated genealogical profile of Alexander's family. This information only serves to confuse identities further rather than clarifying Alexander's personality or motivations, or his connection to the death of Mme. Perlott, a fact underscored by the narrator's flat pronouncement, "it is not of any importance" (*Blood*, 23). At other times, deliberately extraneous information is included and flaunted, perhaps a parody of the detective convention of planting false clues. We learn of a woman who works in the hotel—"she had nothing to do with it" (*Blood*, 21); of the eldest son who fought in the war—"that was not of any importance" (*Blood*, 24); and of the story of Mary M.—"there is no Mary M. in this case but if there were this is what she would do" (*Blood*, 34). As if this were not enough, any faith we might have had in the narrator's ratiocinative powers is undermined by the frank admission from time to time, "I am sure I do not know" (*Blood*, 29), and by statements that are absolutely self-contradictory—"Think how near crime is, and how near crime is not being here at all" (*Blood*, 41). In short, Stein refuses the either/or logic demanded by the traditional detective novel, substituting a both/and logic of contradiction and coincidence that makes totalizing interpretations (interpretation as solution-to-the-mystery) impossible. This is not to say that the text defies meaning; rather as many postmodern texts do, it holds out multiple options for the configuration and reconfiguration of meaning and offers multiple significances no one of which is necessarily definitive.

   Blood on the Dining Room Floor may be seen as a pastiche of detective conventions floating through textual space. Like Polan's description of the text of contemporary mass culture, it is composed of "moments that vaguely hint at meaning, and moments that disavow posited meanings, engage in contradiction, undercut every sense by a subsequent or coincident non-sense."[42] This shifting montage of moments "structures" our experience of the text. While it withholds the more conventional pleasure of solving it, we perhaps learn a new kind of pleasure by being in it. *Blood* disavows any final meaning; like the narrator we do not "know." Yet we do know that, for Stein, crime—"if you know the reason, if you understand the motive, if you understand the character"—is not "interesting." She chooses to leave it interesting.

In suggesting these broad correspondences between Stein's aesthetic program for the twentieth-century composition and some of the heterogeneous structures and iconoclastic artistic practices evident in postmodern culture, I undoubtedly risk distorting a number of things. The complete actual present of late-twentieth-century culture is a complex brew, a historical moment that reflects the social, economic, and technological complexity of life under late capitalism. It differs in its magnitude of complexity from the historical moment in which Stein wrote—the early years of the culture industry. Perhaps it differs in kind as well. Among other things, the mass modes of information transmission that Stein responded to have become enormously more sophisticated, proliferating into a vast, decentered communications network. Here knowledge is replicated and dispersed at blinding speeds, computerized and transformed into an informational commodity, a process that, according to Jean Baudrillard, does not, paradoxically, facilitate greater communication but exhausts it in the staging *of* communication. In a postmodern moment the second order simulation characteristic of the modernist age of mechanical reproduction gives way to a third order of simulation in which the real is no longer even recoverable, in which reality itself becomes hyperreal.[43]

In the global space of the postmodern—the composition in which we live—what counts as lived experience undoubtedly has changed in ways we are still attempting to theorize. As subjects we may well have mutated to the point that Donna Haraway can make the amazing claim, " . . . in our time we are all chimeras, theorized and fabricated hybrids of machine and organism . . . we are cyborgs,"[44] or Laurie Anderson can intone, "I am in my body the way most people drive in their cars"[45]—an interesting wrinkle to Stein's car metaphor. In fact, elsewhere Anderson directly invokes Stein in an effort to distinguish between an early moment in media culture and our present moment, and between the medium of language and the media of film and video.

In "Three Songs for Paper, Film, and Video," part of Anderson's *United States*, she paraphrases Stein's quotation about the modernity of the detective story, acknowledging Stein's recognition of the death of the centered subject in fiction, the loss of a concern for character as personality: "The detective novel is the only novel truly invented in the twentieth century. In the detective novel, the hero is dead at the very beginning. So you don't have to deal with human nature at all." As Anderson's piece continues, this decentered fictional subject becomes a dispersed and less anthropomorphic filmic subject:

> In science fiction films, the hero just flies in at the very beginning. He can bend steel with his bare hands. He can walk in zero gravity. He can see right through lead doors. But no one asks how he is able to do these things. They just say 'Look! He's walking in zero gravity.' So you don't have to deal with human nature at all.

Finally, in Anderson's third song, which describes the hyperspace of video culture, the individual subject disappears entirely, lost in and becoming a disembodied TV signal that itself is traveling in outer space. Here, words are superimposed on and swallowed by the haze of the TV screen, which diffuses to fill the page. Viewer and screen, subject and object, interpenetrate as they do not in the older mediums of print and film—a fact Anderson suggests by having representations of these older forms appear *above* the words of her text. "When t.v. signals are sent out," she says, "they don't stop. They keep going. They pick up speed as they leave the solar system. By now, the first t.v. programs ever made have been traveling for thirty years. . . . All those characters from cowboy serials, variety hours and quiz shows are sailing out. . . . And they sail farther and farther out, intact, still talking."[46] Perhaps it was in the direction of a new medium toward which Stein gestured when she made the following comment, a comment suggesting that she too may have glimpsed the limits of the book to render the speed and movement of the modern: "Think of anything, of cowboys, of movies, of detective stories, of anybody who goes anywhere or stays at home and is an American and you will realize that it is something strictly American to conceive a space that is filled with moving, a space of time that is filled always with moving."[47]

Anderson's piece describes three media and three moments in what has been called postmodern culture. It suggests both the continuity of certain aspects of postmodernism—in this case an emphasis on decentering the subject—and the importance of considering historical differences within it—in this case the differences created through the development of new media. Thus to claim, as I have here and throughout, that Stein embodies aspects of the postmodern—her attitude toward and uses of mass culture being one of these—again does not mean that I necessarily wish to situate her definitively as a full-blown genealogical precursor, a "postmodernist avant la lettre" as Jameson has characterized her. For one thing, this characterization collapses important historical differences between Stein's era and our own, rendering postmodernism as a static monolithic entity rather than an ongoing cultural process, one in which the emergence of mass culture has been central. It also distorts Stein's complexity, as Stein was a richly complex writer and, at times, a richly contradictory one. There are ways in which Stein did identify with and long to be identified with high culture as when she included herself in the company of Homer and Shakespeare. But it is certainly also true that Stein, as a marginalized writer—a woman, a lesbian, a Jew—might well have had less of an investment in maintaining the rigorous separation between high and mass culture so evident in the work of certain male modernists. Perhaps she was simply more able to "use everything," as she put it.

Chapter 7

Postmodern Melodrama and
Simulational Aesthetics in *Ida*

The nomad is not necessarily somebody who moves . . . there are travels in which
one does not move, travels in intensity, and even from a historical point of view,
nomads are not those who move like migrants, on the contrary, they are those
who do not move and who start nomadizing in order to stay in the same place
and free themselves from codes.

—Gilles Deleuze, *Nietzche aujourd'hui*

Nomads wander though they do not always move. In their errancy
(from the root, *iterare*, to travel) they often go astray; errancy slides
quickly into err-ancy. The errancy of the wandering woman—her
travels in intensity, her efforts to free herself from codes—incites
particular anxiety in those who construct them (a fact Deleuze's
nomadology does not overtly recognize). Wandering means:

to move or go aimlessly about without plan or fixed destination;
ramble; roam; 2) to go to a place by any way or at any pace that
suits the fancy; idle; stroll; 3) to turn aside or astray from a path,
course, etc.; to lose one's way; to stray from home, family,
friends, familiar places; 4) to go astray in mind or purpose; to
drift from a subject as in a discussion; to turn away from accepted
thoughts or morals; to go wrong morally or intellectually; to be
disjointed; disordered or incoherent. (*American Heritage Diction-
ary*, 2d ed.)

Wandering gains meaning as the deviant, devalued other side of that
which is linear, coherent, logical. It drifts from the realm of the productive, the purposeful, the responsible, the predictable, the men-
tally, morally, or socially upright and so wandering provokes incom-
prehension, condemnation, the impulse to contain.

Over the course of her career, Gertrude Stein perfected the art of nomadism or textual wandering in order to free herself from the enclosure of literary and social codes that she experienced as outmoded or oppressive. She began her career, however, working within the value system implied in the above definition. In her first novel, *Things As They Are* (*Q.E.D.*), the story of a love triangle, the character Adele wavers between an attempt to maintain what she considers to be a rational, moral position and a desire to comprehend Helen, "her conscience" at odds with "her pain and desire."[1] Adele struggles to explain through logical means an emotional dynamic that resists systematization and to fix herself in an unproblematic noncontradictory relation to it. Ultimately she leaves Helen, choosing to preserve her belief that "nothing is too good or too holy for clear thinking and definitive expression" (*Q.E.D.*, 132).

Wandering desire assumes a more central role in "Melanctha" where Melanctha Herbert vacillates between desires that can find neither full expression nor comfortable resolution in the world of the novel: her "vague," "complicated" wandering after "wisdom" and "excitement," and her desire for a "right position" in which to rest and "live regular." "Melanctha Herbert was always seeking rest and quiet and always she could only find new ways to be in trouble," "new ways to get excited."[2] The nature of Melanctha's desire remains unspoken and unsatisfied, eluding rational categories—as she puts it in talking to Jeff, "it ain't much use to talk about what a woman is really feeling in her" ("M," 135)—and its force constantly overwhelms her until "all the world went whirling in a mad weary dance around her" ("M," 233) and she dies, presumably consumed by the irreconcilable conflict.

The narrator in *A Long Gay Book* shares Adele's impulse to categorize experience, in this case by inventing a vast typology through which to describe "every kind of human being that ever was or is or would be living."[3] Confident at the outset, the narrator begins to waver between a belief in the soundness of her system and doubt that it will ever account for everyone. As she wanders between a desire to fix people through their unchanging essences and her desire to describe their "being," viewed as changeable and in process, her typology begins to admit logics that cannot be comprehended from the perspective of such systematizing urges, logics that disrupt the fixity of their designs. In *A Long Gay Book*, Stein definitively escapes from positivist realist programs and the upright social systems they imply, affirming instead the value of textual wandering over textual systems, and joining for the first time the themes of sexual and textual drifting. Like the idle wandering text, this desire is disordered, incoherent, nonproductive, and nonpredictable from the perspective of a heterosexual (straight) norm. The desire for stasis and rest, and the desire for openness, excitement, and movement, no longer in irresolvable contradiction as they were in "Melanctha," are resolved into a new textual rhythm—evident at the end of *A Long Gay Book* and most fully in *Lucy Church Amiably*, a text in which novelistic space is refigured as primary and the values of immediacy, changeability, and indeterminacy are affirmed.

Ida (1940),[4] Stein's most complex expression and her fullest affirmation of the value of this textual dynamic, reinvokes the figure of the wandering woman as well as the character of the wandering digressive narrator, and joins them to a practice of open-ended textual wandering. Whereas conventional social and narrative scripts prohibited Melanctha from reconciling her desire to wander and her need to rest, Ida wanders among possibilities that remain open, nomadizing in order to stay in the same place, the place where she is always just Ida. Ida is restless and needs to rest; she changes locations unpredictably and reappears unexpectedly; she marries, wanders away from marriage, remarries, and wanders while she is married. Within the logic of this text, all possibilities may potentially be present simultaneously: while Ida is resting she is potentially moving; while she is moving, she contains the potential to be at rest.

Stein refuses to fix Ida *(Ida)*, and thus limit possibilities, affirming instead the superior value of narrative indeterminacy. In order to appreciate Stein's accomplishment we must also desire and affirm this value over the more conventional pleasures of narrative certainty and closure. *Ida* instructs us in the art of textual wandering, teaching us that it is possible to drift through a novel while we simultaneously remain in one place, never advancing in a clear narrative trajectory.

Ida moves to the paradoxical rhythm of the twentieth century (in which if we are all cyborgs, we are certainly also all nomads). As I suggested in the previous chapter, this textual momentum arises in part from Stein's recognition that with the birth of mass culture and processes of mechanical reproducibility "a certain kind of mimesis is destroyed," as Walter Benjamin put it.[5] *Ida* does contain features common to realist texts (especially in comparison to other of Stein's works): a main character (of sorts), a story (of sorts), settings (many of them). Rather than viewing it as her return to realism, however, the novel might more accurately be seen as a miming of mimesis since, as I hope to show, *Ida* is based in an aesthetics of simulation rather than being rooted in an aesthetics of representation. Stein also developed important aspects of her art in dialogue with forms and idioms considered debased from the perspective of elite culture— among them the detective novel, the children's story, and, in the case of *Ida*, the melodrama. In self-consciously mixing these popular modes with avant-garde strategies Stein encouraged a creative inter- action (rather than a hierarchical relation) between the two, using this mixture to open new possibilities for the modern novel. As a means of further exploring Stein's uses of popular materials and her creative transformation of them, I want to approach *Ida* as a postmod- ern melodrama in which particular melodramatic conventions are invoked, transformed, and exceeded through interaction with an aes- thetics of simulation.

As a particular mode of framing experience, melodrama has a long cross-cultural history, beginning in late medieval morality plays and popular forms of oral narrative, such as fairy tales, and reemerging in the Romantic revival of Scott, Byron, Hugo, and others.[6] Melo- drama was an enormously popular mode throughout the nineteenth century, evident in a wide range of cultural practices and formative in the development of twentieth-century mass culture. From the per- spective of elite culture, however, it became in the early twentieth century the very embodiment of an outmoded nineteenth-century (feminized) sensibility within which emotional expressiveness func- tioned as a source and indication of moral value.[7] Denigrated as sentimental, escapist, trivial (associations that persist), melodrama was constituted as an antivalue and the genre repudiated as a form of failed tragedy. High tragedy and realism became cornerstones of elite cultural value in the theater, defining themselves in distinction from mass melodramatic entertainment,[8] part of that widespread pat- tern of repudiating an emerging popular culture and metaphorizing it as female that I discussed in the previous chapter.

As a "particular historically and socially conditioned mode of experience"[9] as well as a genre, melodrama is distinguished by an aesthetics of extremity and exaggeration that sublimates action or dramatic conflict to style and spectacle. In the highly symbolized, emotionally-charged landscape of melodrama, everyday actions intensify or appear in strange, uncanny configurations and pacing is rapid, intense, restless, episodic. Violence, sensationalism, and visual excess predominate through a focus on such plot staples as lurid events, masked relationships or disguised identities, abductions, coincidences, highly polarized moral and emotional states, sudden reversals, or dramatic shifts in mood.[10]

Although aesthetic history suggests the interdependent development of realism and melodrama, and while melodrama shares features with the realist text, their epistemological projects differ in several crucial ways. If realism posits a world capable of full representation and explanation through the organization of experience into coherent structures, melodrama lacks faith in the world's unproblematic decipherability or representability. Instead, if "attests to forces, desires, fears, which, though no longer granted metaphysical reality, nevertheless appear to operate in human life independent of rational explanation."[11] Finding no such explanation available within socially legitimated discourses and possessing no others, melodrama turns to highly stylized relations and events as a means of signifying large inexpressible realms of experience. The formal characteristics of melodrama thus bespeak a crisis in representation in which language is either inappropriate or inadequate to the emotional burden of the subject matter at hand.[12] As Peter Brooks notes in his discussion of melodrama as hysterical text, this suggests the workings of the unconscious that must speak obliquely through physical symptoms in order to give expression to material that evades conscious articulation.[13]

At least in its modern incarnations, the melodramatic mode most often explores themes of identity within the bourgeois family—as do many realist texts. However, it also threatens to expose the "real" conditions of psychic and sexual identity within the family structure, conditions that, pressing too closely to the surface, break the reassuring unity of realist narrative whose business is to contain ideological contradictions and psychic excess.[14] While melodrama does not usually exceed the limitations of the ideologically permissible in any given era, it also foregrounds through style and symbolism demands that trouble the coherence of dominant ideologies. The conditions of this ideological exposure are already apparent in a social system that, as David Rodowick notes, "considers desire to be a fundamental danger to successful socialisation and thus requires the division of sexuality from sociality."[15] This conflict between the constraints of a patriarchal symbolic order and the restlessness of desire constitutes a crisis of representation within melodrama—the central contradiction of the genre, according to Rodowick, and one especially evident in the representation of women. Melodrama's narrative convolutions and stylistic excesses therefore may be read as attempts to negotiate the (impossible) tension between expressing female desire while at the same time remaining within social law.

Melodrama not only assumes a feminized position within the terrain of twentieth-century high culture, it is also perhaps the feminine genre par excellance in that women might be said to stand in a melodramatic relation to culturally dominant patriarchal structures as a point of contradiction or mute unsignifiable excess. Because it foregrounds this culturally negative function, melodrama potentially could dislodge the hegemony of those structures. As Mary Ann Doane argues in her essay on the woman's film, for example, the insistent effort to inscribe female subjectivity in these melodramatic texts provokes ideological crises within them—especially around dramas of looking and seeing—crises made evident in the films' barely containable structural tensions.[16] In the end, however, such films (uneasily) recontain ideological contradictions and immobilize women, illustrating the impossibility of sustaining a coherent representation of female subjectivity within narrative structures so heavily dependent upon masculine spectatorial modes.[17] Clearly, other structures are needed to reconcile melodrama's central ideological contradiction: a woman's desire to wander and her need to rest.

During her first trip to America in more than thirty years, Stein reflected on many aspects of American culture among them the peculiarity of American newspapers:

> What do they want to know in the newspapers . . . and do they want to know what they do want to know [the news] or do they

only think...they want to know what they do want to know.... What they want or think they want to know...is to know every day what happened the day before and so get the feeling that it has happened on that day...and not on the day before. That is what the American newspaper is supposed to do to make it be as if...the things that happened yesterday happen to-day.... The yellow press that is really the American press...had in everyway by headlines by scarelines, by short lines and by long lines, by making all the noise and sound they could with their words and lines tried to invent in every way they could making it be as if the news that had happened on one day had happened...on the newspaper day.[18]

In "making the news that had happened on one day" appear as if it "had happened on the newspaper day," American newspapers do not so much falsely represent reality. Instead, through hyperbole and stylistic excess (noisy words), they simulate the immediacy of real events, substituting melodramatized signs of what happened for the real event itself. Because the American public reads newspapers as if they report the day's news ("this is what they want to know"), the reality of what actually happened is, essentially, beside the point, is, in effect, lost in the process of simulating it.

Stein's observation neatly illustrates Walter Benjamin's argument in "The Work of Art in the Age of Mechanical Reproduction" (also written in 1935, the year of Stein's newspaper essay): with the advent of processes of mechanical reproducibility, the concept of the original and authentic event is destroyed. This fact also affects the authenticity of an individual subject whose sense of personal uniqueness or self-presence—what Benjamin calls "the aura"—fades through an encounter with mechanically produced images of the self. "A feeling of strangeness overcomes the actor before the camera," Benjamin writes, "basically of the same kind as the estrangement felt before one's own image in the mirror."[19] The difference is that with the advent of film the reflected image has become separable from the self and transportable beyond it, creating a situation in which one may be *both* other and oneself. The filmic image of the actor appears before the public, and the actor also is transformed into a "personality," a star, constructed as such by mechanisms of commodification within the film industry. In a manner similar to the spectacular headlines of mass circulation newspapers, the effect of this double simulation is to further estrange any sense of an authentic self or a real event through the "spell of the cult personality," or the generation of the event through public fictions. Stein's comments after first seeing herself on film echo and reinforce Benjamin's.

> One never gets quite used to unexpectedly seeing one's name in print no matter how often it happens to you to be that one, it always gives you a shock of a slightly mixed-up feeling, are you or are you not one. . . . But what is that, imagine what is that compared to never having heard anybody's voice speaking while a picture is doing something, and that voice and that person is yourself. . . . It upset me very much when that happened to me, there is no doubt about that, . . . that was astonishing.[20]

Ida enacts the aesthetic consequences of Stein's recognition that identity itself may be simulated in an age of mechanical reproduction. It is a bildungsroman filtered through the spectacular melodramatic sensibility of the culture of scare lines, movie personalities, and astonishing dislocating shocks to stable identity and coherent representations, such as the one Stein describes above.

In many respects, *Ida* is as histrionic, excessive, and restlessly episodic as any melodrama, and the astonishing things that happen to Ida—plot staples of the genre—begin from the first. She is born with her "twin" to a "sweet and gentle" family, orphaned at an early age, and separated (temporarily) from her twin. After this she lives with a series of relatives (her grandfather, aunts), abruptly and inexplicably moving from one household to another as she later moves—without warning—from place to place. As Ida wanders through the world—figured as an emotionally charged landscape, both ordinary and uncanny—she sees "lots of funny things" that sometimes frighten her and make her "feel funny," a repeated phrase that signals a range of emotions, in much the way key symbols or gestures stand for diffuse emotional terrains in melodrama. These include remarkable appearances and disappearances, alarming reversals of fortune, mysteriously shifting or disguised identities, dramatic abductions, and sensationally violent events, such as the one accompanying Ida's birth. Here a great aunt (who is not "sweet and gentle") becomes pregnant by a soldier and gives birth to stillborn twins that she buries beneath a pear tree.

The emphasis in this episode on personal misfortune and untimely or even violent death is echoed throughout the novel in many of the seemingly digressive stories included in it, which read like pages from the tabloid press. There is an old man whose son shoots his business partner and is condemned to twenty years of hard labor (*I*, 41); a dog eaten by other dogs (*I*, 65); a little boy eaten by a lion (*I*, 68); nuts that are plowed into the ground but do not grow (a gruesome reminder of the stillborn twins) (*I*, 60); even wooden guinea hens whose heads are shot off for sport, a slight episode, worth quoting for its tone, which reinforces the suggestion that melodrama is a way of experiencing the world rather than a specific content as such. Here, an ordinary amusement park activity assumes a tone of menace. "Once upon a time there was a shotgun and there were wooden guinea hens and they moved around electrically, electricity made them move around and as they moved around if you shot them their heads fell off" (*I*, 61).

Incidents such as these cohere through correspondences in their emotional tenor or tone rather than through logical connections. In many ways their operation throughout the text suggests those mechanisms of displacement and transference operating in the symbolic system of dreams. As Thomas Elsaesser puts it in his description of melodrama, this process generates the text as a "highly dynamic, yet discontinuous cycle of non fulfillment."[21] Discontinuity grows from a surface level that seems confused or unreal and an undertone that is emotionally accurate or pervasive, creating a universe of "powerfully emotional but obliquely related fixations."[22]

These fixations, as Elsaesser implies, mime the operations of the unconscious and the workings of certain types of novels, Stein suggests:

A novel is what you dream in your night sleep. A novel is not waking thoughts although it is written and thought with waking thoughts. But really a novel goes as dreams go in sleeping at night and some dreams are like anything and some dreams are like something and some dreams change and some dreams are quiet and some dreams are not. And some dreams are just what

anyone would do only a little different always just a little different and that is what a novel is.[23]

Dreams go on in a multiplicity of ways: like anything, like something,
restlessly, quietly, like *Ida* itself. Dream details, though often recognizable and commonplace—"what anyone would do"—always exceed by their little difference the language of waking thoughts, i.e.,
the plot used to contain them.

Dreams also typically fuse contradictions and, like the movement
of melodrama itself, proceed by abrupt transformations, changes of
episode, spatio-temporal jumps, vaguely or incomprehensibly symbolic acts as in the following episode from early in the novel:

> One day it was not Tuesday, two people came to see her great-
> aunt. They came in very carefully. They did not come in to-
> gether. First one came and then the other one. One of them had
> some orange blossoms in her hand. That made Ida feel funny.
> Who were they? She did not know and she did not like to follow
> them in. A third one came along, this one was a man and he had
> orange blossoms in his hat brim. He took off his hat and he said
> to himself here I am, I wish to speak to myself. Here I am. Then
> he went on into the house. . . . She wondered if she ought to go
> into the house to see whether there was really any one with her
> great aunt, and then she thought she would act as if she was not
> living there but was somebody just coming to visit and so she
> went up to the door and she asked herself is any one at home
> and when they that is she herself said to herself no there is
> nobody at home she decided not to go in. (*I*, 9–10)

The symbolism of the women wearing orange blossoms is mysterious, as it often is if dreams are considered from the perspective of
waking thoughts; clearly, however, the women inspire dread in Ida,
who "does not like to follow them in." When one tries to reconstruct
a sequence of events in this episode, it dissolves into an indeterminate jumble of attraction and repulsion. Ida presumably sees the
women with the orange blossoms enter her great-aunt's house since
she feels "funny" as a result. But she must doubt her perception
because she wonders whether anybody really is with her great-aunt

(a denial of the funny feeling in denying the perception?). As visitor to and occupant of the house, Ida decides that nobody is at home, thereby negating both her earlier perception and her own identity (or an aspect of her identity) since, standing at the threshold of her own home, *she* is at home. The man standing at the door who does go in parallels the actions and inverts the outcome of Ida's threshold experience—literally, she stands at the doorway; metaphorically, she floats between two orders of experience.

As this incident further suggests, several of the funny things that happen to Ida contain vague suggestions of menace at the hands of men: men follow Ida and frighten her (*I*, 9); jump out from behind trees and disappear when she turns to confront them (*I*, 13); stare at Ida (*I*, 15). This supports Doane's suggestion that melodrama is preoccupied with dramas of looking and seeing in which the visible is invested not with desire but with anxiety, horror, or uncanny dread in relation to ordinary places and events. In distinction from Hollywood cinema (and realist fiction), which organizes vision in terms of male pleasure and truth and women's objectification as a spectacle, a certain "despecularization" occurs in these film melodramas, a "deflection of scopophiliac energy" into a free-floating anxiety reinforced by a thematics stressing the gap between concealing and revealing, seen and unseen, known and unknown.[24]

This thematic emphasis on dramas of looking and seeing, along with a melodramatic blending of the commonplace and the fantastic, occurs in two startling episodes of abduction involving Ida's dog, Love. One day Ida is walking and sees a woman carrying a large bundle of wash and a photograph of Love, a fact that Ida finds "astonishing." When Ida tries to grab the photograph from the woman, an auto comes along that stops to see what is happening. Ida snatches the photo, jumps into the car, and is thrown out by the drivers, who speed away, taking Love's photo and dropping a package that Ida retrieves. Several paragraphs later, Ida again sees the wash woman, an auto again comes by, this time carrying Love himself, who has in his mouth the package that Ida had picked up earlier (*I*, 21–22). This section of the novel emphasizes a dreamlike transformation of a representation (the photo of Love) into the "real" Love, who may be only a dream-image of Love and not Love at all. One suspects here too that Stein is embodying the kind of actualization of a play on words common in dreams. Ida literally has and loses love, something that occurs quite frequently, as her many marriages later in the novel suggest.

The identity or existence of Ida's "twin," Winnie, is similarly unstable or uncertain. The opening of the novel suggests that Ida is born "one of two," however later Ida states that she invents her twin because "she is tired of being just one and when I am a twin one of us can go out and one of us can stay in (*I*, 10). Ida's "invention" may suggest that she seeks a way to express contradictory desires in her nature (the desire to stay and to go) or to reconcile a split between public and private selves. The twin might be seen as her alter ego, her unconscious or her unactualized potential. Ida's very name embodies these multiple possibilities: it asserts and affirms an "I," an ego, presence or a putting forth to which it adds "da," a hesitation, holding back, or the return of a presence following its absence in the manner of Freud's "fort-da" story. This drama of presence and absence is reinforced thematically in the opening account of Ida's birth when her mother holds Ida back as she goes forth and in the inverted or absent birth of the stillborn twins (non-I's). As in the Love episode, here the ground of narrative reliability or stability begins to oscillate and slide. Is Winnie actual (i.e., depicted at the same narrative level as Ida herself), but absent? a figment of Ida's imagination (imaginatively present)? or simply an effect of the drama of signification?

An associative link joins this initial episode to a later one in which Ida predicts that "later on they will call me a suicide blond because my twin will have dyed her hair. And then they will call me a murderess because there will come the time when I will have killed my twin which I first made come" (*I*, 11). If Ida eradicates Winnie, is it an act of suicide or murder or neither or both? Ida herself asks "If you make her can you kill her" (*I*, 11) as, analogously, the narrator (who "makes" Ida as she tells her story) wonders "if Ida goes on, does she go on even when she does not go on anymore" (*I*, 154), as the novel both does not and is going on in my act of writing about it.

Winnie disappears as soon as Ida thinks of marriage (begins "waiting for her president to find her" [*I*, 33]) suggesting perhaps that she no longer needs the protection of a symbolic alter ego. Men follow and stare at her still, but she begins to "walk beside them" rather than running away. Yet the gazes of these men—their desire to possess and "know" Ida—still pose a threat: the power to disembody and separate Ida from herself. The following passages suggest this threat with particular directness: "Ida saw herself come then she saw a man come then she saw a man go away then she saw herself go away. And all the time well all the time she said something she said nice little things, she said all right, she said I do" (*I*, 34). In another incident, a soldier asks Ida, "what is it that you like better than anything else . . . and she said I like being where I am. Oh he said excitedly and where are you. I am not here, she said. I am very careful about that. No I am not here (and not [her(e)] who you think I am)." Ida says "I do" several times: to Frank Arthur; to Andrew Hamilton; to Gerald Seaton, with whom Ida lives "almost as if Ida had not been Ida and Gerald Seaton had married any woman" (*I*, 83)—suggesting the interchangeability of women, their easy loss of specific identity. This leads the narrator to conclude that in the world in which Ida moves "everybody might want a king but anybody did not want a queen" (*I*, 39).

Ida is caught within a specular economy that erases woman's identity through the demand that she mimic "nice little things" and mirror for the male the truth of his own dominance, what Luce Irigaray calls mimesis imposed.[25] This involves entry into a system that is not hers and "in which she can appear and circulate only when enveloped in the needs/desires/fantasies of others."[26] As a consequence, woman abandons her "own primal fantasy so that she can inscribe into that of man which in turn becomes the origin of her desire."[27] Within this system, in terms of her own desire, she is "not there" and so Ida continues to wander away, a part of her always remaining elsewhere.

This focus on woman's doubleness as a condition of life in a culture "not of her own making" corresponds to an emphasis on Ida's presence and absence in a contemporary culture of mechanical reproduction and simulation in which identities are created through a display of public images. In 1937, as she was planning the novel that was to become *Ida*, Stein commented "I want to write about the effect on people of the Hollywood cinema kind of publicity that takes away all identity."[28] The constructed public image of the star, as I suggested earlier, takes away identity because simulations are confused for the authentic self, making the ground of selfhood unlocatable, a mistake that makes Ida feel "very faint" (as it did Stein). Ida's numerous appearances and disappearances at least in part reflect this emphasis on the reproduction of images through processes of simulation. People "know" Ida by publicity, by "hearing about" her, and eventually "everybody knew everything about Ida (*I*, 115). However, when people stop talking about her, when she ceases to be a figure of public speculation, Ida herself disappears as her public image fades ("Then they all disappeared not really disappeared but nobody talked about them any more [*I*, 96]).

This link between a scopophilic culture of the male gaze and the culture of identity-as-simulation is worked through the novel at a structural as well as a thematic level. It is one matrix through which the logic of the text is generated: a simulational aesthetic that mimes mimesis rather than enacting it and so replaces the conventional base of realist fiction. Mimetically based fiction, again, posits a stable world capable of accurate or truthful reflection through the transparent medium of language. Word and world, copy and model are coextensive yet clearly distinguishable, the former being in the service of the latter as the copy/mirror that "allows truth to appear beneath the mask."[29] Mimesis always posits an original presence reflected through processes of representation, though the fact of representation itself is erased. Simulation assumes no stable or recoverable truth to be mirrored, no ideal standard or point of origin to be copied. This assumption grows from a recognition that any origin posited, including the self as originary or autonomous, always constitutes a (mis)representation, an imitation, and, further, that in an age of mechanical reproduction the copy has become indistinguishable from the original and is in fact more "real" than the real. In a culture of simulation, as Jean Baudrillard puts it, there is "no more mirror of being and appearance, of the real and its concept . . . the real can be reproduced an infinite number of times . . . and is no longer measured against some ideal instance."[30] The real becomes "hyperreal," and any contradiction or distinction between the real and the imaginary is effaced resulting in "the liquidation of all stable referents."[31] The real becomes not only that which can be reproduced but "that which is already reproduced . . . that of which it is possible to give an equivalent reproduction."[32]

Viewed from this perspective, the opening of *Ida* might be read as a fable of simulation: Ida is born Ida-Ida, duplicated from the first.

As a "reality already contaminated by its simulation,"[33] Ida is constitutionally double and thus impossible to fix as a singular presence. This is a characteristic also of her dog Love, who exists in a text in which a photo of a dog may mutate into the dog himself and back again. After the incident of Love's abduction, Ida feels that Love "did not belong to me he did belong to them. That made me feel very funny, but really it is not true he is here he belongs to me" (*I*, 23). Here, original and reproduction become confused in a "hallucinatory resemblance of the real with itself" (perhaps another way of thinking of the "little difference" of Stein's dream-novel)—a process of mimesis without a true referent, mimesis without truth that generates the text as a "vertigo of realistic simulation."[34]

Baudrillard suggests that this oxymoronic "vertigo of realistic simulation"—expressed in a variety of postmodern aesthetic forms—is enacted formally through a number of maneuvers including those involving multiplication of the object in a series of permutations and those involving duplication of the object in a series of potentially infinite copies. Processes of multiplication and duplication function at many levels in *Ida* to generate the complex simulational aesthetic of the text. At the syntactic level, for example, frequent use of parataxis or additive structures move the novel forward serially rather than according to a more conventional depth model of narrative development. Serial multiplication (through parataxis) and duplication (through repetition) of narrative possibilities also occurs at the level of incidents, repeated actions, and tonal or emotional states as in Ida's comings and goings, her transcontinental slidings from state to state, her series of marriages (no one of which is really distinguishable from any other), the multiplication of funny things that happen to her, and the duplication of phrases like "funny things."

Duplication also extends to less obvious features such as textual rhythms—most often wandering itself—that are reinforced by events only tangentially related on any logical level. In three consecutive paragraphs near the end of part I (first half), for instance, Ida encounters a sick Arab man whose legs are kicking in the air; sees a revival meeting at which a woman slowly walks in a circle, moving her arms; and herself joins a walking marathon—"she kept on moving, sleeping or walking, she kept on slowly moving" (*I*, 17–18). All of these episodes contain references to types of movement that do not ad-

vance anywhere but that, nonetheless, have significance for the par-
ticipants, though we are not told what. The Arab is moving but not
progressing, as the woman at the revival meeting walks in a circle,
as Ida herself "keeps moving" even when she is asleep, as the text
wanders in and out of focus, a textual momentum that corresponds
to the organization of the text as a whole and the larger narrative
technique Stein develops in it.

Even more striking in their apparent gratuitousness are the long
passages on dogs and omens that Stein duplicates from her own earlier
writing. Such a practice of self-quoting contests the promotion of a
single text as originary and thus implicitly challenges the modernist
literary values of uniqueness, autonomy, or stylistic consistency.
Stein's method also suggests that discourses, like media images, are
detachable from their original frames of reference, and capable of
being circulated in a range of other discursive environments—an acknowledgment that finds full expression in a postmodern practice of
generic hybridization and pastiche as I will discuss more fully in this
chapter's final section.

Among the most frequently occurring and entertaining of the
duplicative/multiplicative strategies generated in *Ida* are those arising
from the narrator's gratuitous digressions—her refusal (or inability)
to choose from among narrative options, her desire to multiply rather
than limit descriptive possibilities. The narrator's role in producing
Ida as a comic simulational text is worth stressing, for she contributes
not a little to the indeterminacy and playful paratactic excess of the
novel. A brilliant comic creation whose manner is like a gossip colum-
nist or an avid reader of the *National Enquirer*, she is Ida's other
"twin" and an embodiment of *Ida*'s narrative uncertainty. Unlike the
upright knowledgeable narrator of conventional fiction, whose role
is to report the world objectively, this one shamelessly wanders from
her narrative "responsibility." She omits significant details that might
allow readers to construct an explanation for Ida's behavior or the
"funny things" that happen to her; she includes information whose
relation to the "plot" is unclear or blatantly unrelated, conveying the
impression that she is making it up as she goes along, forgetting
what she has previously said and thus often contradicting herself
along the way. In her repetitions, digressions, exaggerations, distor-
tions, and other displays of poor judgment, she thoroughly under-

mines the position of superior knowledge and certainty traditionally assumed by the narrative persona.

Often the narrator is so tentative that it is impossible to determine whether or not any information has been conveyed:

> Suppose somebody comes in, suppose they say, well, how are we today. Well supposing they do say that. It does not make any difference but supposing they do say that. Somebody else comes in and says that too well how are we today. Well if Ida had not answered the first one she could not answer the second one because you always have to answer the first one before you answer the second one. (*I*, 150)

In this passage we are asked to entertain a hypothetical statement (suppose somebody comes in . . .), a process hindered by the narrator's assertion that it doesn't make any difference whether we do so or not and her suggestion that Ida answers neither one of them. Does "it . . . not make any difference" because the people are not there, because the substance of their statements is unimportant, because Ida does not answer them? Curiously, within this unimportant, hypothetical situation the narrator appeals to propriety ("You always have to answer . . ."), a statement whose self-righteous assurance seems odd in this context. Why worry about behaving correctly around people who may not even be present? In other instances, the narrator seems flatly uninterested in choosing among the possibilities raised and leaves decisions to the reader: "Was she on a train or an automobile, an airplane or just walking. Which was it. Well she was on any one of them . . ." (*I*, 34).

Frequently, the narrator's uncertainty clashes with her effort to be precise: "There he fell in love with a woman, was she older was she younger or was she the same age. She was not older perhaps she was younger, very likely she was not the same age as his age" (*I*, 53). Statements such as this one reflect a general tendency toward the multiplication of information excessive or inessential from the perspective of a reader trying to get on with the plot. Rather than simply omitting the woman's age or stating that she does not know it, the narrator flaunts her uncertainty, preferring to leave the reader bewildered as to the point of the comment.

One important effect of the narrator's gratuitous details and semantic quibbles is to undercut the reader's ability to visualize actions or scenes. The following passage, for example, plays with the arbitrary connection between signifier and signified to spring a semantic trap.

> That was while she was still living with her great aunt. It was not near the water that is unless you call a little stream water or quite a way off a little lake water, and hills beyond it water. If you do not call all these things water then there where Ida was living was not at all near water but it was near a church. (*I*, 12)

In most logical contexts, streams and lakes, no matter how little, would be "called water," unless one uses water to refer only to a significantly sized body of water, in which case they might not be called water—still a logical possibility. But in no commonsense context would hills be called water since they obviously share none of the defining features of water. If hills cannot be called water, then neither can streams or lakes, according to the narrator, thereby proving that Ida does not live near the water. Having gone through this detour, this semantic pile-up that does not add up, we are told the apparently "essential" information that Ida lived near a church anyway. In another respect, the description does convey information about Ida's locale, beyond that deemed important by the narrator: Ida lives near a little stream, a lake, and hills. However, neither this information *nor* the fact that Ida lives near a church seems particularly relevant dramatically (textually significant to set a scene or advance the plot) since Ida changes addresses repeatedly and frequently forgets where she has been ("It was so easy to forget the last address and she really forgot to guess what the next address was" [*I*, 14]).

The narrator's efforts to engage the audience in her own narrative decisions and indecisions frequently lead her to misjudge rather badly what needs to be known: "In Boston the earth is round. Believe it or not, in Boston the earth is round. But they were not in Boston, they were in Washington" (*I*, 62). Often the plot takes a detour that never returns to the main road: "When they got to Ohio, Ohio is a state, it is only spelled with four letters" (*I*, 56). When the narrator does try to interpret information, she comically misses what ought to be her point: "He went away from Montana and he went to Virginia. There he saw trees and he was so pleased. He said I wonder if Ida has ever seen these trees. Of course she had. It was not she who was blind it was her dog Iris [formerly Love]" (*I*, 50). While the character undoubtedly means to pose the question of whether Ida had ever visited Virginia, the narrator, literal to the end, interprets him to mean the capacity for sight and grows indignant at *his* lack of insight.

"When something happens nothing begins. When anything begins then nothing happens," the narrator states, "and you could always say with Ida that nothing [began]. . . . To have anything happen you have to choose and Ida never chose" (*I*, 149). The narrator refuses to choose also, preferring to multiply narrative options, a tendency especially evident at the conclusion of the novel, the precise point at which narrative possibilities usually constrict:

> Every time [Ida] said yes, and she said yes any time she said anything, well any time she said yes it was quite exciting. Ida even was excited, well not altogether but she really was excited . . . And in between, well Ida always did have a tendency to say yes and now she did say, she even sometimes said oh yes . . . Ida was excited but not very excited. At times she was not excited but she always did say yes. (*I*, 147)

Here an assertion about Ida's emotional state is made (Ida was excited), qualified (Ida was not very excited), and negated (at least some of the time Ida is not excited at all), a technique that allows for the existence of all logical possibilities—affirmation, negation, and something in between.

The following passage (also from the novel's concluding section) concerns Ida's position in narrative space, but it could as easily refer to the position in the text held out for the reader:

> one can run away, even if you are resting you can run away. Not necessarily but you can. . . . This could be a thing that Ida would do. She would say yes and she was resting and nothing happened and nothing began but she could run away . . . and she did. . . . She did not really run away, she did not go away. It was something in between. . . . Little by little she was not there she was elsewhere. Little by little. It was little by little and it was all of a sudden. It was not entirely sudden because she was not entirely there before she was elsewhere. (*I*, 151)

The narrator states that Ida is at rest; raises the possibility that she will run away (she potentially is already away if she could run away, just as events are always potentially happening); proclaims that she did run away; and qualifies this statement by suggesting something in between. Ida can "run away" "little by little," an apparent contradiction, because she always contains the potential to be leaving, and part of her is always already elsewhere ("she was not entirely there before she was elsewhere" [*I*, 151]).

"It is wonderful," the narrator gleefully exclaims, "how things pile up even if nothing is added" (*I*, 150). Things *do* "pile up" and multiply indiscriminately in *Ida*, accumulating in intensity as the novel progresses and making it impossible to choose the significant (what would normally advanced the plot) from the insignificant because everything is (only) potential (is significant). The description of Ida in the novel's final paragraph acts to concretize this paratactic excess that joins with the aforementioned techniques for undercutting the visible and the logical, again strategies that Stein employs to preserve narrative indeterminacy:

> If she said anything she said yes. More than once nothing was said. She said something. If nothing is said then Ida does not say yes. If she goes out she comes in. If she does not go away she is there and she does not go away. She dresses, well perhaps in black why not, and a hat, why not, and another hat, why not, and another dress, why not, so much why not. She dresses in another hat and she dresses in another dress and Andrew is in, and they go in and that is where they are. They are there. Thank them. Yes. (*I*, 154)

Here Stein brilliantly combines affirmation and negation, presence and absence, in a joyous celebration of indeterminacy. Ida says "yes"—maybe—since the conditional "if" makes it uncertain whether, at this particular moment, Ida has spoken or not, whether Ida is there or not. Ida also "piles up" with clothes, but cannot be made to "add up"—a woman who could be wearing three dresses and three hats simultaneously is nearly impossible to visualize.

The novel we are reading also "piles up"—to 154 pages of possibilities—without adding up to much of a story. *Ida* thus is also a novel in which "nothing is added" because no one strand of the narrative is fully actualized, and no statement is made that isn't somewhere also ambiguously re-made or even un-made. *Ida* (Ida) realizes and de-realizes it/herself continuously. Although the final lines of the novel state that Ida and Andrew, Ida's last (?) husband "are there" and ask that we be grateful for their "presence" ("thank them"), the overall rhythm of the text suggests that this assertion of presence should not be seen as a final resting place. As Stein puts it in "The Superstitions of Fred Anneday, Annday, Anday A Novel of Real Life," "Inevitably one has to know how a story ends even if it does not."[35] The production of the text *Ida* stops; Andrew and Ida's story "ends." Yet the principle of permanent multiplication of options, an ongoing flow of possibilities for change, which defines Ida and the novel we are reading, suggests that Ida's story could go on indefinitely with or without Andrew, that it does not end, and that we should be thankful for this possibility also.

Unlike most early twentieth-century writers, Stein responded to the modernist imperative to "make it new" in part by using the forms of a developing popular culture as a source for her art and specifically as a means of revitalizing the novel as a genre. I have explored Stein's use of one particular popular genre, melodrama, to detail the effects of the society of the spectacle, and have attempted to specify the creative interaction among a popular genre, certain avant-garde imperatives, and those shifting cultural dynamics arising from processes of modernization. Such an interaction leads to both the extension of these generic conventions—thereby opening new aspects of melodrama as a mode of apprehending experience—and to the subversion/extinction of others—thereby exposing the need to go beyond the social/ideological limitations of these inherited forms.

On one level, *Ida* may be read thematically for its plot, which, as I've suggested, embodies many conventions common to melodrama and, more generally, plot elements common to much nineteenth-century fiction—especially women's domestic fiction.[36] Ida is born and orphaned. She marries unhappily, several times, to men who think they "know" her, before meeting her soul mate, Andrew, her true twin with whom she may enjoy a mutual exchange of selves and with whom she struggles to become ever more herself (depending on how their relationship is interpreted).[37] This plot, overlaid with a melodramatic emphasis on violence, menace, and sensationalism, could—except for the multiple marriages—be the story of *Jane Eyre*. However, Stein complicates the action of *Ida* through the use of a narrative persona sharply at odds with the events narrated, one whose comic digressive wanderings and misrememberings produce a contradictory, even self-cancelling story about a constantly changing character who we are unable to visualize. In this way, the ground of mimetic transparency (that imperative to depict a world in all its plenitude) is undercut through the narrator's informational amplitude that short-circuits visibility. Also undone is the ground of realist objectivity (the demand that fiction make clear, definitive, truthful declarations about the world) through the narrator's flouting of uncertainty and her refusal to choose. Created in the gap between the "funny things" that happen to "poor Ida" and the narrator's account of them are modes of naïve, kitschy humor distinct from melodrama's tragedies and at odds with modernist ironies as well, the more so if we accept Gilles Deleuze's argument that irony implies the possibility of a consistent subject, the coextensiveness of the I with representation.[38] Postmodern humor of the variety found in *Ida* tends toward the childlike or the cartoonish. Engaged in play with sense and nonsense, stable representation and perspective, like the simulational culture it reflects, is an art of

> surfaces and replicas . . . of nomadic singularities and of the aleatory point which is always being moved, the art of static genesis . . . signification, designation, and manifestation being suspended, depth and height abolished.[39]

The narrator's linguistic excess, which leads to a flattening and a short-circuiting of the descriptive power of language, might be compared to melodrama's gestural and stylistic excess. In its theatrical or filmic form melodrama must, paradoxically, use forms of visual excess to inscribe those invisible psychic states or social contradictions that cannot be represented comfortably within conventional modes. Ida's undercutting of the reader's ability to visualize might thus be seen as a logical extension of the drive to despecularization that Doane argues is a product of the genre's attempt to inscribe female subjectivity, and perhaps also Stein's means of refusing those mechanisms that lead to women's objectification and appropriation through sight.

The structural incoherence of melodrama, its troubled excessive surfaces, results from tying to express contradictory demands within a form that requires resolution. This tension is most obvious in those melodramas involving a woman's attempt to embrace self-determination (including sexual self-determination) and escape regulation while at the same time remaining within the social. Nineteenth-century characters are required to choose between wandering outside the law to follow their own desire—which usually leads to death or social ostracism—or integrating that desire within the regulatory mechanisms of the bourgeois family—which may also lead to madness or death as melodrama shows. In *Ida*, the narrator's impulse to multiply options, and her refusal to choose from among them, undercuts the reader's ability to make determinate judgments about Ida's meaning or nature. Through this and other techniques that foreground narrative indeterminacy, Stein generates a text of ongoing possibilities that creates an imaginative nonmimetic space within which a woman may wander and rest, go out and come in. In doing so, she suggests at least one solution to melodrama's central ideological contradiction by shifting the forms that ensure the containment of female desire or demand that it be expressed as an impossible contradiction within processes of representation.

Perhaps it is significant that Stein turned to a genre whose distinctive features bespeak a crisis in representation (and which historically has been most prevalent in times of social crisis) to reflect a dual crisis in early-twentieth-century culture: that crisis in subjectivity arising from processes of mechanical reproduction and simulation, and a crisis in female subjectivity specifically within a culture that (still) renders women as simulations of themselves. Stein's postmodern revisioning of melodrama rehearses these crises thematically and structurally by positing a nonsubject both present and absent—one perhaps doubly absent from herself as a double simulation, but one also doubly capable of wandering away.

My own indeterminacy here reflects the indeterminate status of an ongoing crisis in the stability of the subject that is part of the postmodern condition. The waning of a stable determinate subject position and the metanarratives that have supported its construction may be seen as a cultural pathology, a negative symptom of postmod-

ern fragmentation or "schizophrenia," in Fredric Jameson's formulation. However, from the perspective of those cultural "others" historically denied access to positions of power and privilege, this "crisis" also creates sites of possibility for the construction of new subject
positions. *Ida* is a space of something like pure potential, a site for the
dispersal of regulatory structures, rather than a site for the realization
of a new social subject. This constitutes both the power and the
limitation of *Ida*, a text that, in a larger sense, reflects the possibilities
held out and the limitations inherent within Stein's choice of anti-
mimetic modes in her fiction generally.

Ida also illustrates the fictional possibilities arising from strategies
of appropriation and recoding, practices that are equally prevalent
among postmodern writers and equally doubled and ambivalent in
their use. As one of the distinctive features of a postmodern aesthetic, the practice of appropriation begins, like simulation, by
"bracketing the real altogether, fashion[ing] its artifacts through the
technologies of reproduction and acknowledg[ing] the reiterative already coded status of its own utterance."[40] Such a practice is to be
distinguished from modernist uses of allusion or quotation in which
discursive heterogeneity is most often stylized in relation to a unifying perspective and in which particular discourses are privileged as
modes of representation to the exclusion of others. Postmodern hybridization emerges from and reflects a view of culture as an arena
of competing discourses and styles, no one of which is sufficient or
definitive as a cultural explanation, no one of which is *intrinsically*
more valuable than another, and, thus, all of which might become
the basis for art.

That said, it is equally important to distinguish among the varieties of such appropriative strategies, their multiple effects, and the
complex motivations that inspire them. Strategies that lead to "blank
parody" or "pastiche," a "random cannibalization" of the past—
terms Jameson uses to refer to all of these appropriative strategies[41]—
should be distinguished from those self-conscious strategies for critical appropriation and transformation of inherited discourses evident
in Irigarian mimicry, or Cindy Sherman's staged images of movie
stars, or Kathy Acker and Karen Finley's use of porn conventions,
or Angela Carter's reworking of fairy tales. We need to distinguish
between "Twin Peaks" and Barbara Kruger. As Meaghan Morris puts
it, "When any and every text can be read indifferently as another

instance of strategic rewriting, another illustration of an established general [postmodern] principle, something more and something more specific is needed to argue how and why a particular event of rewriting might matter."[42] Such distinctions require that we specify who produces cultural representations, for whom, who receives them, and in what contexts—to what ends or effects.

If we fail to consider the contexts within which postmodern innovations occur by subsuming all formal disruptions or recodings under a generalized postmodern mode, we risk obscuring important differences among postmodern practitioners, and thus, distorting notions of the postmodern itself. As I have argued throughout this study, such contextualizing moves are equally important in accurately mapping the history of a postmodern literary emergence as it has evolved throughout the twentieth century. If postmodern categories help us to read many of Stein's works more fully, as I believe they do, then Stein's example helps us to read postmodernism more accurately too by helping us to construct understandings capacious enough to account for the complexity and the diversity of postmodern cultural practices.

Notes

Introduction

1. The term *postmodern* has been charted by Andreas Huyssen in *After the Great Divide* (Bloomington: Indiana University Press, 1986); see also Douwe Fokkema and Hans Bertens, eds., *Approaching Postmodernism* (New York: Johns Benjamin, 1986). For general discussions of postmodernism, including especially those developed in relation to literature, see: Jean Baudrillard, *Simulations* (New York: Semiotexte, 1982); Baudrillard, "The Implosion of Meaning in the Media and the Implosion of the Social in the Masses," in *Myths of Information*, ed. Colin McCabe and Kathleen Woodward, 137–48 (Madison, Wis.: Coda Press, 1984); Jim Collins, *Uncommon Cultures* (New York: Methuen, 1989); Terry Eagleton, "Capitalism, Modernism, Postmodernism," *New Left Review* 152 (1985): 60–73; Hal Foster, ed., *The Anti-Aesthetic* (Port Townsend, Wash.: Bay Press, 1983); Foster, *Recodings* (Port Townsend, Wash.: Bay Press, 1985); Harry P. Garvin, ed., *Romanticism, Modernism, Postmodernism* (Lewisberg, Pa.: Bucknell University Press, 1980); Jürgen Habermas, "Modernity—An Incomplete Project," in Foster, *The Anti-Aesthetic*, 3–15; Ihab Hassan, "The Quest of Postmodernism," in Garvin, *Romanticism, Modernism, Postmodernism*, 17–26; Hassan, *The Postmodern Turn: Essays in Postmodern Theory and Culture* (Columbus: Ohio State Press, 1987); Linda Hutcheon, *A Poetics of Postmodernism: History, Theory, and Fiction* (New York: Routledge, 1989); Hutcheon, *The Politics of Postmodernism* (New York: Routledge, 1989); Jean-François Lyotard, *The Postmodern Condition: A Report on Knowledge*, trans. Geoff Bennington and Brian Massumi (Minneapolis: University of Minnesota Press, 1984); Fredric Jameson, "Postmodernism and Consumer Society," in Foster, *The Anti-Aesthetic*, 111–25; Jameson, "Postmodernism, or the Cultural Logic of Late Capitalism," *New Left Review* 146 (1984): 53–92; Jameson, Foreword to Lyotard, *The Postmodern Condition*; Jameson, "Postmodernism and Utopia," in *Utopia Post Utopia: Configurations of Nature and Culture in Recent Sculpture and Photography*, Institute of Contemporary Art Catalog Series (Cambridge, Mass.: MIT Press, 1988); Alice Jardine, *Gynesis: Configurations of Women in Modernity* (Ithaca: Cornell University Press, 1985); Julia Kristeva, "Postmodernism?" in Garvin, *Romanticism, Modernism, Postmodernism*, 136–41; Kristeva, *Desire in Language*, trans. Thomas Gora et al. (New York: Columbia University Press, 1980); Arthur Kroker and David Cook, *The Postmodern Scene: Excremental Culture and Hyper-Aesthetics* (New York: St. Martin's Press, 1986); Larry McCaffery, *Postmodern Fiction: A BioBibliography* (New York: Greenwood Press,

1986); Brian McHale, *Postmodernist Fiction* (New York: Methuen, 1987); Linda Nicholson, ed., *Feminism/Postmodernism* (New York: Routledge, 1990); Andrew Ross, ed., *Universal Abandon?* (Minneapolis: University of Minnesota Press, 1989); Brian Wallis, *Art After Modernism: Rethinking Representation* (Boston: New Museum of Contemporary Art, 1984); Patricia Waugh, *Feminine Fictions: Revisiting the Postmodern* (New York: Routledge, 1989). For readings of Stein that emphasize some postmodern elements in her work (though they are not necessarily named as such) see: Shari Benstock, *Women of the Left Bank* (Austin: University of Texas Press, 1986); Harriet Chessman, *"The Public Is Invited to Dance": Representation, the Body, and Dialogue in Gertrude Stein* (Stanford: Stanford University Press, 1989); Marianne DeKoven, *A Different Language: Gertrude Stein's Experimental Writing* (Madison: University of Wisconsin Press, 1983); Lisa Ruddick, *Reading Gertrude Stein: Body, Text, and Gnosis* (Ithaca: Cornell University Press, 1990); Neil Schmitz, "Gertrude Stein as Postmodernist: The Rhetoric of *Tender Buttons*," *Modern Fiction Studies* 3 (1974): 1203–18; Schmitz, *Of Huck and Alice: Humorous Writing in American Literature* (Minneapolis: University of Minnesota Press, 1983); Catharine Stimpson, "The Mind, the Body, and Gertrude Stein," *Critical Inquiry* 3 (1977): 489–506; Stimpson, "The Somagrams of Gertrude Stein," *Poetics Today* 6, nos. 1–2: 67–80; and Stimpson, "Gertrude Stein and the Transposition of Gender," in *The Poetics of Gender*, ed. Nancy K. Miller, 1–18 (New York: Columbia University Press, 1986).

2. Huyssen, *After the Great Divide*, p. 181.

3. Wendy Steiner, *Exact Resemblance to Exact Resemblance: The Literary Portraiture of Gertrude Stein* (New Haven: Yale University Press, 1978), 28; Richard Bridgman, *Gertrude Stein in Pieces* (New York: Oxford University Press, 1970), xv; John Malcom Brinnin, *The Third Rose: Gertrude Stein and Her World* (Boston: Little, Brown, 1959); Randa Dubnick, *The Structure of Obscurity: Gertrude Stein, Language, and Cubism* (Urbana: University of Illinois Press, 1984); Jayne L. Walker, *The Making of a Modernist: Gertrude Stein from "Three Lives" to "Tender Buttons"* (Amherst: University of Massachusetts Press, 1984); Allegra Stewart, *Gertrude Stein and the Present* (Cambridge, Mass.: 1967); Donald Sutherland, *Gertrude Stein: A Biography of Her Work* (New Haven, Yale University Press, 1951); Harold Bloom, *Modern Critical Views: Gertrude Stein* (New York: Chelsea House Publications, 1986), 4; Shari Benstock, "Beyond the Reaches of Feminist Criticism: A Letter from Paris," *Tulsa Studies in Women's Literature* 2, nos. 1 and 2 (1985): 5–27; Benstock, *Women of the Left Bank*; R. Kostelanetz, Introduction to *The Yale Gertrude Stein* (New Haven: Yale University Press, 1980), xiii–xxxi; Catharine Stimpson, "Gertrude Stein and the Transposition of Gender," in *The Poetics of Gender*, ed. Nancy K. Miller (New York: Columbia University Press, 1986), 1–18; Elizabeth Fifer, "'Is Flesh Advisable?' The Interior Theater of Gertrude Stein," *Signs* 4, no. 3 (Spring 1979): 472–83.

4. This process of refocalization is usefully discussed by McHale, *Postmodernist Fiction*.

5. See for example Pamela Caughie, *Virginia Woolf and Postmodernism: Literature in Quest and Question of Itself* (Urbana: University of Illinois Press, 1991); *Re-Reading the New: A Backward Glance at Modernism*, ed. Kevin J. H. Dettmar (Ann Arbor: University of Michigan Press, 1992); Patricia Waugh, *Feminine Fictions*.

6. For a discussion of the stylistic features generally considered to be postmodern see

especially Fokkema, *Approaching Postmodernism*; McCaffery, *Postmodern Fiction*; McHale, *Postmodernist Fiction*; and Hutcheon, *Poetics of Postmodernism*.

7. Benstock, *Women of the Left Bank*; Carolyn Burke, "Getting Spliced: Modernism and Sexual Difference," *American Quarterly* 39, no. 1 (1987): 98–121; Chessman, "*The Public Is Invited to Dance*"; Janice Doane, *Silence and Narrative: The Early Novels of Gertrude Stein* (Westport, Conn.: Greenwood Press, 1986); DeKoven, *A Different Language*; Ruddick, *Reading Gertrude Stein*; and Jayne L. Walker, *The Making of a Modernist*.

8. See *Uncommon Cultures*; and Bertens, *Approaching Postmodernism*; Huyssen, *After the Great Divide*; McHale, *Postmodernist Fiction*; Hutcheon, *A Poetics of Postmodernism*; and Hutcheon, *The Politics of Postmodernism* for elaborations of the incorporation of popular material into postmodern works.

9. Huyssen, *After the Great Divide*, 53–54.

Chapter 1

1. B. L. Reid, *Art by Subtraction* (Norman: University of Oklahoma Press, 1958), 191.

2. Teresa de Lauretis, *Alice Doesn't: Feminism, Semiotics, Cinema* (Bloomington: Indiana University Press, 1984), 121 and 125.

3. Patricia Tobin, *Time and the Novel: The Genealogical Imperative* (Princeton: Princeton University Press, 1978), 7–8.

4. Roland Barthes, *The Pleasure of the Text*, trans. Richard Miller (New York: Hill and Wang, 1975), 10.

5. Janice Doane, for example, analyzes Stein's early narrative experiments as efforts "to develop a mode of authority that deliberately challenges what she later called 'patriarchal poetry'" (*Silence and Narrative: The Early Novels of Gertrude Stein* [Westport, Conn.: Greenwood Press, 1986] xxvi). For further discussion of Stein as an antipatriarchal writer see Cynthia Secor's "The Question of Gertrude Stein" in *American Novelists Revisited*, ed. Fritz Fleischmann, et al. (Boston: G. K. Hall, 1982) 299–310; Neil Schmitz, *Of Huck and Alice: Humorous Writing in American Literature* (Minneapolis: University of Minnesota Press, 1983); Shari Benstock, *Women of the Left Bank* (Austin: University of Texas Press, 1986). See also numerous articles by Catharine Stimpson, in particular "Gertrude Stein and The Transposition of Gender," in *The Poetics of Gender*, ed. Nancy K. Miller (New York: Columbia University Press), 1–18, and "The Somagrams of Gertrude Stein," in *Poetics Today* 6, nos. 1–2:67–80. Stimpson sees Stein as an antipatriarchal writer with "strong moorings" to the patriarchy.

6. Susan Rubin Suleiman, "Pornography, Transgression, and the Avant-Garde: Batille's *Story of the Eye*," in *The Poetics of Gender*, ed. Nancy K. Miller (New York: Columbia University Press, 1986), 120.

7. Gertrude Stein, *How Writing is Written*, ed. Robert Bartlett Haas (Los Angeles: Black Sparrow Press, 1969), 154.

8. Gertrude Stein, *How to Write* (Craftsbury Common, Vt.: Sherrie Urie Press, 1977), 32.

9. Shari Benstock, "Beyond the Reaches of Feminist Criticism: A Letter from Paris," *Tulsa Studies in Women's Literature* 2, nos. 1 and 2 (1984): 9, 15.

10. Susan B. Anthony's refrain in Stein's play "The Mother of Us All"; see Stein, *Last Operas and Plays*, ed. Carl Van Vechten (New York: Vintage Books, 1975), 52–88.

11. See for example Sandra M. Gilbert and Susan Gubar's discussion of women's writing as a palimpsest in which "surface designs conceal or obscure deeper less accessible (and less socially acceptable) levels of meaning" (*The Mad Woman in the Attic* [New Haven: Yale University Press, 1979], 73); Elaine Showalter's discussion of women's writing as a double-voiced discourse in "Feminist Criticism in the Wilderness," *Critical Inquiry* 8, no. 2 (1981): 179–205; and Nancy Miller's rereading of nineteenth-century women's fiction to disclose in the "implausible twists of plot . . . a fantasy of power that would revise the social grammar in which women are never defined as subjects" (Miller, "Emphasis Added: Plots and Plausibilities in Women's Fiction," *PMLA* 96 [1981], 41). Part of the feminist rereading of Stein has involved the recovery of a coded lesbian subtext in which Stein meditates upon the female body and its relation to a patriarchal culture. Explication of this subtext renders meaningful much of what was previously perceived as nonsense. See Richard Bridgman, *Gertrude Stein in Pieces* (New York: Oxford University Press, 1970); Catharine Stimpson, "The Mind, the Body, and Gertrude Stein," *Critical Inquiry* 3 (1977); Stimpson, "The Somagrams of Gertrude Stein"; Stimpson, "Gertrude Stein and the Transposition of Gender"; Elizabeth Fifer, " 'Is Flesh Advisable?' The Interior Theater of Gertrude Stein," in *Critical Essays on Gertrude Stein*, ed. Michael Hoffman (Boston: G. K. Hall, 1986); Schmitz, *Of Huck and Alice*.

12. Patrocinio Schweickart, "Reading Ourselves: Towards a Feminist Theory of Reading," in *Gender and Reading: Essays on Readers, Texts, and Contexts*, ed. Elizabeth A. Flynn and Patrocinio Schweickart (Baltimore: Johns Hopkins University Press, 1985), 94.

13. For further discussion of the connections between Stein's writing and *l'écriture feminine*, that recovery of the feminine through writing theorized by writers such as Cixous and Irigaray, see Anna Gibbs, "Hélène Cixous and Gertrude Stein: New Directions in Feminist Criticism," *Meanjin* 38:281–93; Marianne DeKoven, *A Different Language: Gertrude Stein's Experimental Writing* (Madison: University of Wisconsin Press, 1983); Shari Benstock, *Woman of the Left Bank*; Lisa Ruddick, "A Rosy Charm: Gertrude Stein and the Repressed Feminine," in *Critical Essays on Gertrude Stein*, ed. Michael Hoffman (Boston: G. K. Hall, 1986).

14. Jane Gallop, *The Daughter's Seduction* (Ithaca: Cornell University Press, 1982), 94.

15. Hélène Cixous, "Castration or Decapitation?" *Signs* 7 (1981): 53.

16. Gertrude Stein quoted in Michael Hoffman, *The Development of Abstractionism in the Writings of Gertrude Stein* (Philadelphia: University of Pennsylvania Press, 1965), 100. The notion of "playing" with language in a tactile sense so that one may use it for one's own purpose is an idea that pervades recent French feminist theory as the following statement by Hélène Cixous suggests: "If woman has always functioned 'within' the discourse of man . . . it is time for her to dislocate this 'within', to explode it, turn it around, and seize it; to make it hers, containing it, taking it in her own mouth, biting that tongue with her very own teeth to invent for herself a language to get inside of" (Cixous, "The Laugh of the Medusa," in *New French Feminisms*, ed. Elaine Marks and Isabelle de Courtiveron [New York: Schocken Books, 1981], 245–64).

17. Schweickart, "Reading Ourselves," xxiv.
18. Schweickart, "Reading Ourselves," 55.
19. Betsy Wing, "Glossary," in *The Newly Born Woman*, by Hélène Cixous and Catherine Clément, trans. Betsy Wing (Minneapolis: University of Minnesota Press, 1986), 165. See also Luce Irigaray, "always one and the other at the same time" ("When Our Lips Speak Together," in *This Sex Which Is Not One*, trans. Katherine Porter [Ithaca: Cornell University Press, 1985], 217); Hélène Cixous, "to love, to watch—think—seek the other in the other . . . a love that rejoices in the exchange that multiplies" ("The Laugh of the Medusa," 264); and Gertrude Stein, "God bless me which is she" ("A Sonatina Followed by Another," in *Bee Time Vine and Other Pieces (1913–1927)* [New Haven: Yale University Press, 1953]).
20. DeKoven, *A Different Language*, 16.
21. Suleiman, "Pornography, Transgression, and the Avant-Garde," 132.
22. Luce Irigaray, "Any Theory of the 'Subject' Has Always Been Appropriated by the 'Masculine'," in *Speculum of the Other Woman*, by Luce Irigaray, trans. Gillian C. Gill (Ithaca: Cornell University Press, 1985), 133–46.
23. Naomi Schor discusses this strategy of doubling in her "Dreaming Dissymmetry: Barthes, Foucault, and Sexual Difference," in *Men in Feminism*, ed. Alice Jardine and Paul Smith (New York: Methuen, 1987). She identifies two feminist positions on the question of difference, the "masculine" that seeks to end sexual difference, and the "feminine" that concedes the "strategic efficacy of undoing sexual oppositions" but at the same time *pursues* the construction of female difference and specificity. The most "active site of the feminine resistance to the discourse of indifferences [desire to end sexual differences] is a certain insistence on doubling" (110), a feminist strategy that she finds in the work of Irigaray, de Lauretis, Gallop and others, including her own double reading strategy ("beyond difference and *for* difference") described in "Reading Double: Sand's Difference," in *The Poetics of Gender*, ed. Nancy K. Miller (New York: Columbia University Press, 1986), 25.
24. Both Gayatri Spivak and Jane Gallop have written about the importance of considering differences between women. See Spivak's "French Feminism in an International Frame," *Yale French Studies* 62 (1981): 154–84, and Gallop's "Annie Leclerc Writing a Letter with Vermeer," in *The Poetics of Gender*, ed. Nancy K. Miller (New York: Columbia University Press, 1986). Gallop says "the problem of écriture feminine is not, . . . its insistence on sexual difference at the expense of some universal humanity, but, rather, . . . its effacement of the differences between women in view of some feminine essence" (154).
25. Gertrude Stein, quoted in Bridgman, *Gertrude Stein in Pieces*, 105–6.
26. Gertrude Stein, *The Geographical History of America* (New York: Random House, 1936), 69.
27. In distinguishing Stein from other modernist writers, Shari Benstock writes that Stein "did what no other writer has had quite the courage to do: to relinquish the right to make language submit to the writer's will." *Women of the Left Bank*, 159.
28. Stein, *The Geographical History of America*, 70.
29. Gertrude Stein, *Tender Buttons*, in *Writings and Lectures, 1901–1945*, ed. Patricia Meyerowitz (Baltimore: Penguin Books, 1967), 195.

30. Julia Kristeva, *Desire in Language*, trans. Thomas Gora et al. (New York: Columbia University Press, 1980), 118.
31. Roland Barthes, *The Pleasure of the Text*, 12–13.
32. Gertrude Stein, *Ida* (New York: Vintage Books, 1968), 63.
33. Barthes, *The Pleasure of the Text*, 10.
34. Gertrude Stein, *Lucy Church Amiably: A Novel of Romantic Beauty and Nature Which Looks Like an Engraving* (New York: Something Else Press, 1969), 27.
35. Stein, *Tender Buttons*, 193.
36. Stein, *Tender Buttons*, 167.
37. Stein, *Tender Buttons*, 169.
38. Kathleen Fraser, quoted in Catharine Stimpson, "Gertrude Stein: Humanism and Its Freaks," *Boundary II* (Spring/Fall 1984): 309.
39. Nancy K. Miller, "Arachnologies: The Woman, the Text, and the Critic," in *The Poetics of Gender*, ed. Nancy K. Miller (New York: Columbia University Press, 1986), 288.
40. Fraser, quoted in Stimpson, "Humanism and Its Freaks," 309.
41. Gertrude Stein, *A Long Gay Book*, in *Matisse, Picasso, and Gertrude Stein, with Two Shorter Stories* (Barton, Vt.: Something Else Press, 1972), 113.
42. Quoted in Gallop, *The Daughter's Seduction*, 102.
43. Luce Irigaray writes of the daughter's feeling of overpowerment by the mother in "And the One Doesn't Stir Without the Other," *Signs* 7 (1981): 60–67. Jane Gallop also discusses this "negative" side of jouissance in her "Beyond the Jouissance Principle," *Representations* 7 (1984). Apropos of my discussion Gallop writes, "If jouissance is defined . . . as a loss of self, disruption of comfort, loss of control, it cannot simply be claimed as an ego-gratifying identity but must also frighten those who 'know' it" (114).
44. Kristeva, *Desire in Language*, 142.
45. DeKoven, *A Different Language*, xxi.
46. Kristeva, *Desire in Language*, 145–46.
47. Gertrude Stein, *Many Many Women* (Barton, Vt.: Something Else Press, 1972), 130.
48. Julia Kristeva, "Psychoanalysis and the Polis," in *The Politics of Interpretation*, ed. W. J. T. Mitchell (Chicago: University of Chicago Press, 1983), 84.
49. Kristeva, *Desire in Language*, 142.
50. Barthes, *The Pleasure of the Text*, 60–61.
51. Fredric Jameson, "Postmodernism, Or the Cultural Logic of Late Capitalism," *New Left Review*, 146 (July/August 1984): 83.
52. Jameson, "Postmodernism, Or the Cultural Logic of Late Capitalism," 91.
53. Gertrude Stein, *A Novel of Thank You* (New Haven: Yale University Press, 1958), 47.
54. Richard Bridgman claims that the novel recounts a "temporary imbalance" in the Stein/Toklas relationship, the intrusion of a "third" (Bridgman, *Gertrude Stein in Pieces*, 153). Shari Benstock links this imbalance to Stein's relationship with Hemingway (Benstock, *Women of the Left Bank*, 171). Bridgman wishes to read *A Novel of Thank You* in terms of the plot of this temporary imbalance; that is, he wishes to narrativize and thus to resolve the tension of incompletion evoked by the text. His attempt to reduce the text to a central idea or event that unfolds in the course of reading not only fails to account for much of the novel's complexity, it

also deflects attention from the ways in which the text radically refuses structuration.

Chapter 2

1. Quoted in John Malcolm Brinnin, *The Third Rose: Gertrude Stein and Her World* (Boston: Little, Brown, 1959), 16.
2. Anne Freadman, "Sandpaper," *Southern Review-Adelaide* 16 (1983) 162.
3. Janice Doane, *Silence and Narrative: The Early Novels of Gertrude Stein* (Westport, Conn.: Greenwood Press, 1986), xxiii–xxiv.
4. Harriet Chessman, *"The Public Is Invited to Dance": Representation, the Body, and Dialogue in Gertrude Stein* (Stanford: Stanford University Press, 1989), 41–53.
5. Michel Picheux, *Language, Semantics, and Ideology: Stating the Obvious*, trans. Harbans Nagpal (London: Macmillan, 1982), 156.
6. Bruce Kawin, *The Mind of the Novel* (Princeton: Princeton University Press, 1982), 252.
7. Jacques Derrida, "The Law of Genre," in *On Narrative*, ed. W. J. T. Mitchell (Chicago: University of Chicago Press, 1980), 55.
8. Gertrude Stein, "The Gradual Making of *The Making of Americans*," in *Lectures in America* (Boston: Beacon Press, 1935), 135–38.
9. Stein, "The Gradual Making of *The Making of Americans*, 139, 142.
10. Quoted in Christopher Nash, *World Games: The Tradition of Anti-Realist Revolt* (London and New York: Methuen, 1987), 310.
11. Flaubert quoted in Nash, *World Games*, 8.
12. Nash, *World Games*, 314.
13. Catherine Belsey, *Critical Practice* (London and New York: Methuen, 1980), 90.
14. Stein, *Lectures in America*, 151.
15. Gertrude Stein, *A Long Gay Book*, in *Matisse, Picasso, and Gertrude Stein, with Two Shorter Stories* (Barton, Vt.: Something Else Press, 1972), 114. Hereafter cited in the text using the abbreviation *LGB*.
16. Susan Stewart, *Nonsense* (Baltimore: Johns Hopkins University Press, 1979), 4–5.
17. Stewart, *Nonsense*, 49–50.
18. Stewart, *Nonsense*, 13.
19. Stewart, *Nonsense*, 200.
20. Stewart, *Nonsense*, 118.
21. Patricia Tobin, *Time and the Novel: The Genealogical Imperative* (Princeton: Princeton University Press, 1978), 6.
22. Stewart, *Nonsense*, 171.
23. Belsey, *Critical Practice*, 110.
24. Nash, *World Games*, 41.
25. Gertrude Stein quoted in Michael Hoffman, *The Development of Abstractionism in the Writing of Gertrude Stein* (Philadelphia: University of Pennsylvania Press, 1965), 100.
26. Marianne DeKoven, "Gendered Doubleness and the Origins of Modernist Form," *Tulsa Studies in Women's Literature* 8 (1989): 21.
27. Nash, *World Games*, 34.
28. Nash, *World Games*, 36.

29. Jean-François Lyotard, *The Postmodern Condition: A Report on Knowledge,* trans. Geoff Bennington and Brian Massumi, Theory and History of Literature, vol. 10 (Minneapolis: University of Minnesota Press, 1984), 81.
30. Brian McHale, *Postmodernist Fiction* (New York: Methuen, 1987), 6.

Chapter 3

1. Gertrude Stein, *How Writing Is Written,* ed. Robert Bartlett Haas (Los Angeles: Black Sparrow Press, 1974), 151.
2. Gertrude Stein, *A Novel of Thank You* (New Haven: Yale University Press, 1958), 31. Hereafter cited in text using the abbreviation *ANOTY.*
3. Gertrude Stein, *Lectures in America* (Boston: Beacon Press, 1935), 55.
4. Gertrude Stein, "What Are Master-pieces and Why Are There So Few of Them," in *Writings and Lectures, 1909–1945,* ed. Patricia Meyerowitz (Baltimore: Penguin, 1967), 150.
5. Gertrude Stein, "How Writing is Written," 157.
6. Gertrude Stein, "Plays," in *Lectures in America* (Boston: Beacon Press, 1935), 118.
7. Stein, *Lectures in America,* 55.
8. Gertrude Stein, *Narration* (Chicago: University of Chicago Press, 1935), 17.
9. Stein, *Narration,* 23.
10. Stein, *Narration,* 23.
11. Phillipe Sollers, *Writing and the Experience of Limits,* ed. David Hayman, trans. Philip Barnard with David Hayman (New York: Columbia University Press, 1983).
12. Neil Schmitz, "Gertrude Stein as Postmodernist: The Rhetoric of *Tender Buttons,*" *Modern Fiction Studies* 3 (1974): 1204.
13. Patricia Waugh, *Feminine Fictions: Revisiting the Postmodern* (New York: Routledge, 1989), 10.
14. Waugh, *Feminine Fictions,* 12.
15. Roland Barthes, *S/Z,* trans. Richard Miller (New York: Hill and Wang, 1974), 95.
16. Waugh, *Feminine Fictions,* 20.
17. Carolyn Burke, "Getting Spliced: Modernism and Sexual Difference," *American Quarterly* 39, no. 1 (1987), 102–3.
18. Harriet Chessman, *"The Public Is Invited to Dance": Representation, the Body, and Dialogue in Gertrude Stein* (Stanford: Stanford University Press, 1989), 65.
19. Quoted in Richard Bridgman, *Gertrude Stein in Pieces* (New York: Oxford University Press, 1970), 171.
20. Marianne DeKoven, *A Different Language* (Madison: University of Wisconsin Press, 1983), 115.
21. Bridgman, *Gertrude Stein in Pieces,* 173.
22. Janice Doane, *Silence and Narrative: The Early Novels of Gertrude Stein* (Westport, Conn.: Greenwood Press, 1986), xxiii.
23. Stein, *Lectures in America,* 200.
24. Patricia Tobin, *Time and the Novel: The Genealogical Imperative* (Princeton: Princeton University Press, 1978), 7–8.
25. Jacques Derrida, "The Ends of Man," in *Language and Human Nature,* ed. P. Kurtz (St. Louis: Warren H. Green, 1971), 205.

Chapter 4

1. Hans Bertens, "The Postmodern Weltanschauung and Its Relation with Modernism: An Introductory Survey," in *Approaching Postmodernism*, ed. Douwe Fokkema and Hans Bertens (Amsterdam and Philadelphia: Johns Benjamins, 1986), 9–51.

2. Raymond Federman, "Fiction Today or the Pursuit of Non-Knowledge," *Humanities in Society* 1, 2 (1978): 122.

3. Bertens, "The Postmodern Weltanschauung," 24.

4. Ihab Hassan, "Ideas of Cultural Change," in *Innovation/Renovation: New Perspectives on the Humanities*, ed. Ihab Hassan and Sally Hassan (Madison: University of Wisconsin Press, 1983), 29.

5. Gertrude Stein, "Plays," in *Lectures in America* (Boston: Beacon Press, 1935), 125.

6. Teresa de Lauretis, *Alice Doesn't: Feminism, Semiotics, Cinema* (Bloomington: Indiana University Press, 1984), 140–42.

7. de Lauretis, *Alice Doesn't*, 142.

8. Gertrude Stein, *Lucy Church Amiably: a Novel of Romantic Beauty and Nature Which Looks Like an Engraving* (New York: Something Else Press, 1969), 47. Hereafter cited in the text using the abbreviation *LCA*.

9. Luce Irigaray, *Speculum of the Other Woman*, trans. Gillian C. Gill (Ithaca: Cornell University Press, 1985), 127.

10. Roland Barthes, *S/Z*, trans. Richard Miller (New York: Hill and Wang, 1978), 215–16.

11. Gertrude Stein, *Narration* (Chicago: University of Chicago Press, 1935), 10.

12. Alice Jardine, *Gynesis: Configurations of Women in Modernity* (Ithaca: Cornell University Press, 1985), 25.

13. Irigaray, *Speculum of the Other Woman*, 230–31. In its most simple meaning *ana* is a prefix meaning up, upward, throughout, backward, back again, or anew with connotations of excessiveness. More specifically, *anamorphosis* is a distorted or monstrous project or representation of an image or a plane or a curved surface that, when viewed from a certain point—as by reflection from a curved mirror—appears regular and in proportion. Irigaray in using anamorphosis to refer to the textually, culturally, and physically feminine is drawing on the male association of femaleness with monstrosity and suggesting that a change in perspective/proportion, a change in the viewing instruments, is in order.

14. Michel Benamou, "Presence and Play," in *Performance in Postmodern Culture*, ed. Michel Benamou and Charles Caramello (Madison, Wis.: Coda Press, 1977), 3.

15. Jerzy Kutnik, *The Novel as Performance: The Fiction of Ronald Sukenick and Raymond Federman* (Carbondale: University of Illinois Press, 1986), 231.

16. Kutnik, *The Novel as Performance*, 10.

17. Richard Poirier, *The Performing Self* (New York: Oxford University Press, 1971), 87.

18. Josette Féral, "Performance and Theatricality: The Subject Demystified," *Modern Drama* 25 (1982): 171.

19. Féral, "Performance and Theatricality," 177.

20. Féral, "Performance and Theatricality," 178.

21. Barthes, *S/Z*, 197.

22. Alain Robbe-Grillet, *For a New Novel* (London: John Calder, 1970), 27.

23. Féral, "Performance and Theatricality," 175.

24. Harriet Chessman, *"The Public Is Invited to Dance": Representation, the Body, and Dialogue in Gertrude Stein* (Stanford: Stanford University Press, 1989), 126. Harriet Chessman reads the novel as promoting "a mythos of continual and unordered linguistic birth" (126), and a model of creativity as democratic, dialogic, and female, while Marianne DeKoven argues that what I am calling the novel's unrestrained metonymy emerges from a return to "the pre-Oedipal continuity with the mother's body as representative of the natural, physical world that constitutes in patriarchy the repressed female mode" (DeKoven, *A Different Language: Gertrude Stein's Experimental Language* [Madison: University of Wisconsin Press, 1983], 136).

25. Edward Said, "Contemporary Fiction and Criticism," *Tri-Quarterly* 33 (1975): 244–45.

26. Ulla Dydo, "Landscape Is Not Grammar: Gertrude Stein in 1928," *Raritan* 7, no. 1 (1987): 97–118. See especially 103ff. Marianne DeKoven argues that in these years Stein moved toward a greater acceptance of her femaleness and that this enabled the female vision of the novel (Marianne DeKoven, *A Different Language*, 137). In a similar vein, Harriet Chessman reads the text as Stein's attempt to resuscitate a "profoundly 'amiable' or loving female creator" (Chessman, *"The Public Is Invited to Dance,"* 132). I take issue with aspects of these readings later in this discussion.

27. Gertrude Stein, *Lectures in America* (New York: Vintage, 1973), 125.

28. Fredric Jameson, "Postmodernism and Utopia," in *Utopia Post Utopia: Configurations of Nature and Culture in Recent Sculpture and Photography* (Boston: Institute of Contemporary Art, 1988).

29. Gertrude Stein, "An American in France," in *What Are Masterpieces* (New York: Pitman, 1970), 64.

30. Kutnik argues for this "fundamental irreconcilability" (*The Novel as Performance*, 31) between these two traditions. His elaboration of the nonmimetic foundation of performance art has been extremely useful to my analysis of Stein's nonmimetic performative text. As an example of the ways in which making mimetic standards the basic criteria for judging art distorts the nature of the performative text see Victoria Maubrey-Rose, *The Anti-Representational Response: Gertrude Stein's "Lucy Church Amiably"* (Uppsala, Sweden: Studia Anglistica Upsaliensia, 1985). Although she has many useful insights into the workings of the novel and the literary-philosophical contexts from which it emerges, Maubrey-Rose's preoccupation with Stein's deviations or "annihilations" of sense causes her to judge the novel as a qualified failure.

31. Victor Turner, "Frame, Flow and Reflection: Ritual and Drama as Public Liminality," in *Performance in Postmodern Culture*, ed. Michel Benamou and Charles Caramello (Madison, Wis.: Coda Press, 1977), 33.

32. Natalie Davis, quoted in Turner, "Frame, Flow and Reflection," 40–41.

33. Turner, "Frame, Flow and Reflection," 41.

34. Turner, "Frame, Flow and Reflection," 50–51.

35. Luce Irigaray, *Speculum of the Other Woman*, 346.

36. Julia Kristeva, "Women's Time," trans. Alice Jardine, *Signs* 7, no. 1 (1981): 33–34.

Chapter 5

1. Gertrude Stein, *Everybody's Autobiography* (New York: Vintage, 1973), 153.
2. David Carroll, *The Subject in Question: The Languages of Theory and the Strategies of Fiction* (Chicago: University of Chicago Press, 1982), 119.
3. Janice L. Doane, *Silence and Narrative: The Early Novels of Gertrude Stein* (Westport, Conn.: Greenwood Press, 1986), 91.
4. Doane, *Silence and Narrative*, 117.
5. Harriet Chessman, *"The Public Is Invited to Dance": Representation, the Body, and Dialogue in Gertrude Stein* (Stanford: Stanford University Press, 1989), 41.
6. Gertrude Stein, *The Geographical History of America* (New York: Random House, 1936), 105.
7. Gertrude Stein, *Mrs. Reynolds and Five Earlier Novelettes* (New Haven: Yale University Press, 1952), 167. Hereafter cited in the text using the abbreviation *MR*.
8. Hayden White, "The Value of Narrativity in the Representation of Reality," *Critical Inquiry* 7 (1980): 14.
9. Fernand Braudel, *On History*, trans. Sarah Matthews (Chicago: University of Chicago Press, 1980), 3.
10. Julia Kristeva, "Women's Time," *Signs* 7, no. 1 (1981): 16–17.
11. Braudel, *On History*, 3–4.
12. Kristeva, "Women's Time," 17.
13. Carroll, *The Subject in Question*, 124.
14. Jean-François Lyotard, *The Postmodern Condition: A Report on Knowledge*, trans. Geoff Bennington and Brian Massumi, Theory and History of Literature, vol. 10 (Minneapolis: University of Minnesota Press, 1984), 95. See also the works of Michael de Certeau, Dominick La Capra, Fredric Jameson, Edward Said, Joan Kelly, and Elizabeth Fox-Genovese.
15. Carroll, *The Subject in Question*, 139.
16. For early Stein studies that regarded her in this way see, for example, B. L. Reid's *Art by Subtraction* (Norman: University of Oklahoma Press, 1958) and reviews in *Critical Essays on Gertrude Stein*, ed. Michael J. Hoffman (Boston: G. K. Hall, 1986), especially those by Michael Gold and Edmund Wilson.
17. See, for example, Shari Benstock, *Women of the Left Bank* (Austin: University of Texas Press, 1986); Elizabeth Fifer, " 'Is Flesh Advisable?' The Interior Theater of Gertrude Stein," in Hoffman, *Critical Essays*; Lisa Ruddick, "A Rosy Charm: Gertrude Stein and the Repressed Feminine," in Hoffman, *Critical Essays*; Cynthia Secor, "The Question of Gertrude Stein," in *American Novels Revisited*, ed. Fritz Fleischmann et al. (Boston: G. K. Hall, 1982); Neil Schmitz, *Of Huck and Alice: Humorous Writing in American Literature* (Minneapolis: University of Minnesota Press, 1983); numerous essays by Catharine Stimpson, in particular "Gertrude Stein and the Transposition of Gender," in *The Poetics of Gender*, ed. Nancy K. Miller (New York: Columbia University Press, 1986), and "The Somagrams of Gertrude Stein," *Poetics Today* 6, nos. 1–2:67–80. Stimpson sees Stein as an antipatriarchal writer with "strong moorings" to the patriarchy. Marianne DeKoven analyzes Stein's writing as antipatriarchal to the extent that all experimental writing is antipatriarchal, but she asserts that Stein never intended to be antipatriarchal in

her writing (*A Different Language: Gertrude Stein's Experimental Writing* [Madison: University of Wisconsin Press, 1983]). The issue of how deliberate Stein's critique of patriarchy was remains open to debate; nonetheless it seems clear that she is currently regarded as a much more socially aware writer than she was previously. Interestingly, Stein's critical reception follows the pattern established in Woolf criticism: early accounts in which Woolf was pictured as a refined empress disengaged from life and more recent studies—many of them feminist—that see Woolf as a trenchant social critic.

18. Maurice Blanchot, "Everyday Speech," *Yale French Studies* 73 (1987): 12–20.
19. James R. Mellow, *Charmed Circle: Gertrude Stein and Company* (New York: Praeger, 1974), 443.
20. Quoted in Richard Bridgman, *Gertrude Stein in Pieces* (New York: Oxford University Press, 1970), 314. In addition to reading the English classics during the war, Stein read nightly from Leonardo Blake's book of astrological predictions. Astrology also is a system that depends on a presumed causal link between natural phenomena and human behavior.
21. Neil Schmitz, for example, finds the central motive of Stein's writing to be the desire to escape from the fixation of a particular identity—the power of the name (Schmitz, *Of Huck and Alice*). See also Harriet Chessman's discussion of the ways in which the doubleness of female identity affects Stein's literary form (Chessman, *"The Public Is Invited to Dance": Representation, the Body, and Dialogue in Gertrude Stein* [Stanford: Stanford University Press, 1989]).
22. Quoted in Bridgman, *Gertrude Stein in Pieces*, 325.
23. White, "The Value of Narrativity," 24.
24. Gertrude Stein, *Narration* (Chicago: University of Chicago Press, 1935), 19.
25. Chessman discusses Stein's lifelong resistance to "explanation" associated with unquestioned or absolute truth claims and with monologic discourse that closes down potentially contestatory voices. I agree that this resistance is deeply political as Chessman claims, but as *Mrs. Reynolds* shows, it is also deeply problematic (Chessman, *"The Public Is Invited to Dance,"* 47ff.).
26. I mean the word *tactic* in the sense that Michael de Certeau uses it. Unlike tactics, he says, strategies partake of "the calculus of force relationships." They are exercised by subjects of will and power who speak from "a place that can be circumscribed as proper," that can be isolated from an environment. Rational, hierarchical systems—metanarratives (politics, economics, science, history)—are constructed on this strategic model that "works to conceal beneath objective calculations their connection with the power that sustains them" (de Certeau, *The Practice of Everyday Life*, trans. Steven F. Rendall [Berkeley: University of California Press, 1984]). A tactic, however, is a calculus that cannot count on a "proper" (institutionalized) location. Concealed by these forms of rationality, these systems of power, but existing within them as alternatives, a tactic is an operational logic that must manipulate events in order to turn them into opportunities. It must "make do" with what is at hand. Thus a tactic does not/cannot propose itself as a permanent solution—it is "not a discourse" de Certeau says, but rather is the manner in which an "opportunity" is seized that defines a tactical maneuver. Nonetheless, tactics

can operate to erode the systems of power by dislocating and potentially reorganiz-
ing the "place from which discourse is produced" (xix).

27. Blanchot, "Everyday Speech," 12.
28. Gertrude Stein, "What are Master-pieces and Why Are There So Few of Them,"
    in *Writings and Lectures 1909–1945*, ed. Patricia Meyerowitz (Baltimore: Penguin,
    1967), 156.
29. Chessman, *"The Public Is Invited to Dance,"* 115.
30. Thomas Foster, "'The Very House of Difference': Gender as 'Embattled' Stand-
    point," *Genders* 8 (1990): 23.

Chapter 6

I wish to thank the Bowling Green State University Faculty Research Committee for
their award of a Summer Research Grant that enabled me to draft this chapter. Portions
of it were delivered at the 1988 Midwest Modern Language Association Conference
and at the Reconstructing Cultural Criticism Conference (Milwaukee, Wis., April,
1989). For her helpful comments on the drafts of this chapter and for her continuing
support of my work, I wish to thank Vicki Patraka.

1. Those who have suggested that Stein embraced certain postmodern tendencies
   include: Shari Benstock in *Women of the Left Bank* (Austin: University of Texas Press,
   1986); Marianne DeKoven in *A Different Language: Gertrude Stein's Experimental Writing* (Madison: University of Wisconsin Press, 1983); Fredric Jameson in "Postmodernism, Or the Cultural Logic of Late Capitalism," *New Left Review* 146 (July/August
   1984): 53–92; and Neil Schmitz in "Gertrude Stein as Postmodernist: The Rhetoric
   of *Tender Buttons*," *Modern Fiction Studies* 3 (1974): 120–18. Many other recent studies of Stein are informed by varieties of poststructuralist theory, itself a manifestation of a postmodern impulse, according to Jameson and others. See, for example,
   Anna Gibbs, "Hélène Cixous and Gertrude Stein: New Directions in Feminist
   Criticism," *Meanjin* 38: 281–93; Lisa Ruddick, "A Rosy Charm: Gertrude Stein and
   the Repressed Feminine," in *Critical Essays on Gertrude Stein*, ed. Michael Hoffman
   (Boston: G. K. Hall, 1986) 225–40; Catharine Stimpson, "Gertrude Stein and the
   Transposition of Gender," in *The Poetics of Gender*, ed. Nancy K. Miller (New York:
   Columbia University Press, 1986) 1–18; and Harriet Chessman, *"The Public Is Invited
   to Dance": Representation, the Body, and Dialogue in Gertrude Stein* (Stanford: Stanford
   University Press, 1989).
2. Andreas Huyssen, *After the Great Divide* (Bloomington: Indiana University Press,
   1986), 53–54.
3. Huyssen, *After the Great Divide*, 49. See also Benstock's discussion in *Women of the
   Left Bank* and that of Sandra M. Gilbert and Susan Gubar in *No Man's Land: The
   Place of Women in the Twentieth Century* (New Haven: Yale University Press, 1988).
4. Huyssen, *After the Great Divide*, 53.
5. Lawrence W. Levine, *Highbrow/Lowbrow: The Emergence of Cultural Hierarchy in
   America* (Cambridge: Harvard University Press, 1988), 177. It is interesting to
   speculate on the significance of the metaphoric overlap among early assessments
   of Stein's literary worth, the modernist feminization and denigration of mass cul-

ture, and the modernist desire to exclude the cultural productions of real women. Like mass culture, Stein's texts were seen as being childish, trivial, monstrous, degenerate, and threatening to the establishment of literary standards (meaning a particular notion of the literary). One might postulate then that the critical repudiation of Stein arose in part from a desire to promote a particular notion of the modern, one built on a firm repudiation of mass culture, a notion that Stein's work contests, as I hope to show.

6. Ezra Pound, *The Literary Essays of Ezra Pound* (New York: New Directions, 1954), 281.

7. Iain Chambers, *Popular Culture: The Metropolitan Experience* (London: Methuen, 1986), 193.

8. Jameson, "Postmodernism, Or the Cultural Logic of Late Capitalism," 53–54.

9. I borrow this concept from Jim Collins, whose excellent study of popular culture and postmodernism, *Uncommon Cultures* (New York: Routledge, 1989), has been helpful to my own analysis. See especially chapter 1 for his theory of postmodern culture as decentered and composed of multiple competing discourses.

10. Roland Barthes, "From Work to Text" in *Textual Strategies: Perspectives in Poststructuralist Criticism*, ed. Josue Harari (Ithaca: Cornell University Press, 1979), 77.

11. Fredric Jameson, *The Political Unconscious: Narrative as a Socially Symbolic Act* (Ithaca: Cornell University Press, 1981), 207.

12. While I am concerned here to distinguish Stein's position from the modernist aesthetic as it has been defined through successive canonizations, distinctions also should be made between Stein's uses of and attitudes toward mass culture and those of the historical avant-garde. In distinction from the more traditional modernist notions of the autonomous work of art and the specialized status of the aesthetic, the early-twentieth-century avant-garde intended to undermine "institution" art and to merge art and life. Walter Benjamin, the Russian avant-garde, and various Dada and surrealist groups had as their utopian goal the development of an emancipatory mass culture (culture for the masses) based on a revolutionary reorganization of everyday life. Although Stein shared their interest in mass culture and their belief that the experience of an increasingly technologized life had altered culture in important ways, she had no such political program. The creation of a socialist avant-garde for the masses was never her intention; her revolution was purely textual. It is also the case that Stein did not deliberately appeal to a popular audience though she used popular forms and often rooted her writing in the daily and the domestic. Her work never had a widespread popular appeal— with the exception of *The Autobiography of Alice B. Toklas*—and, on the whole, Stein was ambivalent over the prospect of popular success. Of course, it is also true that she never had widespread critical acceptance either—she was barred from the museum.

13. Gertrude Stein, "How Writing Is Written," in *How Writing Is Written*, ed. Robert Bartlett Haas (Los Angeles, Black Sparrow, 1974), 153.

14. Gertrude Stein, "Composition as Explanation," in *Gertrude Stein: Writing and Lectures, 1909–1945*, ed. Patricia Meyerowitz (Baltimore: Penguin Books, 1967), 24.

15. Stein, "How Writing Is Written," 151.

16. Walter Benjamin, "The Work of Art in the Age of Mechanical Reproduction," in

Film Theory and Criticism, 3d ed., ed. Gerald Mast and Marshall Cohen (New York: Oxford University Press, 1985), 679.

17. Raymond Williams defines structures of feeling as "social experiences in solution, as distinct from other social semantic formations which have been precipitated and are more evidently and more immediately available. . . . Yet, this specific solution is never mere flux. It is a structured formation which, because it is at the very edge of semantic availability, has many of the characteristics of a pre-formation, until specific articulations—new semantic figures—are discovered in material practice" (Raymond Williams, *Marxism and Literature* [New York: Oxford University Press, 1972], 133–34).

18. Gertrude Stein, "Portraits and Repetition," in *Lectures in America*, 177.

19. Gertrude Stein, *Many Many Women*, in *Matisse, Picasso, and Gertrude Stein, with Two Shorter Stories* (Barton, Vt.: Something Else Press, 1972), 100–101.

20. Gertrude Stein, *The Geographical History of America* (New York: Random House, 1936), 70.

21. Benjamin, "The Work of Art," 689–90.

22. Gertrude Stein, *Narration* (Chicago: University of Chicago Press, 1935), 29.

23. Gertrude Stein, "Portraits and Repetition," in *Lectures in America* (Boston: Beacon Press, 1935), 195.

24. Gertrude Stein, *The Autobiography of Alice B. Toklas* (New York: Random House, 1933), 206.

25. Gertrude Stein, *A Novel of Thank You* (New Haven: Yale University Press, 1958), 20–21.

26. This phrase is Cecelia Tichi's in *Shifting Gears: Technology, Literature, Culture, in Modernist America* (Chapel Hill: University of North Carolina Press, 1987). Tichi's valuable study explores the influence of "gear and girder" technology on literary form in the work of Hemingway, Dos Passos, and Williams. These writers, she argues, wrote machine-age texts defined as "a functional system of component parts designed to transmit energy" that "obeys the design rules for sound structures and efficient machines" (Tichi, *Shifting Gears*, 16). Like Hemingway, Dos Passos, and Williams, Stein used new technologies as the basis for new literary forms, forms created in response to those new perceptual values that arose from an increasingly technologized life. There are ways in which she too wrote "machines made of words," by exploring language as a "functional system of component parts designed to transmit energy." Stein differs from them, it seems to me, in other aspects of her aesthetic. She was more interested in textual energy as disruptive of form rather than in the form that contains this energy. Hers is not an aesthetics of the sound structure, the efficient machine. She also was more eclectic in her approach toward mass culture, embracing motor cars *and* funny papers, the cinema *and* the cowboy.

27. Gertrude Stein, "What Are Master-pieces," in *Gertrude Stein: Writings and Lectures, 1909–1945*, ed. Patricia Meyerowitz (Baltimore: Penguin Books, 1967), 150.

28. Stein, "How Writing Is Written," 157.

29. Gertrude Stein, *Everybody's Autobiography* (New York: Vintage, 1973), 69.

30. Stein, *Lectures in America*, 195–96.

31. Benjamin, "The Work of Art," 690.

32. Dana Polan, "Brief Encounters: Mass Culture and the Evacuation of Sense," in *Studies in Entertainment*, ed. Tania Modleski (Bloomington: Indiana University Press, 1986), 179.

33. Polan, "Brief Encounters," 168.

34. Stein, *Lectures in America*, 166.

35. Polan, "Brief Encounters," 182.

36. Chambers, *Popular Culture*, 12.

37. Stein, *Lectures in America*, 161.

38. Stein, "What Are Master-pieces," 151.

39. Stein, *How Writing Is Written*, 104–5.

40. Seymour Chatman, *Story and Discourse: Narrative Structure in Fiction and Film* (Ithaca: Cornell University Press, 1978), 48.

41. Roland Barthes, *The Pleasure of the Text*, trans. Richard Miller (New York: Hill and Wang, 1975), 10.

42. Polan, "Brief Encounters," 182.

43. Jean Baudrillard, *Simulations*, trans. Paul Foss, Paul Patton, and Philip Beitchman (New York: Semiotexte, 1983).

44. Donna Haraway, "A Manifesto for Cyborgs: Science, Technology, and Socialist Feminism in the 1980s," *Socialist Review* 15 (1985): 66.

45. Quoted in Fred Pfeil, "Postmodernism as a 'Structure of Feeling'," in *Marxism and the Interpretation of Culture*, ed. Cary Nelson and Lawrence Grossberg (Urbana: University of Illinois Press, 1988), 384.

46. Laurie Anderson, *United States* (New York: Harper and Row, 1984), unpaginated.

47. Stein, *Lectures in America*, 161.

Chapter 7

1. Gertrude Stein, *Q.E.D. (Things As They Are)* (New York: Liverright, 1971), 137. Hereafter cited in the text with the short title *Q.E.D.*

2. Gertrude Stein, "Melanctha," in *Three Lives* (New York: Vintage, 1936), 92. Hereafter cited in the text using the abbreviation "*M.*"

3. Gertrude Stein, *Lectures in America* (Boston: Beacon Press, 1935), 142.

4. Gertrude Stein, *Ida* (New York: Vintage, 1971). Hereafter cited in the text with the abbreviation *I.*

5. Walter Benjamin, "The Work of Art in the Age of Mechanical Reproduction," in *Film Theory and Criticism*, 3d ed., ed. Gerald Mast and Marshall Cohen (New York: Oxford University Press, 1985), 688.

6. Thomas Elsaesser, "Tales of Sound and Fury, Observations on the Family Melodrama," in *Home Is Where the Heart Is: Studies in Melodrama and the Women's Film*, ed. Christine Gledhill (London: British Film Institute, 1987), 44–45. See also Peter Brooks, *The Melodramatic Imagination: Balzac, Henry James, and the Mode of Excess* (New Haven: Yale University Press, 1976); and Christine Gledhill's introduction to *Home Is Where the Heart Is*, "The Melodramatic Field: An Investigation," 5–39.

7. Gledhill, *Home is Where the Heart Is*, 19–22.

8. Gledhill, *Home is Where the Heart Is*, 26–27.

9. Elsaesser, "Tales of Sound and Fury," 268.

10. The aesthetics of melodrama are discussed by Brooks, Elsaesser, and Gledhill, among others.

11. Gledhill, *Home is Where the Heart Is*, 31.

12. Gledhill, *Home is Where the Heart Is*, 33.

13. Brooks, *The Melodramatic Imagination*, 35.

14. David N. Rodowick, "Madness, Authority and Ideology: The Domestic Melodrama of the 1950s," in Gledhill, *Home is Where the Heart Is*, 270ff.

15. Rodowick, "Madness, Authority and Ideology," 272.

16. Mary Ann Doane, "The 'Woman's Film': Possession and Address," in Gledhill, *Home is Where the Heart Is*, 285–87.

17. Doane, "The 'Woman's Film'," 290.

18. Gertrude Stein, "American Newspapers," in *How Writing Is Written*, ed. Robert Bartlett Haas (Los Angeles: Black Sparrow Press, 1974), 89.

19. Benjamin, "The Work of Art," 685.

20. Gertrude Stein, "I Came and Here I Am," in *How Writing Is Written*, ed. Robert Bartlett Haas (Los Angeles: Black Sparrow Press, 1974), 68.

21. Elsaesser, "Tales of Sound and Fury," 62.

22. Elsaesser, "Tales of Sound and Fury," 62–63.

23. Gertrude Stein, "The Superstitions of Fred Anneday, Annday, Anday: A Novel of Real Life," in Haas, *How Writing is Written*, 25.

24. Doane, "The 'Woman's Film'," 286.

25. Luce Irigaray, *Speculum of the Other Woman*, trans. Gillian C. Gill (Ithaca: Cornell University Press, 1985), 52.

26. Luce Irigaray, "Questions," in *This Sex Which is Not One*, trans. by Katherine Porter (Ithaca: Cornell University Press, 1985), 134.

27. Irigaray, *This Sex Which Is Not One*, 137.

28. Quoted in Richard Bridgman, *Gertrude Stein in Pieces* (New York: Oxford University Press, 1970), 306.

29. Luce Irigaray, *Speculum of the Other Woman*, 266.

30. Jean Baudrillard, *Simulations*, trans. Paul Foss, Paul Patton, and Philip Beitchman (New York: Semiotexte, 1983), 3–4.

31. Baudrillard, *Simulations*, 142.

32. Baudrillard, *Simulations*, 146.

33. Baudrillard, *Simulations*, 149.

34. Baudrillard, *Simulations*, 142–43.

35. Stein, *How Writing is Written*, 30.

36. For an elaboration of connections among the woman's film, melodrama, and women's domestic fiction of the nineteenth century see E. Ann Kaplan's "Mothering, Feminism and Representation: The Maternal in Melodrama and the Women's Film 1910–1940," in Gledhill, *Home Is Where the Heart Is*, 113–37.

37. Because recent readings of *Ida* have tended to emphasize its feminist thematics, a somewhat greater importance is given to the Andrew-Ida relationship than I give here. Neil Schmitz reads the novel as a meditation on the status of women in a patriarchal world, specifically their inability to enter a patriarchal symbolic order. The Andrew-Ida relationship illustrates "the complexity of the political struggle in a love affair" (Schmitz, *Of Huck and Alice: Humorous Writing in American Literature*

[Minneapolis: University of Minnesota Press, 1983], 236). Harriet Chessman views *Ida* as Stein's most overtly feminist novel in which she proposes a model of "twin-ship" to replace the appropriative structures of a male symbolic. The relationship with Andrew suggests the liberating possibilities of a nonhierarchical, nonopposi-tional liaison outside the confines of the traditional romantic quest. See Chessman *"The Public Is Invited to Dance": Representation, the Body, and Dialogue in Gertrude Stein* (Stanford: Stanford University Press, 1989), 166–98.

38. Quoted in Regis Durand, "The Disposition of the Voice," in *Performance in Postmod-ern Culture*, ed. Michel Benamou and Charles Caramello (Madison, Wis.: Coda Press, 1977), 105.

39. Quoted in Durand, "The Disposition of the Voice," 105.

40. Abigail Solomon-Godeau, "Beyond the Simulation Principle," in *Utopia Post Utopia: Configurations of Nature and Culture in Recent Sculpture and Photography* (Cambridge, Mass.: MIT Press, 1988), 83.

41. Fredric Jameson, "Postmodernism, or the Cultural Logic of Late Capitalism," *New Left Review* 146 (July/August 1984): 65, 67.

42. Meaghan Morris, *The Pirate's Fiance: Feminism, Reading, Postmodernism* (London: Verso, 1988), 5.

Bibliography

Anderson, Laurie. *United States.* New York: Harper and Row, 1984.

Bakhtin, Mikhail. *Rabelais and His World.* Trans. Hélène Iswolsky. Bloomington: Indiana University Press, 1984.

Barth, John. "The Literature of Exhaustion." *Atlantic* 222:2 (1967): 29–34.

Barthes, Roland. *The Pleasure of the Text.* Trans. Richard Miller. New York: Hill and Wang, 1975.

———. *S/Z.* Trans. Richard Miller. New York: Hill and Wang, 1978.

Baudrillard, Jean. "The Implosion of Meaning in the Media and the Implosion of the Social in the Masses." In *Myths of Information*, ed. Colin McCabe and Kathleen Woodward, 137–48. Madison, Wis.: Coda Press, 1984.

———. *Simulations.* Trans. Paul Foss, Paul Patton, and Philip Beitchman. New York: Semiotexte, 1983.

Belsey, Catherine. *Critical Practice.* London and New York: Methuen, 1980.

Benamou, Michel. "Presence and Play." In *Performance in Postmodern Culture*, ed. Michel Benamou and Charles Caramello. Madison, Wis.: Coda Press, 1977.

Benjamin, Walter. "The Work of Art in the Age of Mechanical Reproduction." In *Film Theory and Criticism*, 3d ed., ed. Gerald Mast and Marshall Cohen, 675–94. New York: Oxford University Press, 1985.

Benstock, Shari. "Beyond the Reaches of Feminist Criticism: A Letter from Paris." *Tulsa Studies in Women's Literature* 2, nos. 1 and 2 (1984): 5–27.

———. *Women of the Left Bank.* Austin: University of Texas Press, 1986.

Berger, John. *The Look of Things.* New York: Viking Press, 1984.

Bertens, Hans. "The Postmodern Weltanschauung and Its Relation with Modernism: An Introductory Survey." In *Approaching Postmodernism*, ed. Douwe Fokkema and Hans Bertens, 9–51. Amsterdam and Philadelphia: Johns Benjamins, 1986.

Blanchot, Maurice. "Everyday Speech." *Yale French Studies* 73 (1987): 12–20.

Braudel, Fernand. *On History.* Trans. Sarah Matthews. Chicago: University of Chicago Press, 1980.

Bridgman, Richard. *Gertrude Stein in Pieces.* New York: Oxford University Press, 1970.

Brinnin, John Malcolm. *The Third Rose: Gertrude Stein and Her World.* Boston: Little, Brown, 1959.

Brooks, Peter. *The Melodramatic Imagination: Balzac, Henry James, and the Mode of Excess.* New Haven: Yale University Press, 1976.

Burke, Carolyn. "Getting Spliced: Modernism and Sexual Difference." *American Quarterly* 39, no. 1 (1987): 98–121.

Carroll, David. *The Subject in Question: The Languages of Theory and the Strategies of Fiction.* Chicago: University of Chicago Press, 1982.

Caughie, Pamela. *Virginia Woolf and Postmodernism: Literature in Quest and Question of Itself.* Urbana: University of Illinois Press, 1991.

Chambers, Iain. *Popular Culture: The Metropolitan Experience.* London: Methuen, 1986.

Chatman, Seymour. *Story and Discourse: Narrative Structure in Fiction and Film.* Ithaca: Cornell University Press, 1978.

Chessman, Harriet. *"The Public Is Invited to Dance": Representation, the Body, and Dialogue in Gertrude Stein.* Stanford: Stanford University Press, 1989.

Cixous, Hélène. "Castration or Decapitation?" *Signs* 7 (1981): 41–55.

———. "The Laugh of the Medusa." In *New French Feminisms,* ed. Elaine Marks and Isabelle de Courtiveron, 245–64. New York: Schocken Books, 1981.

Collins, Jim. *Uncommon Cultures: Popular Culture and Post-Modernism.* New York: Routledge, 1989.

Davis, Natalie. *Society and Culture in Early Modern France.* Stanford: Stanford University Press, 1975.

de Certeau, Michael. *The Practice of Everyday Life.* Trans. Steven F. Rendall. Berkeley: University of California Press, 1984.

DeKoven, Marianne. *A Different Language: Gertrude Stein's Experimental Writing.* Madison: University of Wisconsin Press, 1983.

———. "Gendered Doubleness and the 'Origins' of Modernist Form." *Tulsa Studies in Women's Literature* 8 (1989): 19–42.

de Lauretis, Teresa. *Alice Doesn't: Feminism, Semiotics, Cinema.* Bloomington: Indiana University Press, 1984.

Deleuze, Gilles. *Nietzsche aujourd 'hui?.* Paris: U. G. E., 1973.

Derrida, Jacques. "The Ends of Man." In *Language and Human Nature,* ed. P. Kurtz. St. Louis: Warren H. Green, 1971.

———. "The Law of Genre." *Glyph* 7:202–29.

Dettmar, Kevin J. H., ed. *Re-Reading the New: A Backward Glance at Modernism.* Ann Arbor: University of Michigan Press, 1992.

Doane, Janice. *Silence and Narrative: The Early Novels of Gertrude Stein.* Westport, Conn.: Greenwood Press, 1986.

Doane, Mary Ann. "The 'Woman's Film': Possession and Address." In *Home Is Where the Heart Is: Studies in Melodrama and the Women's Film,* ed. Christine Gledhill, 283–89. London: British Film Institute, 1987.

Dubnick, Randa. *The Structure of Obscurity: Gertrude Stein, Language, and Cubism.* Urbana: University of Illinois Press, 1984.

DuPlessis, Rachel Blau. *Writing Beyond the Ending: Narrative Strategies of Twentieth-Century Women Writers.* Bloomington: Indiana University Press, 1985.

Durand, Regis. "The Disposition of the Voice." In *Performance in Postmodern Culture,* ed. Michel Benamou and Charles Caramello, 99–112. Madison, Wis.: Coda Press, 1977.

Dydo, Ulla. "Landscape is Not Grammar: Gertrude Stein in 1928." *Raritan* 7, no. 1 (1987): 97–113.

Eagleton, Terry. "Capitalism, Modernism, Postmodernism." *New Left Review* 152 (1985): 60–73.

Elsaesser, Thomas. "Tales of Sound and Fury, Observations on the Family Melodrama." In *Home Is Where the Heart Is: Studies in Melodrama and the Women's Film*, ed. Christine Gledhill, 43–69. London: British Film Institute, 1987.

Federman, Raymond. "Fiction Today or the Pursuit of Non-Knowledge." *Humanities in Society* 1, no. 2 (1978): 115–31.

Féral, Josette. "Performance and Theatricality: The Subject Demystified." *Modern Drama* 25 (1982): 170–81.

———. "The Powers of Difference." In *The Future of Difference*, ed. Hester Eisenstein and Alice Jardine, 88–94. Boston: G. K. Hall, 1980.

Fifer, Elizabeth. " 'Is Flesh Advisable?' The Interior Theater of Gertrude Stein." In *Critical Essays on Gertrude Stein*, ed. Michael Hoffman, 160–70. Boston: G. K. Hall, 1986.

Fokkema, Douwe, and Hans Bertens, eds. *Approaching Postmodernism*. New York: Johns Benjamin, 1986.

Foster, Hal, ed. *The Anti-Aesthetic: Essays on Postmodern Culture*. Port Townsend, Wash.: Bay Press, 1983.

———. *Recodings*. Port Townsend, Wash.: Bay Press, 1985.

Foster, Thomas. " 'The Very House of Difference': Gender as 'Embattled' Standpoint." *Genders* 8 (1990): 17–37.

Foucault, Michel. "Of Other Spaces." *Diacritics* 16 (1986): 22–27.

Frankenberg, Lloyd. Introduction to *Mrs. Reynolds and Five Earlier Novels*, by Gertrude Stein. New Haven: Yale University Press, 1952.

Freadman, Anne. "Sandpaper." *Southern Review-Adelaide* 16 (1983): 161–73.

Friedman, Ellen G., and Miriam Fuchs, eds. *Breaking the Sequence*. Princeton: Princeton University Press, 1989.

Gallop, Jane. "Annie Leclerc Writing a Letter with Vermeer." In *The Poetics of Gender*, ed. Nancy K. Miller, 137–56. New York: Columbia University Press, 1986.

———. "Beyond the Jouissance Principle." *Representations* 7 (1984): 110–15.

———. *The Daughter's Seduction*. Ithaca: Cornell University Press, 1982.

Garvin, Harry P., ed. *Romanticism, Modernism, Postmodernism*. Lewisberg, Pa.: Bucknell University Press, 1980.

Gibbs, Anna. "Hélène Cixous and Gertrude Stein: New Directions in Feminist Criticism." *Meanjin* 38: 281–93.

Gilbert, Sandra M. and Susan Gubar. *The Madwoman in the Attic*. New Haven: Yale University Press, 1979.

———. *No Man's Land: The Place of the Woman Writer in the Twentieth Century*. 2 vols. New Haven: Yale University Press, 1988.

Gledhill, Christine. Introduction to *Home Is Where the Heart Is: Studies in Melodrama and the Women's Film*, ed. Christine Gledhill, 5–39. London: British Film Institute, 1987.

Gold, Michael. "Gertrude Stein: A Literary Idiot." In *Critical Essays on Gertrude Stein*, ed. Michael J. Hoffman, 76–78. Boston, G. K. Hall, 1986.

Habermas, Jürgen. "Modernity—An Incomplete Project." In *The Anti-Aesthetic: Essays on Postmodern Culture*, ed. Hal Foster, 3–15. Port Townsend, Wash.: Bay Press, 1983.

Haraway, Donna. "A Manifesto for Cyborgs: Science, Technology, and Socialist Feminism in the 1980s." *Socialist Review* 15 (1985): 65–107.

Haas, Robert Bartlett, ed. *How Writing Is Written*. Los Angeles: Black Sparrow Press, 1974.

Hassan, Ihab. "Ideas of Cultural Change." In *Innovation/Renovation: New Perspectives on the Humanities*, ed. Ihab Hassan and Sally Hassan. Madison: University of Wisconsin Press, 1983.

———. *The Postmodern Turn: Essays in Postmodern Theory and Culture*. Columbus: Ohio State University, 1987.

———. "The Quest of Postmodernism." In *Romanticism, Modernism, Postmodernism*, ed. Harry P. Garvin, 17–26. Lewisberg, Pa.: Bucknell University Press, 1980.

Hoffman, Michael, ed. *Critical Essays on Gertrude Stein*. Boston: G. K. Hall, 1986.

———. *The Development of Abstractionism in the Writings of Gertrude Stein*. Philadelphia: University of Pennsylvania Press, 1965.

Hutcheon, Linda. *A Poetics of Postmodernism: History, Theory, and Fiction*. New York: Routledge, 1989.

———. *The Politics of Postmodernism*. New York: Routledge, 1989.

Huyssen, Andreas. *After the Great Divide*. Bloomington: Indiana University Press, 1986.

Irigaray, Luce. "And the One Doesn't Stir Without the Other." *Signs* 7 (1981): 60–67.

———. *Speculum of the Other Woman*. Trans. Gillian C. Gill. Ithaca: Cornell University Press, 1985.

———. "This Sex Which Is Not One." In *This Sex Which Is Not One*, trans. Catherine Porter. Ithaca: Cornell University Press, 1985.

———. "When Our Lips Speak Together." In *This Sex Which Is Not One*, trans. Catherine Porter. Ithaca: Cornell University Press, 1985.

Jameson, Fredric. *The Political Unconscious: Narrative As a Socially Symbolic Act*. Ithaca: Cornell University Press, 1981.

———. Foreword to *The Postmodern Condition: A Report on Knowledge*, by Jean-François Lyotard. Trans. Geoff Bennington and Brian Massumi. Theory and History of Literature, volume 10, vii–xxi. Minneapolis: University of Minnesota Press, 1984.

———. "Postmodernism and Consumer Society." In *The Anti-Aesthetic: Essays on Postmodern Culture*, ed. Hal Foster, 111–25. Port Townsend, Wash.: Bay Press, 1983.

———. "Postmodernism and Utopia." In *Utopia Post Utopia: Configurations of Nature and Culture in Recent Sculpture and Photography*, 11–34. Catalog Series. Cambridge, Mass.: MIT Press, 1980.

———. "Postmodernism, Or the Cultural Logic of Late Capitalism." *New Left Review* 146 (July/August 1984): 53–92.

Jardine, Alice. *Gynesis: Configurations of Women in Modernity*. Ithaca: Cornell University Press, 1985.

Kaplan, E. Ann. "Mothering, Feminism and Representation: The Maternal in Melodrama and the Women's Film, 1910–1940." In *Home Is Where the Heart Is: Studies in Melodrama and the Women's Film*, ed. Christine Gledhill, 113–37. London: British Film Institute, 1987.

Kawin, Bruce. *The Mind of the Novel*. Princeton: Princeton University Press, 1982.

Kristeva, Julia. *Desire in Language*. Trans. Thomas Gora et al. New York: Columbia University Press, 1980.

———. "Postmodernism?" In *Romanticism, Modernism, Postmodernism*, ed. Harry P. Garvin, 136–41. Lewisberg, Pa.: Bucknell University Press, 1980.

———. "Psychoanalysis and the Polis." In *The Politics of Interpretation*, ed. W. J. T. Mitchell, 83–98. Chicago: University of Chicago Press, 1983.

———. "Women's Time." *Signs* 7, no. 1 (1981): 13–35.

Kroker, Arthur and David Cook. *The Postmodern Scene: Excremental Culture and Hyper-Aesthetics.* New York: St. Martin's Press, 1986.

Kutnik, Jerzy. *The Novel as Performance: The Fiction of Ronald Sukenick and Raymond Federman.* Carbondale: University of Illinois Press, 1986.

Levine, Lawrence W. *Highbrow/Lowbrow: The Emergence of Cultural Hierarchy in America.* Cambridge: Harvard University Press, 1988.

Lyotard, Jean-François. *The Postmodern Condition: A Report on Knowledge.* Trans. Geoff Bennington and Brian Massumi. Theory and History of Literature, volume 10. Minneapolis: University of Minnesota Press, 1984.

McCaffery, Larry. *Postmodern Fiction: A BioBibliography.* New York: Greenwood Press, 1986.

McHale, Brian. *Postmodernist Fiction.* New York: Methuen, 1987.

Maubrey-Rose, Victoria. *The Anti-Representational Response: Gertrude Stein's "Lucy Church Amiably."* Uppsala, Sweden: Studia Anglistica Upsaliensia, 1985.

Mellow, James R. *Charmed Circle: Gertrude Stein and Company.* New York: Praeger, 1974.

Miller, Nancy K. "Arachnologies: The Woman, the Text, and the Critic." In *The Poetics of Gender,* ed. Nancy K. Miller, 270–96. New York: Columbia University Press, 1986.

———. "Emphasis Added: Plots and Plausibilities in Women's Fiction." *PMLA* 96 (1981): 36–48.

Nash, Christopher. *World Games: The Tradition of Anti-Realist Revolt.* London and New York: Methuen, 1987.

Nicholson, Linda, ed. *Feminism/Postmodernism.* New York: Routledge, 1990.

Pfeil, Fred. "Postmodernism as a 'Structure of Feeling'." In *Marxism and the Interpretation of Culture,* ed. Cary Nelson and Lawrence Grossberg, 381–403. Urbana: University of Illinois Press, 1988.

Picheux, Michel. *Language, Semantics, and Ideology: Stating the Obvious.* Trans. Harbaus Nagpal. London: Macmillan, 1982.

Poirier, Richard. *The Performing Self.* New York: Oxford University Press, 1971.

Polan, Dana. "Brief Encounters: Mass Culture and the Evacuation of Sense." In *Studies in Entertainment,* ed. Tania Modleski, 167–87. Bloomington: Indiana University Press, 1986.

Pound, Ezra. *The Literary Essays of Ezra Pound.* New York: New Directions, 1954.

Reid, B. L. *Art by Subtraction.* Norman: University of Oklahoma Press, 1958.

Rodowick, David N. "Madness, Authority and Ideology: The Domestic Melodrama of the 1950s." In *Home Is Where the Heart Is: Studies in Melodrama and the Women's Film,* ed. Christine Gledhill, 268–80. London: British Film Institute, 1987.

Robbe-Grillet, Alain. *For a New Novel.* London: John Calder, 1970.

Ross, Andrew, ed. *Universal Abandon?* Minneapolis: University of Minnesota Press, 1989.

Ruddick, Lisa. *Reading Gertrude Stein: Body, Text, and Gnosis.* Ithaca: Cornell University Press, 1990.

———. "A Rosy Charm: Gertrude Stein and the Repressed Feminine." In *Critical Essays on Gertrude Stein,* ed. Michael Hoffman, 225–39. Boston: G. K. Hall, 1986.

Said, Edward. "Contemporary Fiction and Criticism." *Tri-Quarterly* 33 (1975): 231–56.

Schmitz, Neil. "Gertrude Stein as Postmodernist: The Rhetoric of *Tender Buttons.*" *Modern Fiction Studies* 3 (1974): 1203–18.

———. *Of Huck and Alice: Humorous Writing in American Literature*. Minneapolis: University of Minnesota Press, 1983.

Schor, Naomi. "Dreaming Dissymmetry: Barthes, Foucault, and Sexual Difference." In *Men in Feminism*, ed. Alice Jardine and Paul Smith, 98–110. New York: Methuen, 1987.

———. "Reading Double: Sand's Difference." In *The Poetics of Gender*, ed. Nancy K. Miller, 248–69. New York: Columbia University Press, 1986.

Schweickart, Patrocinio. Foreword to *Gender and Reading: Essays on Readers, Texts, and Contexts*, edited by Elizabeth A. Flynn and Patrocinio Schweickart. Baltimore: Johns Hopkins University Press, 1985.

———. "Reading Ourselves: Towards a Feminist Theory of Reading." In *Gender and Reading: Essays on Readers, Texts, and Contexts*, ed. Elizabeth A. Flynn and Patrocinio Schweickart. Baltimore: Johns Hopkins University Press, 1985.

Secor, Cynthia. "The Question of Gertrude Stein." In *American Novelists Revisited*, ed. Fritz Fleischmann et al., 299–310. Boston: G. K. Hall, 1982.

Showalter, Elaine. "Feminist Criticism in the Wilderness." *Critical Inquiry* 8, no. 2 (1981): 179–205.

Sollers, Phillipe. *Writing and the Experience of Limits*. Ed. David Hayman. Trans. Philip Barnard with David Hayman. New York: Columbia University Press, 1983.

Solomon-Godeau, Abigail. "Beyond the Simulation Principle." In *Utopia Post Utopia*, 83–100. Institute of Contemporary Art Catalog Series. Cambridge, Mass.: MIT Press, 1988.

Spivak, Gayatri Chakravorty. "French Feminism in an International Frame." *Yale French Studies* 62 (1981): 154–84.

Stein, Gertrude. "An American in France." In *What Are Master-pieces*. New York: Pittman, 1970.

———. "American Newspapers." In *How Writing Is Written*, ed. Robert Bartlett Haas. Los Angeles: Black Sparrow Press, 1974.

———. *The Autobiography of Alice B. Toklas*. New York: Random House, 1933.

———. *Blood on the Dining Room Floor*. Berkeley: Creative Arts Book Co., 1982.

———. "Composition As Explanation." In *Writing and Lectures, 1909–1945*, ed. Patricia Meyerowitz, 21–30. Baltimore: Penguin Books, 1967.

———. *Everybody's Autobiography*. New York: Vintage, 1973.

———. *The Geographical History of America*. New York: Random House, 1936.

———. "The Gradual Making of *The Making of Americans*." In *Lectures in America*, 135–61. Boston: Beacon Press, 1935.

———. *How to Write*. Craftsbury Common, Vt.: Sherrie Urie Press, 1977.

———. "How Writing Is Written." In *How Writing Is Written*, ed. Robert Bartlett Haas, 151–60. Los Angeles: Black Sparrow Press, 1974.

———. "I Came and Here I Am." In *How Writing Is Written*, ed. Robert Bartlett Haas, 67–72. Los Angeles: Black Sparrow Press, 1974.

———. *Ida*. New York: Vintage Books, 1968.

———. *Lectures in America*. Boston: Beacon Press, 1935.

———. *A Long Gay Book*. In *Matisse, Picasso, and Gertrude Stein, with Two Shorter Stories*. Barton, Vt.: Something Else Press, 1972.

―――. *Lucy Church Amiably: A Novel of Romantic Beauty and Nature Which Looks Like an Engraving*. New York: Something Else Press, 1969.

―――. *Many Many Women*. In *Matisse, Picasso, and Gertrude Stein, with Two Shorter Stories*. Barton, Vt.: Something Else Press, 1972.

―――. *The Mother of Us All*. Ed. Carl Van Vechten, 52–88. New York: Vintage, 1975.

―――. *Mrs. Reynolds and Five Earlier Novelettes*. New Haven: Yale University Press, 1952.

―――. *Narration*. Chicago: University of Chicago Press, 1935.

―――. *A Novel of Thank You*. New Haven: Yale University Press, 1958.

―――. "Plays." In *Lectures in America*, 93–131. Boston: Beacon Press, 1935.

―――. "Portraits and Repetition." In *Lectures in America*, 165–206. Boston: Beacon Press, 1935.

―――. *Q.E.D. (Things As They Are)*. New York: Liverright, 1971.

―――. "A Sonatina Followed by Another." In *Bee Time Vine and Other Pieces (1913–1927)*. New Haven: Yale University Press, 1953.

―――. "The Superstitions of Fred Anneday, Annday, Anday: A Novel of Real Life." In *How Writing Is Written*, ed. Robert Bartlett Haas, 24–30. Los Angeles: Black Sparrow Press, 1974.

―――. *Tender Buttons*. In *Gertrude Stein: Writings and Lectures, 1909–1945*, ed. Patricia Meyerowitz. Baltimore, Md.: Penguin Books, 1967.

―――. *Three Lives*. New York: Vintage, 1971.

―――. "What Are Master-pieces and Why Are There So Few of Them." In *Gertrude Stein: Writings and Lectures, 1909–1945*, ed. Patricia Meyerowitz, 148–56. Baltimore: Penguin, 1967.

Steiner, Wendy. *Exact Resemblance to Exact Resemblance: The Literary Portraiture of Gertrude Stein*. New Haven: Yale University Press, 1978.

Stewart, Susan. *Nonsense*. Baltimore: Johns Hopkins University Press, 1979.

Stimpson, Catharine. "Gertrude Stein and the Transposition of Gender." In *The Poetics of Gender*, ed. Nancy K. Miller, 1–18. New York: Columbia University Press, 1986.

―――. "Gertrude Stein: Humanism and Its Freaks." *Boundary II* (Spring/Fall 1984): 301–19.

―――. "The Mind, the Body, and Gertrude Stein." *Critical Inquiry* 3 (1977): 489–506.

―――. "The Somagrams of Gertrude Stein." *Poetics Today* 6, nos. 1–2: 67–80.

Suleiman, Susan Rubin. "Pornography, Transgression, and the Avant-Garde: Batille's *Story of the Eye*." In *The Poetics of Gender*, ed. Nancy K. Miller, 117–36. New York: Columbia University Press, 1986.

Tichi, Cecelia. *Shifting Gears: Technology, Literature, Culture, in Modernist America*. Chapel Hill: University of North Carolina Press, 1987.

Tobin, Patricia. *Time and the Novel: The Genealogical Imperative*. Princeton: Princeton University Press, 1978.

Turner, Victor. "Frame, Flow and Reflection: Ritual and Drama as Public Liminality." In *Performance in Postmodern Culture*, ed. Michel Benamou and Charles Caramello, 33–55. Madison, Wis.: Coda Press, 1977.

Wallis, Brian. *Art After Modernism: Rethinking Representation*. Boston: New Museum of Contemporary Art, 1984.

Walker, Jayne L. *The Making of a Modernist: Gertrude Stein from "Three Lives" to "Tender Buttons."* Amherst: University of Massachusetts Press, 1986.

Waugh, Patricia. *Feminine Fictions: Revisiting the Postmodern.* New York: Routledge, 1989.

White, Hayden. "The Value of Narrativity in the Representation of Reality." *Critical Inquiry* 7 (1980): 5–27.

Wing, Betsy. "Glossary." In *The Newly Born Woman,* by Hélène Cixous and Catherine Clément, trans. Betsy Wing, 163–68. Minneapolis: University of Minnesota Press, 1986.

Williams, Raymond. *Marxism and Literature.* New York: Oxford University Press, 1972.

Wilson, Edmund. "Things As They Are." In *Critical Essays on Gertrude Stein,* ed. Michael J. Hoffman, 58–61. Boston: G. K. Hall, 1986.

Index